NAZI GERMANY AND THE AMERICAN HEMISPHERE, 1933–1941

by Alton Frye

As Hitler's armies swept through Paris in the early summer of 1940, rumors flew thick and fast as to where the Führer's legions would turn next. The fall of France changed the attitude of the Western hemisphere from one of relative indifference toward the Third Reich to one of anxiety. Throughout the United States and Latin America troubled citizens asked: Would Hitler invade the New World?

Wading through the morass of espionage, half-truth, artifice, and controversy, Alton Frye has arrived at a viable answer to this question. Through his examination of Nazi activities in the Americas and the evidence made available since the capture of German archives, Mr. Frye concludes that National Socialist Germany did pose a distinct threat to the Western hemisphere. The massive Nazi propaganda apparatus, he finds, was unwieldy and undiplomatic, but stubbornly effective, particularly in Latin America. The leaders of the Nazi party, especially Hitler, were dedicated to expanding the Third Reich's boundaries to include the whole world, and had formulated elaborate schemes for the infiltration of the Western hemisphere. And the German military force, with its superior technology and execution, was capable of widespread conquest. In a provocative concluding chapter Mr. Frye demonstrates that a successful Nazi invasion of Britain might well have been followed by an equally successful attack upon the American hemisphere.

Yale Historical Publications, Miscellany 86.

A member of the research staff of the RAND Corporation, Mr. Frye has taught at U.C.L.A. and Harvard University, where he completed this study as research associate of the Center for International Affairs.

Yale Historical Publications

MISCELLANY 86

Published under the direction

of the Department of History

NAZI GERMANY AND THE AMERICAN HEMISPHERE

1933-1941

by Alton Frye

New Haven and London, Yale University Press, 1967

Library of Congress catalog card number: 67-13433

Published with assistance from
the Louis Stern Memorial Fund.

TO PATRICIA

Preface

What were Nazi Germany's ultimate intentions regarding the New World? If the Third Reich had been victorious in Europe, would conquest of the Western Hemisphere have come next? These questions continue to perplex historians. Answers conclusive enough to remove the nagging doubts that persist in certain quarters have so far eluded us. Some writers have been content with the ambiguous evidence on these issues, since it permits them to justify one or another preconceived notion. Yet even if scholars cannot and should not eliminate all the ambiguity of their data, they are obligated to reduce it so far as possible.

This study seeks to throw some light on these questions by reviewing Nazi activities in the Western Hemisphere from 1933 to 1941. During this period the Reich's actions in the New World revealed much about its attitudes and intentions toward the American republics. By various methods Berlin sought to gain influence in the Western Hemisphere and to channel the policies of the American nations into directions compatible with the Fuehrer's vision of a new world order.

If the concept of national security includes, as surely it must, security against foreign intervention in a nation's domestic affairs, then the countries of the New World were under attack long before the outbreak of war in Europe. Like other totalitarian regimes, Hitler's government placed great reliance on its ability to exploit the open politics of democratic states, in the Americas no less than in Europe. The present work is concerned primarily with such Nazi attempts to undermine the integrity of American political systems. These efforts to manipulate the political processes of American states were themselves the most suggestive evidence of the Reich's true disposition toward this hemisphere. Whether they were the prelude to more direct intervention by the Third Reich at some later date is one of the imponderables of history, but it is difficult to escape the conclusion that, had the Nazis achieved enduring victory in the Old World, the nations of the New would have faced an unending succession of political assaults. And hindsight confirms what important elements in the Reich hierarchy had already come to expect—that technological progress would certainly make feasible a transatlantic attack in the near future.

The author's interest in this subject stems from his concern with contemporary American foreign policy. None can deny that U.S. participation in the anti-fascist conflict from 1941 to 1945 has had immeasurable influence on the subsequent course of world affairs. Yet there have been lingering disputes, recalled here in the opening chapter, over whether that participation was justified or unjustified, wise or unwise. No one can presume to resolve this issue simply and definitively, but an examination of Nazi activities in the Western Hemisphere illuminates some factors that are both relevant and relatively neglected in recent historiography.

There is a special reason for desiring further research in this area. In the maze of literature dealing with the role of the United States in the Second World War there emerges a pointed and discouraging moral for those concerned with the value of history and the issue of objectivity in historical research. Many of the American writers who have produced important works since the end of the war were prominent in the bitter debate between isolationists and interventionists during the nineteen-thirties. It is testimony to the influence of personal predispositions and perspectives that, in spite of the tons of documents which have become available for the more complete evaluation of the problem, none of the major contributors to either side of the argument has reversed his prewar position because of more recent investigations.[1]

This fact, needless to say, does not reflect favorably on the reliability of these historical interpretations. It does afford prima facie evidence that, if we are ever to have reasonable confidence that our understanding of the period is not seriously colored by the bias of writers who were themselves active in the events being studied, new analyses by persons not directly involved in the prewar disputes will be required. It is in light of this observation that the writer, who achieved his maturity some time after the end of the war, offers this essay.

This study concentrates on Nazi propaganda activities in the New World and on the diplomatic crises which they generated between Berlin and the American governments. It relies primarily on captured files of the German Foreign Ministry, both published and unpublished, supplemented by other sources pertaining to the Nazis which are discussed in the bibliography.

1. Unlike the principal historians of America's role in the war, a number of leading political figures did alter their initial stands. Senator Arthur Vandenberg and Chester Bowles, for example, abandoned isolationism to support the United States' new responsibilities in international affairs.

It is a genuine privilege to acknowledge one's intellectual debts. From the time I began an earlier study of this subject as part of a doctoral program at Yale University, my principal and most welcome obligation has been to Samuel Flagg Bemis for the sustenance of his untiring interest over the years, as well as for the inspiration of his own prodigious example. In addition, Karl Deutsch and Hajo Holborn, also of Yale, have been most generous with their time and valuable suggestions.

Among my colleagues at the RAND Corporation, I have been especially stimulated by the distinguished work of Alexander L. George and Hans Speier, pioneers in the systematic analysis of propaganda. Their studies make one sensitive to the operational significance of activities which are examined here mainly from the standpoint of planning and organization.

Boyd Schafer, formerly Executive Secretary of the American Historical Association, proved a knowledgeable adviser, and I am especially grateful to him for directing me to Willard Fletcher, then director of the American Historical Association project filming portions of the voluminous Nazi Party and other records in Alexandria, Virginia. Dr. Fletcher lent a gracious and learned guiding hand in my foraging expedition into that paper jungle. I should also like to thank Ezekiel Lifschutz of the Yivo Institute for Jewish Research in New York City for his assistance; and Bernard Noble, former Chief of the State Department's Historical Office, for providing me a copy of an important report on Nazi activities in Latin America prepared by the Department in 1938. Finally, I must express sincere gratitude to the staffs of the several divisions of the National Archives and the Library of Congress, who were unsparing in their willingness to help, and to the Center for International Affairs, Harvard University, which provided a most hospitable setting for completing the manuscript.

A. F.

Washington, D.C.
September 1966

Contents

Agency Abbreviations

AO   *Auslandsorganisation* (Foreign Organization of the Nazi Party)

APA   *Aussenpolitisches Amt* (Foreign Policy Office of the Nazi Party)

DAI   *Deutsches Ausland-Institut* (German Foreign Institute of Stuttgart)

DNB   *Deutsches Nachrichtenbuero* (German News Bureau)

NSDAP   *Nationalsozialistische Deutsche Arbeiterpartei* (National Socialist German Labor Party)

PROMI   *Propagandaministerium* (Reich Ministry For Public Enlightenment and Propaganda)

TO   *Transozean* (Transocean News Service)

VDA   *Volksbund fuer das Deutschtum im Ausland* (League For Germandom Abroad)

CHAPTER 1

America's Role in the Second World War: Wisdom or Folly?

The historic debate over America's role in the Second World War began long before the war itself.[1] It is scarcely an exaggeration to say that the argument started in the nineteen-twenties with the publication of such books as C. Hartley Grattan's *Why We Fought* and revisionist condemnations of America's entry into the conflict of 1914–1918. The putative lesson was clear: the United States should refrain from any participation in future European wars. As the tempo and intensity of the debate increased and as ominous murmurs began to disturb Europe after January 30, 1933, historical reconsiderations of the First World War merged into the interventionist–isolationist controversy over the events leading up to the Second. Very much the same divisions have continued to the present day in the literature concerning America's entry into the second great conflict of this century.

Harry Elmer Barnes, a recognized leader of the revisionists after both wars, has emphasized the continuity of revisionism in this lament:

> For the sad state of the world today, the entry of the United States into two world wars has played a larger role than any other single factor. Some might attribute the admittedly unhappy conditions of

1. For intelligent considerations of the historiography of the subject see Wayne S. Cole, "American Entry into World War II: A Historiographical Appraisal," *Mississippi Valley Historical Review,* 42 (March 1957), 595–617; Eugene C. Murdock, "Zum Eintritt der Vereinigten Staaten in den Zweiten Weltkrieg," *Vierteljahrshefte fuer Zeitgeschichte,* 4 (January 1956), 93–114; Ernest R. May, *American Intervention, 1917 and 1941* (Washington, D.C., 1960); Louis Morton, "Pearl Harbor in Perspective: A Bibliographical Survey," *United States Naval Institute Proceedings,* 81 (April 1955), 461–68. "Neo-revisionist" is used here to designate works and authors dealing with the Second, as opposed to the First, World War. Throughout this study "America" and "the United States" serve as synonyms. The adjective "American," when used to modify "Hemisphere" or such nouns as "nations" or "republics," refers collectively to the countries of North and South America. The precise meaning should always be clear from the context.

our time to other items and influences than world wars and our intervention in them. No such explanation can be sustained. Indeed, but for our entry into the two world wars, we should be living in a far better manner than we did before 1914. . . . The rise and influence of Communism, military state capitalism, the police state, and the impending doom of civilization, have been the penalty exacted for our meddling abroad in situations which did not materially affect either our security or our prestige. Our national security was not even remotely threatened in the case of either world war. There was no clear moral issue impelling us to intervene in either world conflict. The level of civilization was lowered rather than elevated by our intervention.[2]

By contrast Samuel Eliot Morison, reviewing an early neo-revisionist volume by Charles A. Beard, gave imaginative expression to the thoughts of many of the opponents of such views:

> If all the books on the war before 1942 but Beard's should perish from the earth, the curious reader in the far future would have to infer that a dim figure named Hitler was engaged in a limited sort of war to redress the lost balance of Versailles; that Japan was a virtuous nation pursuing its legitimate interests in Asia; and that neither threatened or even wished to interfere with any legitimate American interest.[3]

Within the broad position outlined by Barnes, revisionist authors have developed a number of specific themes concerning the United States and the Second World War. The most important of these propositions are, explicitly:

    1. The Axis powers did not in fact constitute a threat to American security.

2. Harry Elmer Barnes, ed., *Perpetual War For Perpetual Peace* (Caldwell, Idaho, 1953), p. 6. This volume brings together in some 700 pages the most extensive treatment of various aspects of the question by the leading neo-revisionists. It renders virtually all of their many other publications redundant. May, *American Intervention,* pp. 18–19, repudiates the single-track revisionist interpretation by his discussion of the essential differences among the issues and circumstances of the two world wars.

3. Samuel Eliot Morison, "Did Roosevelt Start The War?—History Through a Beard," *Atlantic Monthly, 182* (August 1948), 97. This is Professor Morison's review of Beard's *President Roosevelt and the Coming of the War, 1941* (New Haven, 1948).

2. The policies of the Roosevelt Administration were largely responsible for the war and almost entirely to blame for United States participation in it.

3. The President practiced calculated deception on the American people to disguise his intentions toward the developing European conflict.

4. Roosevelt's policies before and during the war contributed significantly to the subsequent rise of an even graver menace than Nazi Germany: Soviet Russia.

The question of whether the Axis, and specifically Nazi Germany, was an actual danger to the New World is obviously basic to any assessment of American policy vis-à-vis Hitler's Reich, since that policy was predicated on the belief that a threat existed. From the very beginning isolationist–revisionist writers have argued steadfastly that there was no serious danger to the Western Hemisphere from the European military imbroglio. In the prewar period, appraisals by such military experts as Hanson Baldwin and George Eliot bolstered the argument. Capture of many German archives has provided it with what some have considered an even stronger prop: the revisionists can now point to the fact that no detailed Nazi war plans for the Americas have been discovered. Further, they can call up the testimony of General George Marshall, in his final report as Chief of Staff (1945), that the Axis lacked any coordinated scheme for world domination. The Axis allies, neo-revisionists point out, did not even have well-defined plans for cooperation among themselves.[4]

Even if the Nazis had devised war plans for action against the Western World, the revisionists contend that there would still have been no danger sufficient to justify American entry into the war. They declare that a transatlantic invasion would have required a gigantic naval force which Hitler did not have and could not get. They scorn the possibility that the

4. This discussion is based on a number of neo-revisionist volumes, including most notably Barnes, *Perpetual War;* Charles A. Beard, *President Roosevelt and the Coming of the War, 1941,* and *American Foreign Policy in the Making, 1932–1940* (New Haven, 1946); Charles C. Tansill, *Back Door to War* (Chicago, 1951); Frederick C. Sanborn, *Design for War* (New York, 1951); and William Henry Chamberlin, *America's Second Crusade* (Chicago, 1950). For a favorable bibliographical survey of many other pertinent works, see *Select Bibliography of Revisionist Books Dealing with the Two World Wars and Their Aftermath* (Oxnard, California, n.d.). No author is listed for the latter pamphlet, but it appears to be the work of Harry Elmer Barnes. The most extreme of all revisionist works has only recently appeared: David L. Hoggan, *Der erzwungene Krieg* (Tuebingen, Germany 1963).

Fuehrer might have gained adequate naval power through an early conquest of France and England, with their substantial fleets and ship-building capacity.

Neo-revisionists depict Hitler's intentions as pacific even toward Great Britain. Almost unanimously these writers lay much of the blame for the outbreak of hostilities at the doors of Britain and France for attempting to fulfill their obligations to Poland. Charles Tansill argues that the Polish question, especially as regarded Danzig and the Corridor, was bound to be settled in favor of Germany. Barnes further states that Hitler's demands on Poland were the most reasonable he had yet made. These considerations, for this group of historians, mean that the British and French should not have assumed commitments to the Poles.

Furthermore, they point to Hitler's peace offers during the period of the "twilight war" and after the fall of France. They suggest that the Fuehrer's generous restraint in allowing the British to evacuate their forces from Dunkirk demonstrated his great esteem for that nation. The Third Reich would never have fought Britain, much less the United States, aver the revisionists, if the Germans had been permitted to pursue their real interests in a war against Russia. William Henry Chamberlin particularly argues that the character of Nazi military training, with its emphasis on mobility, light tanks, and armor, was plainly designed for operations to the East across the Russian heartland. In sum, the neo-revisionists hold that Hitler's real intentions looked to purely continental expansion and that there was no danger that he would ever have attacked the Western Hemisphere.

In their second major argument, revisionist historians contend that the policies of Franklin Roosevelt, which eventually resulted in the calamitous entry of the United States into the war, played a major role in precipitating it. They contend that Roosevelt meddled extensively and without warrant in European affairs. By their standards the President was the archsupporter of the Munich appeasement and they suggest that Chamberlain might not have been so ready to give in to Hitler if Washington had not exerted pressure in that direction. In turn, had the British Prime Minister not made the fateful journey to Munich, revisionists speculate that the well-known army plot to overthrow the German dictator in September 1938 would probably have materialized and European politics would have taken on quite a different complexion. All the evils associated with the failure of appeasement revisionists attribute to Franklin Roosevelt's interference.

Yet they also claim that Britain, France, and Poland would have been much more conciliatory in September 1939 if Roosevelt had not pressed them to stand firm in rejecting Hitler's demands. According to this view, ambassadors such as Joseph Kennedy in London and William Bullitt in Paris led the British, French, and Poles to believe they could count on American intervention, sooner or later, should they become involved in a military contest with Nazi Germany. C. C. Tansill stresses an isolated passage in *The Forrestal Diaries* and the *German White Paper* on Poland to show that Chamberlain and Daladier were told they could expect American aid in any subsequent general war *only* if they stood by Poland in her hour of need. Tansill does report that both Kennedy and Bullitt deny that they ever submitted any such idea to France and England, but he dismisses their statements on the matter as mere whitewashes.[5]

Neo-revisionists are not in perfect agreement as to the reasons for Roosevelt's alleged volte-face between 1938 and 1939. Tansill advances most ingeniously the view usually favored. With a strong second from Barnes, he concludes that there is only one possible explanation for Roosevelt's contradictory stands on Munich and on the Polish invasion a year later. In September 1938 Nazi Germany would have been opposed by a strong, well-organized Czech army, as well as by Britain and France and possibly the Soviet Union. Any war which might have erupted at the time of the Munich settlement would thus have brought the prompt defeat of Hitler, without the possibility of American intervention.

But by September 1939 the situation was utterly different. The Czech army was no more and Czechoslovakia's valuable Skoda Works were producing arms for Germany; Russia had given Germany carte blanche by the pact of August 23; the relative armaments posture of the Germans and the democracies, particularly in the aviation sector, had shifted drastically in Hitler's favor. All these factors made it highly probable that the prospective conflict would not end abruptly. Therefore, Tansill submits, Roosevelt approved a rigid stand against Berlin in 1939 because he was confident the ensuing war would drag on long enough for the United States to get involved. This is the reasoned judgment of the acknowledged revisionist authority on the European phase of the Second World War.

While revisionists are convinced that Roosevelt's known interventionist tendencies reinforced the Anglo-French decision for war, they are even

---

5. See Tansill, *Back Door to War,* pp. 450 ff.; and his essay on the European aspects of the war in Barnes, *Perpetual War,* pp. 165–70.

more outraged at the policies he initiated in the months that followed. They interpret almost every move taken by the President during the next twenty-six months as a premeditated step along the road to war, rather than a necessary measure to defend American interests. Chief among the departures from neutrality were the destroyer-bases agreement and the Lend-Lease Act. The revisionists stigmatize both these actions as deplorable violations of international law. The late Edwin Borchard, Yale law professor and ardent partisan of neutrality legislation, denounced the diplomatic swap of destroyers to Britain in exchange for bases in her Western Hemisphere possessions as simply incompatible with neutrality. Frederick Sanborn, another international lawyer, holds similar views regarding Lend-Lease, which he thinks was mainly the product of clever British manipulation. The Administration misrepresented these and other Machiavellian stratagems in its attempt to conceal the facts from the people.

This leads to the third outstanding accusation against Roosevelt, viz., that he dissembled to an unprecedented degree in his relationship with the electorate. By any measure, it is the most viable theme voiced by neo-revisionists. All revisionist writers emphasize this aspect of the attack, but the most substantial indictment comes from Charles Austin Beard. Few public figures are more vulnerable in this respect than Mr. Roosevelt. Beard makes a telling case by highlighting the disparities between Administration words and deeds. Because of this chasm between appearances and realities, the "Devil theory of war," discounted by Beard as responsible for bringing the United States into the First World War, leads this distinguished historian and his colleagues to impute base motives to the Squire of Hyde Park.

It is their contention that Roosevelt maneuvered the United States into war in order to promote partisan political aims, to distract the American people from domestic failures of the New Deal. Others suggest that dastardly British machinations duped the President into intervention. Somewhat more generously, William Henry Chamberlin feels that Roosevelt's ambition to be a great wartime leader in a troubled world enticed him into the conflict. At any rate, all revisionists consider Roosevelt's motives as personal ones not related to true American interests.

Finally, this school of writers blames Roosevelt for the postwar tension and bipolarization of world politics between Moscow and Washington. They put forward the proposition that Russia became an infinitely more serious threat than the Third Reich and that its rise could have been prevented had not the United States stupidly waged war on the Nazis. Specifically, they assert that Germany and Russia should have been allowed to fight it out, thus depleting their resources and crippling one another. This, they insist, was Germany's real concern—to gain *Lebensraum* at the expense of the Soviet Union. Furthermore, they stress that there was no ethical distinction between Hitler and Stalin; both represented the vilest manifestations of government by terror. American and British policy-makers should have stood by while the conflict raged on the central plains of the world island. True statesmen, in Tansill's phrase, would have welcomed both bloody-handed dictators to hospitable graves. The regrettable war alliance with Russia has only redounded to the benefit of Communism and has resulted in the emasculation of a virile Germany, the one power in Europe strong enough to have contained the Red peril. Neo-revisionists attribute all of these deplorable consequences to the bankrupt policies of Franklin Delano Roosevelt.

Before concentrating attention on the fundamental issue in the dispute, that is, whether Nazi Germany really threatened the security of the United States and the Western Hemisphere, let us note some of the principal responses other historians have made to the charges just discussed. To begin with, the fact that no German plans for an attack on the New World turned up in the captured archives is scarcely proof that no danger existed. To an extraordinary degree one man alone dictated the basic policies of the Third Reich, a man subject to the most volatile emotions. That erratic individual, whose shifts of policy were notorious throughout his rule, concentrated important decisions almost exclusively in his own hands.[6] Given the nature of the regime and its demonstrated ruthlessness in the quest for power, no nation could be secure.

The aggressive paths to Hitler's New Order were unpredictable; the only certain conclusion was that any nation unwilling to satisfy the demands of Berlin would be subjected to military compulsion. Russo-German relations amply illustrate this point. In less than two years after Ribbentrop's famous flight to Moscow to conclude the non-aggression pact with Molotov on August 23, 1939, German armies began a crush-

6. See especially Eric H. Boehm, "Policy-Making of the Nazi Government" (unpublished Ph.D. dissertation, Yale University, 1951). Also useful on this point is Franz Neumann, *Behemoth: The Structure and Practice of National Socialism* (New York, 1942). Still the most distinguished treatment of the Fuehrer and his career is Alan Bullock, *Hitler: A Study in Tyranny* (rev. ed., New York, 1964).

ing assault on the Soviet Union. Germany had no war plans for "Operation Barbarossa" until after France and Western Europe had been subdued. Hitler first ordered the preparation of such plans in the summer of 1940, only months before the second eastern campaign began.

Thus, had one examined German archives in June 1940, there would have been no documentary indication that Hitler would attack the Soviet Union within a year. Yet no one would argue that the absence of war plans constituted incontrovertible evidence of the Fuehrer's peaceful intentions toward Russia in the long run. It is just as fallacious to assert that the absence of specific plans for military action against the United States proves that Nazi Germany would never have attacked this country.[7]

And the attack on Russia was but the latest in a series of aggressions, each of which Hitler proclaimed to be his final ambition. To the world he had declared successively: Give me military parity and I shall be satisfied. Let me occupy the Rhineland and I shall ask no more. Permit the *Anschluss* with Austria and my greatest dreams will be fulfilled. Return the *Sudetendeutschen* to the fatherland and Germany will rest content. Grant me the remainder of Czechoslovakia and the Third Reich will have no further cause for complaint. Allow me to remove the Polish thorn from my side and there will remain no other item of contention to disturb the peace. Simply recognize my conquest of Norway, Denmark, Holland, Belgium, and France, and the English can retain their freedom, their fleet, and their empire. By this time Hitler's dulcet request was being directed to the United States: Do not interfere in my subjugation of Britain and you can remain secure in the New World, for there I have no interests.

Could any reasonable citizen, not to say responsible public official, have accepted the comfort of these specious assurances? In view of the record, posterity would have condemned any such gullible person as stupid, insane, or supremely pusillanimous.

7. Even more abrupt was Hitler's decision to invade Yugoslavia in April 1941; planning did not begin until late March 1941. On the Russian case see Gerhard L. Weinberg, "Der Deutsche Entschluss zum Angriff auf die Sowjetunion," *Vierteljahrshefte fuer Zeitgeschichte*, 1 (April 1953), 303–13, and his book, *Germany and the Soviet Union, 1939–1941* (Leiden, 1954). Hitler's directive for the assault on Russia is dated December 18, 1940.

We may collect at this point several of the major contributions on which the discussion rests: William Langer and S. Everett Gleason, *The Challenge to Isolation* and *The Undeclared War* (New York, 1952 and 1953); Hans L. Trefousse, *Germany and American Neutrality, 1939–1941* (New York, 1951); Basil Rauch, *Roosevelt: From Munich to Pearl Harbor* (New York, 1950); and Donald F. Drummond, *The Passing of American Neutrality, 1937–1941* (Ann Arbor, Mich., 1955). The last-named book, though seldom cited, is one of the most thorough and substantial efforts.

To the revisionist view that Hitler lacked sufficient naval power to invade the New World, even if he wanted to do so, other students point out that there was always the dangerous possibility that the Nazis would gain control of the French and/or British fleets. In spite of French pledges never to surrender their fleet, Vichy was an unknown quantity and no one could overlook the contingency that the notorious Pierre Laval, the aging Marshal Pétain, or the inconstant Admiral Darlan might reach an agreement exchanging the fleet for concessions from Germany. Similarly, although Churchill had publicly declared his intention to carry on the war from the colonies if driven from the British Isles, there was no certainty that he would always be at the helm. As he himself ominously suggested to President Roosevelt, undoubtedly to stir the United States to stronger action, no one could guarantee that Nazi assaults on Great Britain might not bring about the downfall of his government. If a new group gained ascendancy in Britain, one more willing to deal with the Germans, they would naturally consider the fleet their chief bargaining point in seeking a settlement with Hitler.[8]

If the Nazis gained possession of either or both fleets, and the industrial base to multiply ship construction quickly, they would be in a position to extend their military operations across the Atlantic. This might be facilitated by the collaboration of the large aggregations of Germans already living in the New World, many of whom were prepared to assist the fatherland in its endeavors to gain a foothold in this hemisphere. The United States could not even concentrate its still feeble military power against a prospective move by the Reich, because of the comparable menace of Japan in the Pacific.

These considerations were not unwarranted. The German government in fact contemplated expansion of its naval forces. As Gerhard L. Weinberg has written, "The German navy in July, 1940, was planning a program for the large scale construction of battleships *after* the defeat of England—for use against whom?"[9] Those charged with the security of

---

8. Winston Churchill, *Their Finest Hour* (Boston, 1949), pp. 188 f., for the Prime Minister's letter to Roosevelt of June 14–15, 1940. See also Churchill's dispatch to Lord Lothian, Britain's Ambassador in Washington, dated June 6, 1940, and instructing Lothian to press these points home to Secretary of State Hull and the President, pp. 400 f.

9. Weinberg cites evidence presented at Nuremberg in "German Colonial Plans and Policies, 1938–1942," in *Geschichte und Gegenwartsbewusstsein: Historische Betrachtungen und Untersuchungen, Festschrift fuer Hans Rothfels zum 70. Geburtstag, dargebracht von Kollegen, Freunden und Schuelern,* ed. Waldemar Besson and Friedrich Frhr. Hiller v. Gaertringen (Goettingen, 1963), n. 48, p. 474. Italics in original.

the United States would have been grievously derelict in their duty if they had not weighed these possibilities and acted accordingly.

As for the contention that Roosevelt bears the primary responsibility for the Munich policy of appeasement, it is sophistical. True enough, the American government expressed the belief that there was universal relief that a settlement had been reached without resort to war. But throughout the President's correspondence with the European leaders involved at Munich, his stated concern was only that the powers resolve their differences by negotiation. Doubtless he had opinions about the issues determined at the conference, but in each of his communications to Chamberlain, to Hitler, to Mussolini, to Daladier, he carefully refrained from passing on the merits of the points in dispute. When British Foreign Secretary Lord Halifax tried to align the United States with his country's policy of appeasement, he received a prompt disclaimer of such intention by the Under Secretary of State, Sumner Welles. Welles pointedly informed the British Ambassador that the United States had not indicated approval of the British course of action in any of its communications. As he stated, America's sole interest in the European situation was that a solution be attained by peaceful means, in accord with the Kellogg-Briand Pact and other obligations of the parties. On being so informed, the British Ambassador acknowledged that he had perhaps misled his superiors by dispatches stressing America's good will toward Britain.[10] At any rate, the President's messages appear to have had little effect on the decisions reached at Munich.

Regarding the charge that Roosevelt was largely to blame for the outbreak of war in 1939 because he urged a strong stand by Britain and France in support of Poland, most writers agree that the President did oppose further appeasement. This is hardly surprising since Hitler had exhibited his absolute faithlessness in the intervening eleven months. But there is no convincing evidence that Roosevelt promised American intervention in any subsequent general hostilities. The sympathy of the United States was plainly not with Germany, but there was no commitment to future active support of the democracies. The American ambassadors in London and Paris, Joseph P. Kennedy and William C. Bullitt, deny that

10. A relevant discussion of this topic is John McVickar Haight, Jr., "France, the United States and The Munich Crisis," *Journal of Modern History*, 32 (December 1960), 340–58. The best examination of the relation of the United States to the Munich settlement remains that of Langer and Gleason, *The Challenge to Isolation*, pp. 26–35, which quotes Welles' memorandum of his conversation with British Ambassador Sir Ronald Lindsay.

they were ever instructed to inform Britain and France that America would aid them only if they lived up to their obligations to Poland. American influence on the Anglo-French resistance to Hitler's invasion of Poland was not of great significance. Chamberlain and Daladier had at last concluded that the Nazi dictator must be stopped at all costs.[11] Their decision to take military measures was independent of the American attitude.

Tansill's assertion that Roosevelt wanted war in 1939, as opposed to his desire for peace in 1938, because a conflict in the later year would stretch on long enough for this nation to become engaged, is probably the most extreme of all neo-revisionist sophistries. To attribute such calculations to the President would, in the first place, credit him with sheer clairvoyance concerning the duration of military hostilities. The fact is that with the French army reputed to be the finest in Europe, and the British fleet able to blockade Germany, the President expected that the Allies would be able to handle the situation by themselves. At the outset of the Polish campaign he foresaw no need for American involvement and certainly did not wish it.

It was only in the spring and summer of 1940, with the stunning defeat of France and the Low Countries and the development of the Battle of Britain, that Roosevelt genuinely began to fear for his own country's safety. His actions in the following months were not intended to take this nation into war but to keep the violence as far as possible from American shores. When it became apparent that Britain, without French cooperation, could not produce all the implements necessary to her survival and to the containment and eventual elimination of Axis aggression, Roosevelt vainly sought to limit the United States' role to that of the "arsenal of democracy." If that failed to suffice, he was determined that the country would be in a better position to defend the Western Hemisphere. This accounts for the occupation of Iceland, the inter-American coordination of defense, and similar undertakings during 1940 and 1941. Revisionist efforts to depict these policies as deliberate steps to war are plainly mountain labor.

11. Of interest on this point is the work of a prominent English revisionist whose work deals only with the European aspects of the war that began in 1939; A. J. P. Taylor, *The Origins of the Second World War* (New York, 1962), pp. 212 ff. Taylor carefully dissociates himself from the U.S. revisionists, noting that their works are unimpressive from a scholarly standpoint and characterizing them as "survivors of the campaigners after the first world war, who still regard their own government as more wicked than any other."

It is in their criticism of Roosevelt's deception of the American public that the neo-revisionists perform their most valid function. There can be no unqualified defense of his actions in this regard, and authors who support the President's policies as necessary to national security do not strain themselves as apologists for his disingenuousness. The argument most commonly cited in his behalf is that of Thomas A. Bailey. In his book, *The Man in the Street,* Bailey compares the President's relationship to the people with that of a physician to his patient; at times, the doctor deems it wise to withhold the truth in the interest of the patient.[12] This is a feeble justification for Roosevelt's behavior.

Langer and Gleason do not hesitate to indict him for his reluctance to take his case forthrightly to the people. Their view is that, had he revealed more of the facts of the perilous situation into which the nation had fallen, the public would have been willing to follow his lead in all necessary measures. The Chief Executive, however, with a politician's acute sense of the mutability of the electorate, felt he could not take the chance that the people would refuse to heed his warnings. Bearing the awesome responsibility for the protection and preservation of the nation, he thought his duty compelled him to act as he did. Even those who grant the wisdom of his actions question whether the deceptive means he occasionally employed were necessary and proper. On balance, prevailing opinion tends to accord with Samuel Flagg Bemis' appraisal: "It will be Franklin D. Roosevelt's claim to statesmanship as compared with that of Woodrow Wilson, that, whatever his initial vacillations and his campaign deceptions, he came to see the American *raison d'état,* the vital relation of the United States to the balance of power at the advent of the Second World War."[13]

In their fourth major condemnation of the Roosevelt Administration, that mistaken American policy in the Second World War helped to create in Soviet Russia a menace greater than Hitler's Germany, revisionists illustrate why Maitland once said, "It is very hard to remember that events now long in the past were once in the future." They fail to place themselves in the position of the statesmen who had to make the fateful decisions at the time. These writers claim that but for the intervention of the United States, Germany and Russia would have conducted a mutually debilitating war in Europe. Apart from disregarding the plight of the

---

12. Thomas A. Bailey, *The Man in the Street* (New York, 1948), pp. 11–12.

13. Samuel Flagg Bemis, "The Shifting Strategy of American Defense and Diplomacy," in *Essays in History and International Relations in Honor of George Hubbard Blakeslee* (Worcester, Mass., 1949), p. 11.

lands already under Nazi subjugation, this charge rests on assumptions quite different from those on which the political leaders of the democracies in 1939, 1940, and 1941 had to act.

At that time the general apprehension was that Hitler might very well succeed where Napoleon had failed. After all, did not the Nazis demonstrate their mastery of modern, mobile warfare by overrunning Poland in three weeks and Western Europe in six? On the other hand, had not the Russian military organization revealed glaring weaknesses in its almost ineffectual attack on tiny Finland? If the Finns by themselves could sorely tax the might of Russian arms, most military experts could scarcely expect the Soviets to fare well against a massive German onslaught. Churchill and Roosevelt had to reckon with the possibility—and some advisers termed it a probability—that the Soviet Union would prove an easy prey for Hitler, like France with its highly-touted army. Then the Reich's troops could turn westward once more to complete the task already begun and to extend their dominion across the water without fear of difficulties in their rear. These were the imminent prospects which Great Britain and the United States had to envision.

Indeed, the Soviet Union might have collapsed had it not been for American Lend-Lease. No one knew for sure how greatly Russia had suffered until the 1959 census showed that between fifteen and twenty million of her citizens died in the war. It is questionable whether the Soviet Union could have withstood much more. While no citizen of the Free World can be pleased with Russia's vast augmentation of power in the aftermath of the war, the Western democracies had no choice but to support her if the crucial eastern front was to be maintained long enough for them to prepare the forces necessary to defeat Hitler. In Churchill's picturesque metaphor of 1941, "If Hitler invaded Hell, I would make at least a favorable reference to the Devil in the House of Commons."[14]

Detailed refutations of this fourth revisionist argument are unnecessary, for it is clearly a feckless attempt to convict Roosevelt on invalid, ex post facto grounds. There was no way accurately to foretell the astonishing rise of the Soviet Union. The succinct expression of Eugene Murdock fits the case well: "The development of this new danger is no argument against the liquidation of the old."[15]

Such then is the context of historical disputation over America's entry

14. Churchill, *The Grand Alliance* (Boston, 1950), p. 370. Data from the 1959 Soviet census appear in the *New York Times*, May 11, 1959, p. 1; see also the analysis by Harry Schwartz in the issue of May 17, 1959, Sec. 4, p. 6.

15. Murdock, "Zum Eintritt," p. 100.

into the Second World War. At the heart of the controversy lies the question of national interest, especially that most basic interest, the security of the Western Hemisphere. The substance of the central revisionist charge is that the rise of Nazi Germany did not in fact jeopardize the security of the United States and its neighbors. It is to this issue that the following chapters are directed.

Granted that no specific war plans for an invasion of the New World have turned up among the bounteous collections of captured documents, what other information bearing on this matter can one glean from Nazi sources? In particular, recognizing that the actions of the Third Reich reflected to a phenomenal extent the will of one man, what can one discover of Hitler's underlying attitude toward the American nations? What was the nature, scope, and purpose of the widespread Nazi activity in the Americas in the years before the United States entered the conflict? Of the utmost interest are propaganda and political activities, directed largely from Berlin, Hamburg, and Munich, which sought to influence the shape of public policy and the course of events in the Western Hemisphere. To what extent do these intrigues reveal the aims of Hitler and his followers? We may begin by examining the ways and means through which Nazi Germany sought to penetrate the republics of the New World.

CHAPTER 2

The Vehicles of Nazi Penetration

Throughout the nineteen-thirties the United States and other American nations grew increasingly apprehensive about possible Nazi intentions in the Western Hemisphere. These anxieties related most directly to the racial doctrines of National Socialism. German immigrants and their descendants made up sizable percentages of the American populations. Would the pernicious Nazi dogma infect them?

Nazi activities among German groups in the New World became the subject of frequent representations to Berlin by diplomats from many American countries. Although Reich officials consistently denied anything more than cultural relations with such German groups, these denials were designed to soothe American sensitivities while the work of organizing and gaining control of racial Germans continued. In 1937, when United States Ambassador to France William C. Bullitt visited Berlin, he warned Hermann Goering against the reported Nazi efforts to indoctrinate German-Americans. The Reichsmarschall's reply, although asserting once more that such reports were erroneous, was surprisingly frank and revealing:

> It is true that certain persons in our Government here believe that we should attempt to organize the Germans, especially of the Middle West, because they feel that if Germany should again become involved in war with France and England, there would come a moment when the United States might again consider entering such a war against Germany and they believe that such groups of organized Germans in the United States might throw their influence decisively against a declaration of war and might prevent the United States entering such a conflict.[1]

1. Report from Bullitt to the Secretary of State, Nov. 27, 1937, *Foreign Relations of the United States,* 1937, I (Washington, D.C., 1954), 174. (This series will be hereafter cited as *FR,* along with the year and volume number.) Goering's statement came only three weeks after Hitler, before a small group of leading German officials, had set forth plans for territorial expansion which were in fact to precipitate another

This guarded statement by Goering, perfectly in line with Hitler's own views on weakening an opponent from within, summed up a central tenet of Nazi policy toward the Western Hemisphere. During the years leading up to American involvement in the war, Nazi propaganda and other undertakings in this hemisphere were often directed toward enervating and incapacitating American governments.

The complexity of German activities abroad during the Hitler period is baffling, and one must attempt early to bring some order out of the confusion of ministries, departments, organizations, institutes, leagues, and academies which engaged in foreign enterprises. When the Nazi Party came to power, Hitler and his associates inherited a wide assortment of unofficial instruments which had extensive contacts among German communities in other countries. These agencies were readily adapted to propagate National Socialist racial views in both the Old World and the New. Generally related in their origins to the old Pan-German movement, they dedicated themselves to working for the retention of German language and culture among Germans who had left the fatherland. The original Pan-German League, or *Alldeutscher Verband,* had itself formed local units among some of the German colonies in South American countries during the early years of the twentieth century.[2]

Of the agencies still operating when Hitler proclaimed the Third Reich, the most important was the *Volksbund fuer das Deutschtum im Ausland* (VDA) with headquarters in Berlin. Founded in 1880, the VDA claimed two million members in 1932, many of whom resided in the Americas. Initially it had devoted its efforts to preserving German schools in certain areas of mixed nationality within Austria. The *Volksbund* continued its

---

world war. The Fuehrer's remarks at this famous meeting, recorded in the so-called Hossbach Memorandum of November 5, 1937, must have been fresh in Goering's mind as he spoke to the ambassador.

Bullitt aptly countered Goering's assertion by recalling the similar views of the German government in the First World War, when Acting Secretary of State Zimmermann of the Reich Foreign Ministry had declared to United States Ambassador James Gerard that America would not enter the war because there were five million Germans in the United States who would prevent American intervention by force if necessary. Gerard retorted acidly that, if there were five million Germans in the United States, there were *five million and one lamp-posts.*

After the war, Goering testified further that Hitler had relied on the isolationists to weaken the Roosevelt Administration and keep the United States out of the struggle. See below, Chapters 9 and 10.

2. See Ralph E. Bischoff, *Nazi Conquest Through German Culture* (Cambridge, Mass., 1942), p. 73.

work after the First World War, arranging correspondence among German school children in foreign countries and those in Germany, supplying textbooks, and otherwise promoting the retention of bonds between émigrés and the homeland. To thousands of German families in the United States and other American republics the VDA annually sent illustrated calendars depicting activities among various German communities around the world, as well as special blue candles which were to be burned at Christmas as a symbol of each family's links with the fatherland and other racial comrades. The organization's principal propaganda vehicles were three periodicals: *Volksdeutsche, Deutsche Welt,* and *Deutsche Arbeit,* widely circulated among German-speaking residents of this hemisphere.

The VDA welcomed the advent of the Nazi regime and was prepared to cooperate immediately in the promotion of the racial principles it shared with the Hitler movement. Although the Nazis treated the VDA and its personnel in a particularly benevolent fashion, they completely reorganized the agency under the Fuehrer concept. Dr. Hans Steinacher became director of the VDA in May 1933 and shortly thereafter a special agreement brought the members of the Hitler Youth into the organization. Even more important was the fact that the VDA did not receive an official status. An independent organization was an invaluable asset for certain racial endeavors. If the traditional position of the VDA could be maintained, at least to all outward appearances, then it could carry on the work among foreign Germans in areas "where the government and the Party are not able and may not do this on account of political reasons."[3]

Comparable in importance to the VDA and more diverse in its activities was the *Deutsches Ausland-Institut* (DAI), founded in 1917 to maintain contact with German emigrants. Partly because large numbers had emigrated from southwestern Germany, the DAI operated from Stuttgart where it erected an impressive museum and cultural center, *Das Haus des Deutschtums,* as its headquarters. The DAI prepared extensive records on the family histories of migrant Germans, with special reference to their continued racial integrity. In addition to cultural activities similar to those of the VDA, the DAI was active in the economic sphere as a private coordinating agency for German business firms engaged in foreign commerce. It also took a prominent role in the procedural work connected with emigration, seeking to channel Germans to appropriate countries, to obtain for them satisfactory positions, and generally to help them get es-

3. Otto Schaefer, *Sinn und Wesen des V.D.A.* (Frankfurt, 1933), p. 21. This official VDA publication is a principal source for the discussion.

tablished abroad while retaining their ties with the fatherland. Largely because of its more far-ranging interests and connections, the DAI eventually superseded the VDA as the number one "private" agency active among foreign Germans. Its private status was a fiction, of course, following its "coordination," as the Nazis euphemistically termed their subjugation of such organizations.[4]

Supplementing the two major unofficial organizations in their activities abroad were myriad other agencies. The *Deutsche Akademie* of Munich, a research institute which had fallen under the dominant influence of Karl Haushofer and his peculiar science, was increasingly important among German communities in foreign countries, as was its affiliate, the Goethe Institute. More prominent in the New World was the *Ibero-amerikanisches Forschungsinstitut* of Hamburg which published a great many works pertaining to Latin America and provided valuable connections among educated and influential elements in this hemisphere. Working from that same city, the *Fichtebund* was yet another agency engaged in cultural and propaganda activities in many countries of North and South America.

The role of organizations like these in the New Order was the subject of many deliberations and some controversy in the opening months of the Hitler era. In October 1933 Rudolf Hess, acting as the Fuehrer's deputy and the number two man in the Nazi Party, proclaimed the establishment of the *Volksdeutsche Mittelstelle*. This was to be a deliberative and executive organ under Hess's mentor, Dr. Haushofer, and was to coordinate activities among Germans abroad in order to strengthen and unify Germandom. In an effort to make the most effective use of existing agencies

---

4. The *Gleichschaltung* of the DAI was somewhat more difficult for the Nazis than that of the VDA, for Stuttgart was a center of anti-Nazi sentiment and local influence had tended to be supreme in DAI. However, DAI was reorganized in 1933 by a committee headed by Hans Steinacher. Although Dr. Richard Csaki, who was brought in from a German organization in Rumania in July 1933, retained his position as the institute's general director, Dr. Karl Stroelin, whom the Nazis had appointed mayor of Stuttgart in spite of his recent electoral defeat, assumed overall authority. Materials from the Reich Ministry of Interior, in the archives of the Yivo Institute for Jewish Research in New York, file NFI–18, are most useful for this crucial change in the status and composition of DAI. They also reveal that the budget of the DAI doubled between 1932 and 1937, rising to approximately RM 400,000 per annum, after state agencies were obligated by the Hitler regime to lend financial support to the organization. See also Raymond Murphy et al., *National Socialism* (Washington, 1943), pp. 122–27; and Arthur L. Smith, *The Deutschtum of Nazi Germany and the United States* (The Hague, 1965), pp. 1–26.

and to disguise their connections with the Party, the Haushofer office was to function only in secret.

The Hess announcement brought a prompt reaction from the Foreign Ministry. Foreign Minister Konstantin von Neurath pointed out the close relation of the new organization's work to the general conduct of foreign policy, and he insisted that the *Mittelstelle* should act only as an advisory body. Hess momentarily appeared to agree, but in December he unequivocally informed an interministerial committee which had recently been created to deal with questions of nationality and minorities that he and the Haushofer bureau "assumed jurisdiction over all unofficial organizations active in *volksdeutschen* questions."[5] There were to be many disputes over the work of the new office in the next few years.

As the chief Party administrator, Hess already had gained impressive authority in the sphere of foreign operations by his control of the several Party offices active abroad. Most important of these was the *Auslandsorganisation.* The Party had set up a section in 1931 to coordinate the work of members who happened to be in foreign countries or on board ship, and to establish and expand Party groups abroad. In May 1933 Ernst Wilhelm Bohle, a Hess protégé, became head of the section and in October it was placed directly under Hess, with Bohle a member of his staff. At that time Hess elevated the status of the section and appointed Bohle *Gauleiter*; a Party order of February 1934 gave it the title of *Auslandsorganisation* (AO). This was to be the most aggressive of all agencies operating abroad during the Hitler period. Its zeal in promoting Nazism among German communities in foreign countries would lead to serious and recurrent conflict with the Foreign Ministry's efforts to maintain normal diplomatic relations abroad.[6]

Other Party offices also engaged in foreign propaganda. The *Amt Auslandspresse,* headed for a time by Harvard graduate Ernst Hanfstaengl, developed voluminous correspondence with a fantastic assortment of propagandists in the United States, Canada, and other American states. Hanfstaengl himself promoted a favorable press for the Reich through extensive contacts with correspondents and news representatives in Berlin. As a

5. The circumstances surrounding the creation of this new body are disclosed in a number of documents published in *Documents on German Foreign Policy, 1918–1945,* Series C (Washington, D.C., 1953; cited hereafter as *DGFP–C*), 2, 49, 107, 255–59.

6. Emil Ehrich, *Die Auslandsorganisation der NSDAP* (Berlin, 1937), provides a detailed history of the origins and organization of the AO. See also the *Organisationsbuch der NSDAP* (Munich, 1940), pp. 143–45.

counterweight to the uncertain state bureaucracy which remained from the
Weimar years, Hitler had established yet another Party office, the *Aussenpolitisches Amt* (APA), under Alfred Rosenberg. The APA was intended
to become a central agency in the formation of German foreign policy,
paralleling the *Auswaertiges Amt.* Rosenberg did in fact send his own
agents to the Americas, although the role of the party's foreign office
never developed as expected.[7]

While Hess was gathering these sprawling bureaucracies of the Party
and unofficial organizations under his control, the early months of the
Third Reich saw battle joined between the Foreign Ministry and a specifically Nazi state agency, the *Reichsministerium fuer Volksaufklaerung
und Propaganda,* for control of propaganda *policy* in foreign countries.
In May 1933 a conference of Propaganda Ministry officials had agreed
that the Press Department of the Foreign Ministry, along with the funds
which financed its work, should be transferred to the newly created propaganda agency. The Propaganda Minister, Joseph Goebbels, pressed this
argument on the Fuehrer, who finally called a conference of department
heads in the Reich government to settle the matter. Goebbels stated his
position vigorously. All control over foreign propaganda should be concentrated in the Propaganda Ministry. An increase in funds for this purpose would be required immediately, for an effective campaign abroad
would be much more costly than domestic propaganda. Goebbels proposed that attachés, similar to military attachés, should serve in the
principal Reich missions abroad to supervise these activities. Von Neurath
feebly replied that the Foreign Ministry simply could not get along without its own Press Department. This uninspired rejoinder did not appre-
ciably affect the outcome of the meeting, which resulted in a significant
shift of powers to PROMI, as the Goebbels ministry was known in Nazi
jargon.

Hitler gave high priority to an effective propaganda establishment, and
he decided that the discussion indicated the need for a new organization.
"In future the Press Department of the Foreign Ministry will limit itself to
its previous traditional activity [i.e., reporting facts from abroad as a basis
for Ministry decisions]. Active propaganda abroad is taken over by the
Reich Ministry for Public Enlightenment and Propaganda which is setting

---

7. Ernst Hanfstaengl, *Unheard Witness* (New York, 1957), pp. 234–63. I have
also found the papers of Rolf Hoffmann, Hanfstaengl's aid and the key man in the
Amt Auslandspresse, of interest; they are available on microfilm at the U.S. National
Archives, micro-copy T–81, rolls 25–31 and 35–37.

up a press office of its own."[8] The new Chancellor implemented this decision by a decree dated June 30, 1933, which transferred from the Foreign Ministry to PROMI information and propaganda services abroad, together with all matters related to artistic exhibitions, films, and sports in foreign countries. Likewise, jurisdiction over economic and commercial propaganda, expositions, fairs, and general publicity went to Goebbels, as did control of tourist propaganda and all radio transmissions to foreign states. For the next six years this divorce of foreign propaganda from the control of the Foreign Ministry and its officers in other countries worked havoc with the efficient functioning of the Reich's official foreign service.

Even before Goebbels had obtained formal authority over German propaganda abroad, he had begun sending secret instructions to Reich representatives and other agents in the Americas. These preliminary orders, which PROMI issued monthly after April 1933, were superseded by a general directive of September 20, 1933. Although this fundamentally important document was strictly confidential, the ramshackle Nazi security provisions suffered one of their frequent failures and the orders fell into the hands of anonymous anti-Nazis who smuggled them out of Germany. Their publication in Paris aroused something of a furor there, but the Western Hemisphere, to which the document had primary reference, scarcely took notice, probably because the utter brazenness of the directive made it seem incredible to those not yet attuned to Hitlerian blatancy.[9]

The September instructions constituted nothing less than a master plan

8. Minutes of the conference of heads of departments, May 24, 1933, *DGFP–C, 1*, 483 ff.

9. See Louis de Jong, *Die deutsche fuenfte Kolonne im Zweiten Weltkrieg* (Stuttgart, 1959), pp. 18–20. (This is a German translation, carried out under the auspices of Munich's *Institut fuer Zeitgeschichte*, of an important study commissioned by UNESCO. The work appeared originally in Dutch.) On November 18, 1933, Goebbels publicly denied the truth of the Paris reports, *claiming he had no authority abroad*, a statement we know to be false. The passage of time has confirmed the Paris version, for the detailed procedures followed by Nazi propagandists in the New World corresponded to those prescribed by the directive to a degree beyond that which one may rationally attribute to chance. As but a single example, the German consulate general in New York was specified as the principal propaganda center in the United States and inquiries from Latin America pertaining to propaganda were to be directed there rather than to the embassy in Washington. This was actually the case during most of the nineteen-thirties. I have used the text published in the original German, with French translation, as *Les Instructions Secrètes de la Propagande Allemande* (Paris, 1933, cited hereafter as *Instructions*). After the war began an English-language journal finally gave limited attention to the documents; cf. Ernst Kris, "German Propaganda Instructions of 1933," *Social Research, 9* (February 1942), 46–81.

for German propaganda in the Americas. A major and explicit premise was that public opinion in both North and South America was especially susceptible to a carefully executed campaign. Goebbels also took note of the generally greater importance of public opinion among the American democracies than in Europe, and pointed to the dependence of American governments on popular support. Viewing the hostile environment into which the New Germany had been born, Goebbels proposed to cultivate a favorable attitude toward Germany among the masses in the Western Hemisphere, hoping thereby to exert a corresponding pressure on American governments. The directive recognized the prevalence of an anti-German attitude in most countries of the New World, and it repeatedly exhorted Nazi operatives to use the utmost caution in order to mask the sources and intentions of the propaganda. It then proceeded to set forth in some forty pages the principles and methods to be followed in a massive assault on public opinion all over the Americas, indicating that the campaign would be heavily subsidized and not limited by financial considerations.

For German propaganda in the Western Hemisphere the central task would be to develop sympathy for the Reich's foreign policy. For that reason the operatives in the field received a brief, general survey of the new regime's guiding principles in its relations with other countries. The principal goal of Reich foreign policy would be the revision of the Versailles *Diktat,* by negotiation if possible, by other means if necessary. In the pursuit of this aim France would be Germany's irreconcilable adversary, with England the strongest and most dangerous associate of the French. Although Germany had in no way abandoned her claims in the East, the Reich had adopted for the moment a conciliatory attitude toward Poland. Ultimately, National Socialist policy called for the reincorporation of all territories bordering on Germany in which there existed a German minority; the return of German colonies, unencumbered by the legal forms of a League of Nations mandate; and true equality for the Reich in the matter of armaments, excluding any international arms control.[10] It seems unlikely that the cautious von Neurath had helped the Propaganda Minister elaborate this set of political goals, but Goebbels had no doubt relied on knowledge of the Fuehrer's private plans in preparing this summary for Nazi agents in the Western Hemisphere.

Having thus mapped out the political foundations for all German

---

10. *Instructions,* pp. 9–14.

propaganda, Goebbels turned to the specifics of his plans for the New World. Germany's peaceful intentions were always to be stressed, and those opposing the Reich's legitimate demands should appear as responsible for preventing peaceful accord. To disseminate this opinion Germany would employ various media of which the most important were the press services controlled by the Reich. After the advent of Hitler, the dispatches of the *Deutsches Nachrichtenbuero* (DNB), an official agency which Goebbels had created to provide authentic reports of German governmental actions and statements, supplemented those of *Transozean* (Transocean or TO), a service which had been operating internationally for several years. But Berlin realized that DNB and Transocean would be insufficient for the tasks facing German propaganda, "because their sources are suspect." Transocean, in spite of all efforts to maintain its private appearance, had come to be considered by the world press as a semi-official agency and important papers like *La Prensa* of Buenos Aires printed its dispatches with ever-decreasing frequency. Previously newspapers served by Transocean had carried an average of 75 percent of its reports, but this percentage was steadily declining, because of growing suspicion of propaganda content and because many foreign bureau chiefs had warned their papers against Transocean.

Still Transocean and DNB were especially useful for German-language newspapers in the Americas and their operations were to be extended. Since these services transmitted dispatches largely via radiotelegraph, Goebbels required his agents to report on the best periods of the day and the most satisfactory wavelengths for transmissions to the various American countries. "In cities in which many papers are served by our agencies, we should consider establishing a central bureau for the reception of these transmissions by a technician and for the distribution of copies of the services among subscribing newspapers."[11]

In small towns where few papers were served and expenses were beyond their means, they might be reimbursed, or, alternatively, they could be provided with the services gratuitously through intermediaries appointed by the official Reich representative in the region. In the latter case, the persons appointed by the local Reich official should be Nazi Party members and preferably wireless operators recruited from German ship lines. Agents could make similar concessions to larger papers in major cities if the journals undertook to publish Transocean and DNB dispatches

11. Ibid., p. 16.

without abridging them. To take account of the extent to which the recipients actually used the services, PROMI directed local agents to maintain exact records of the number of dispatches sent and the number printed by individual papers. Papers that received the material under special concessions and who failed to use certain reports would have to indicate why they did not carry the particular items.

To the most important newspapers Goebbels proposed a more subtle enticement. "A special press service under an absolutely neutral flag can be placed at the disposition of these papers, which in its operations would flatter the predilection of many American papers for 'special correspondents.' "[12] In the future all German and foreign representatives of German news services would be available without expense to such papers. Thus different dispatches would not emanate from Germany, but from "special correspondents" in France, England, Austria, and so on. PROMI would assume the costs of these operations, provided the circulation and influence of the newspapers involved justified the expenditures.

It was obvious, the instructions continued, that offers of such "special services" should only go to papers which were not anti-German in outlook, and then only through the most discreet intermediaries. If special correspondents were reporting to several papers within a single city or area, the responsible German representative must exercise care to see that the content of the dispatches was distinct and varied in order to avoid duplication. Journals which for one reason or another were not amenable to such an approach were not to be neglected; agents should cultivate personal friendships with their editors and publishers. At suitable moments, agents could use their friendly relations with these persons to recommend a special correspondent who would be willing to write for relatively little in order to build up his reputation and authority in the respective country. For example, the confidential agent might call a publisher's attention to the work of a reporter whose articles were already being carried by a local paper under one of the secret understandings just described. Thus the several approaches would be self-reinforcing and, by such devious routes, German influence could worm its way into the independent press.

Another method which Goebbels hoped to exploit also relied on personal relations. Agents were to develop their contacts among employees of certain non-German press services. Although Goebbels warned his sub-

12. Ibid., p. 17.

ordinates not to attempt to bribe regional directors of such organizations, the Propaganda Minister suggested that a favorable attitude on the part of lower-ranking employees might be gained in return for appropriate considerations. One advantage which the Nazis foresaw in such contacts with the field agents of foreign press services was possible advance information on the dispatches which they were transmitting. With prior knowledge of reports which the following day's papers would print, German agencies could initiate immediate countermeasures, should it prove necessary. In this connection PROMI ordered its agents to file regular reports with detailed statistics on the degree to which publications in the Americas employed foreign news sources. "It will naturally be necessary to point out unceasingly and in every place the economies which the papers can realize, if they use the generally free official or unofficial German services, instead of spending so much for foreign services."[13]

Goebbels was particularly wary of the extreme hostility of the Associated Press and he forbade all German agents to associate with AP executives. Similarly, they should observe strict restraint in any relations with agents of the French and British services, Havas and Reuters. Newspapers which made unduly frequent use of Havas or other such hostile services should be denied, so far as practicable in the various localities, all revenues from German-financed advertising. Withdrawal of German advertisements from these papers should be gradual and unobtrusive, avoiding any suggestion of a boycott.

The directive took into consideration the fact that it would not be possible to implement this part of the instructions in every situation. In some areas the most important papers drew heavily on Havas, for example, and Germany could not afford to risk alienating them. In such cases agents were to make recommendations as to how relations between these papers and foreign news agencies might be disturbed. PROMI already had one promising method in mind: Goebbels intended to leak false documents to antagonistic press services in order to embarrass them by public refutation of their reports.

> The purpose of this action is publicly to bring into question the credibility of hostile foreign news agencies and above all to disturb so far as possible the relations between these opposition news sources and prominent foreign papers. A major paper, for example, which uses Havas or Reuters to supplement United Press, will always find

13. Ibid., p. 20.

it very awkward if it must print a retraction of one of their dispatches which it has published. Without a doubt it will make known its complaint to the appropriate news source in each case of a retraction, and in this way relations between such a paper and the news service concerned can gradually be disrupted.[14]

Both official and unofficial representatives of the Reich would be of great value in this enterprise by providing spurious documents and information to foreign press services. For instance, agents could indirectly supply Havas with a story on an alleged political affair in Brazil which would be offensive to Brazilians. When newspapers in other countries published the Havas reports on the matter, Brazilians would consider them an attack on their prestige and the French agency would fall into disrepute in Brazil. German news agencies must of course exploit these episodes, as well as other items from foreign press services, critical of the domestic situation in any American country and likely to offend its inhabitants if published abroad. Goebbels declared that all such means redounded to Germany's benefit and that no measure should be overlooked which could improve the Reich's position in the battle for world opinion. "Every interference in the good relations between other states is indirectly an advantage for Germany! Every weakening of foreign news influence is a great gain for Germany!"

To supplement the daily activities of German press agencies and the related efforts just described, the September directive announced the creation of a new organization, *Korrespondenz- und Artikel-Nachrichten-dienst* (KAN). This would provide to journals, magazines, and reviews in the Americas materials dealing in detail with specific issues, especially the Versailles arrangements. It would translate articles into Spanish, Portuguese, and English for distribution in the New World, and would adapt its presentations so as to be most effective in the different countries.

One of the outstanding questions with which KAN would deal was that of German minorities in foreign countries, and on this subject very diverse tactics were necessary in the Americas, as compared with the themes employed in Europe. In Argentina, Brazil, Chile, and elsewhere, the governing circles were naturally pursuing policies designed to promote the assim-

14. Ibid., p. 23. This technique was perhaps responsible for the notorious case of Alfred Mueller and the alleged plan for German seizure of Patagonia, which provided fuel for much Nazi counter-propaganda when Mueller was acquitted by an Argentine court in 1940. This incident is discussed below, Chapter 7.

ilation of desirable immigrants. For propaganda purposes KAN would stress the distinctions between the Germans who had voluntarily immigrated to North and South America and those who had been forced to accept foreign rule as a result of the annexations by Germany's neighbors after the World War. This was one example of the need to adjust propaganda to the different situations prevailing in the Western Hemisphere.

KAN would not prepare merely a single article on a given subject, but many articles approaching the topic from various points of view. This would help prevent undesirable duplication, for the campaign would only be weakened if several publications in the same area repeated an identical article. In order to bolster political maneuvers by the Reich, the new office would prepare preliminary articles for release on specified dates in connection with current foreign policies. However, there would be instances in which advance notice of political moves could not be given and agents would have to improvise prompt local action without waiting for instructions. In these urgent situations they should never apologize for decisions by the Reich government. For example, in regard to disarmament policy, in which "surprises or other unexpected developments" might be forthcoming, agents should consistently argue that the course of events is logically a product of the attitude of the other side. Operatives must always bear in mind the general guides laid down in previous directives, whenever they found independent action necessary.

Tourist and cultural propaganda was to assume greater significance in the future and Germany would make good use of it for political ends. In areas where there were no PROMI agents these campaigns would proceed under the general direction of German shipping lines, which would afford guarantees of tight German control. To exemplify the values of such propaganda for political indoctrination of foreign populations, the directive described a brochure on the Rhineland which would recall in passing the sufferings of the German people there under the occupation and would mention the demilitarization of the region, noting that it had left the country open to foreign aggression. It would also allude to other areas which had been taken from Germany, notably Alsace-Lorraine and the Saar. Nazi propagandists must keep these political references to a minimum in advertisements or articles published in papers or travel journals in the Western Hemisphere, so that editors would not reject the material as propaganda. Related to these activities were lectures accompanied by lantern slides and other exhibits dealing with tourism, science, and culture in the Reich. Official Reich representatives and other agents should make these lectures available without charge to appropriate groups in the New World.

In all important centers where there were not yet German radio hours they should be immediately organized. PROMI would allot special funds for this purpose and agents already possessed ample material for such broadcasts, including adaptations of plays, lectures, and special scripts which were suitable for propaganda. There should be no overt political broadcasts in violation of local laws and programs should include announcements in the local language, as well as music and songs suited to the taste of the population. The Propaganda Ministry had already established good relations with a certain Mr. Jankielewicz, the owner of several stations in Argentina. Even though he was a Jew, he appeared ready to collaborate for possible commercial gain, and German agents were to take full advantage of this opportunity.

Motion pictures would also play an expanded part in the bid for public opinion in the Americas. To enhance the attractiveness of films produced in Germany, especially documentaries, the Nazi government was providing liberal subsidies so that exhibitors could obtain them at quite modest prices or even at no expense. Preferably these films would serve as filler material at theaters in major cities. Where there remained the practice of showing advertisements between features, operatives should encourage German merchants to make use of film commercials and to support motion picture houses which ran German documentaries. To achieve a unified impact PROMI would coordinate film and radio propaganda with other materials on tourism, culture and the New Germany.

Nor did these exhaust the possibilities the Propaganda Ministry intended to exploit. Art expositions and book displays were among the most prominent auxiliary means to impress the American peoples with the virtues and accomplishments of the Third Reich. Already preparations were under way for a touring exhibition to visit Latin America, featuring sections on the graphic arts and modern German literature. Goebbels was especially interested in disseminating National Socialist works, both in German and in foreign tongues, which would be directed mainly at university students and professors, important political factors in Latin America. They might also find a receptive audience among native fascist organizations, "Germany's natural allies."

From this elaborate discussion of the means by which the Nazis would conduct their campaign to win public opinion in this hemisphere, the directive turned to the special problem of adapting German propaganda in the Americas to the mentalities of the different countries. The Propaganda Minister emphasized the basic distinction between the Anglo-Saxon countries, Canada and the United States, and the nations of Latin America. In the former states propaganda and mass media operations had attained considerable sophistication and German propaganda would need to be very astute. Of fundamental importance was the fact that the United States had been an adversary of Germany during the last war and belligerent attitudes had persisted even to the present. Since German immigrants were rapidly assimilated in North America, "great caution is in order in the selection of all collaborators in German propaganda. This is also advisable because of the Jewish influence which is much stronger in the public life of North America than elsewhere."[15]

Several factors in the United States would be useful to German propagandists. First of all was the tendency of the people to be disinterested in European affairs and their recognition that their sacrifices in the World War had gone unrewarded. Although there was widespread sympathy for devastated France, Germany could effectively counter this by stressing the French refusal to continue payment of war debts to the United States. It would be vain to attempt to arouse enmity against Great Britain by analogous arguments, but the Germanic origins of both the English and the Americans would be valuable as a wedge in opening up a more favorable disposition toward the Reich. Goebbels sternly reminded Nazi representatives that this theme was purely for propaganda purposes, since the North Americans, unlike the British, had gravely adulterated their superior racial heritage through long years of melting pot existence. Still the racial emphasis would serve a useful function in aiding Americans to identify themselves with Germany and in developing bad feeling toward the countries of Eastern Europe. The Nazis were sure they already detected strong currents of sentiment in the United States which considered Poles and other Slavic peoples as definitely inferior to Anglo-Saxons.

Other themes could also fit into the Nazi program. As a moral argument, Goebbels' operatives would point out that the United States had not kept the pledge which President Wilson made to Germany with the

---

15. Ibid., p. 38. Assimilation of German immigrants in the United States, greatly accelerated by the events of the First World War, was a decisive difference between North and South America. For suggestive data see below, Chapter 4, p. 54 and n. 11; Chapter 6, p. 86.

Fourteen Points and his subsequent declarations. Certain influential circles, centering around Senator Borah and his associates, appeared susceptible to such an argument.

> The most important argument, however, is the view that the resurrection of a lasting prosperity in the United States is dependent on a reorganization of Europe, which can be attained only by means of a revision, that is to say a removal, of the Versailles *Diktat, because Germany would not participate in any other, insufficient reorganization.*[16]

The Propaganda Ministry expected the most telling case would be one stressing the economic advantages which the United States could secure by a cooperative posture toward Hitler's Germany. It would not be wise to protest that Germany's rights were being violated, but rather that world economy and world order were best served by Germanophile policies. Even with financial assistance from the Reich, it would be unlikely that Nazi agents could gain truly significant influence over the American press, but they could at least turn the tide of public opinion.

In Latin America Germany would have to devise its propaganda with great care in order not to disturb the Reich's delicate relations with the United States. Germany's policy of economic expansion in South America could even derive benefit from North American capital investment. The principal fact for German propagandists in Latin America to note was the Latin extraction of the population, which produced a general "sensuality" and "vanity," characteristics readily exploited. Although there was much sympathy in Latin America for downtrodden Germany, the Reich would have to combat at every opportunity the region's racial and cultural affinity for France.

The press in the area was presently anti-Reich, but Goebbels credited this to opposition to National Socialism rather than Germanophobia. He was confident that adroit propaganda could alleviate such hostility. Major papers had maintained a certain reserve toward the new Reich, but the popular press was controlled by strongly anti-Nazi groups. For this reason, agents should collaborate with local fascist organizations in Latin America to discredit the "boulevard press," making it appear that these opposition papers had sold out to Jews or other adversaries of progress. In concluding these fundamental instructions on propaganda in the Americas,

16. Ibid., p. 40. Italics in original.

the Propaganda Minister warned his representatives that they must never confide secret materials to the ordinary mails, especially in Argentina. They should dispatch all letters and confidential reports by German vessels only, and cables on urgent matters should always be in code. In the Rio de la Plata area, agents were to channel all cables through Montevideo.

These, then, were the substantial plans of the Propaganda Ministry when it assumed authority over German propaganda in the Western Hemisphere. Together with the brief review of the other principal agencies involved in German propaganda in the New World, they suggest the two central goals of the Nazi campaign:

> 1. In accord with the racial doctrines of National Socialism, to consolidate, gain control over, and enhance the power position of German elements in the several American states.
>
> 2. To win influence over public opinion in the Western Hemisphere in order to improve Germany's international position, and to weaken the power of American governments to provide effective opposition to Nazi policies and actions.

These aims were not perfectly compatible and, broadly speaking, Germany's efforts to attain the first seriously compromised attempts to achieve the second. It was to be expected that doctrines which sought to inculcate the idea of racial supremacy in one part of the population in the American nations would breed a reaction among groups relegated by Nazi theorists to an inferior status. The tendency of public opinion in the New World to be suspicious of Nazi influence among German elements in this hemisphere was amplified by the ominous course of European politics in the late nineteen-thirties and eventually played a major role in the development of a hemispheric front against the Axis menace. That Nazi propaganda ultimately failed in its efforts to influence American governments through popular opinion is obvious from the participation of the American republics in the Second World War. That it was designed to do so, however, is apparent from the master propaganda plan just discussed. To the intrigues through which the Third Reich sought to implement this design for subversion we now turn.

CHAPTER 3

Unser Amerika—A Bad Beginning

The rise of National Socialism in Germany had been paralleled by the spread of the Hitler movement among Germans in foreign countries, although the Nazi Party received its greatest impetus abroad only after Hitler came to power in the Reich. After the failure of the Beer Hall Putsch in 1923, one of the Fuehrer's devoted lieutenants, Kurt Georg Wilhelm Ludecke, fled to the United States where he became a vigorous proponent of Hitler's views. Operating independently and without financial support from the Party in Germany, Ludecke carried on a one-man propaganda campaign to enlist sympathy for the Nazi movement among Germans in the United States and the public at large, although he opposed formation of Nazi cells in this country.

Ludecke's principal task was to solicit funds for the Party's work in Germany. Noting the anti-Semitic tone of the *Dearborn Independent,* a publication controlled by Henry Ford, the Nazis hoped to gain substantial backing from the famous manufacturer. Within a month after he reached the United States in January 1924, Ludecke had wangled an interview with Ford. The meeting quickly dashed the German's dreams of tapping the tycoon's money and prestige. Although he listened with interest to Ludecke's description of the Nazi movement, the industrialist had no intention of aiding so dubious an enterprise. "The more I mentioned the word [money], the more Henry Ford cooled down from idealist to business man."[1] Ludecke was obliged to turn to less eminent figures in his search for financial support; even then, the returns were paltry and infrequent.

Other young German immigrants, impressed by Nazi racial theory and practices, sought to emulate the Hitler organization which was growing in the fatherland. Under the leadership of Fritz Gissibl a small group of hyphenates formed "Teutonia, Incorporated," an Illinois corporation with headquarters in Chicago, which adopted the basic forms and tenets of the

---

1. Kurt G. W. Ludecke, *I Knew Hitler* (New York, 1937), p. 200. Ford later abandoned his public efforts to propagate anti-Semitism, apparently because such activities proved harmful to his business interests. See also below, Chapter 11, n. 10, pp. 172–73.

Nazi Party in Germany. Although details are obscure, this group soon received the sanction of the Party and eventually became the Nazi Party, U.S.A., with locals in New York, Detroit, Milwaukee, Boston, Philadelphia, Chicago, and several other cities. Once accepted into the Party, the group took its directions from Germany. It established an official organ, *Amerika's Deutsche Post,* and began to seek converts among German communities in this country.[2]

In June 1932, while street fighting raged in Germany between Nazis, Communists, and assorted other factions, Ludecke's voluntary efforts in the United States earned him appointment as official representative of the Party in this country, as well as press representative of several Party newspapers. At the same time, however, and despite Ludecke's known opposition to such attempts, Gregor Strasser named a certain Dr. Neyland as his personal emissary to German groups in the United States. A principal contestant for power within the NSDAP, Strasser instructed Neyland to stimulate the organization of Party locals in this country as a potential source of funds for the political battles being waged in the homeland. Joseph Goebbels had wrested control of the Party's Berlin organization from Strasser, who may have hoped to revive his political fortunes by winning support among Germans living abroad.

The immediate development of strong anti-German sentiment in the United States after Hitler's designation as Chancellor on January 30, 1933, brought a sharp change of tactics by the Party. In March of that year, to avoid friction with the United States government, Berlin ordered the local Nazi cells in this country to dissolve. This did not signify the abandonment of Nazi aims to organize both Americans of German origin and German citizens resident in the United States. After conferences with Rudolph Hess, Robert Ley, and other prominent Party leaders, Heinz Spanknoebel, former leader of the Nazi group in Detroit, returned to this country in May with full authority and plans for an organization to succeed the Party. The new oganization, to be known as Friends of the New Ger-

---

2. This chapter is based largely on an extensive file of several thousand Foreign Ministry documents dealing with political and cultural propaganda in the United States, 1933–36. It is available on microfilm at the U.S. National Archives, Foreign Affairs Branch, micro-copy T–120, serials K1052–K1054, containers 4614–16. Citations will henceforth refer merely to serial and frame numbers, along with a brief description of the documents filmed. For reports on Ludecke and the origins of the Nazi Party, U.S.A., cf. serial K1054, frames K270037–52; see also House of Representatives, *Historical Sketch on Origin and Extent of Nazi Activities in the United States* (Washington, D.C., 1933), pp. 1–5.

many (*Bund der Freunde des neuen Deutschlands*), would attempt to unify the various German groups in America under Spanknoebel, who now held the title of Fuehrer of the Nazi Party in the United States. The new American Fuehrer had received assurances from Hess and his associates that the Bund would be the only officially recognized National Socialist body in the United States and Canada.[3]

During May 1933, while preparations were under way to launch the new Nazi front organization, the Hitler regime sought to soothe American apprehensions over developments in Germany, especially those concerning the persecution of Jews. Hjalmar Schacht, president of the Reichsbank, visited the United States and made a point to confer with prominent Jewish citizens who were beginning to call for a voluntary boycott on trade with Germany. Schacht sought to assure them that there was no cause for alarm over the situation of German Jews, but his declarations rang hollow in face of the abundant evidence of anti-Semitic outbursts that had already occurred in the Reich. He did not help his cause when he added a warning against outside pressure in behalf of the German Jews.[4]

As the summer of 1933 wore on, Germany's efforts to reverse the unfavorable trend of American public opinion increased. Goebbels had designated the consulate general in New York as headquarters for German propaganda in the United States and the widely respected consul general, Dr. Otto Kiep, carried out a number of measures designed to improve the German position. In May the Propaganda Ministry granted Kiep $5,000 to engage a competent advisor and a public relations firm, as well as to support the activities of a small bureau disseminating pro-German information. The consul promptly enlisted the services of George Sylvester Viereck, well-known propagandist of the World War and a man to whom we shall have frequent reference. The firm of Carl Byoir and Associates also contracted to work for the Germans, and Kiep financed the operations of Colonel Edwin Emerson, a former friend of Ernst Hanfstaengl who wished to work in behalf of the New Germany. Emerson prepared a series of news bulletins for American newspapers and magazines, discussing progress in the Reich and favoring increased German-Ameri-

---

3. Information on the formation of the Bund is contained in serial K1052, frames K269100–37; see also the Rolf Hoffmann papers, National Archives, micro-copy T–81, roll 27, frames 23970–87. See also Joachim Remak, " 'Friends of the New Germany': The Bund and German-American Relations," *Journal of Modern History*, 29 (1957), 38–41.

4. Schacht's report of his conversations with American Jewish leaders is printed in *DGFP–C, 1*, 423 f.

can trade. At the same time the colonel founded an organization named Friends of Germany (not to be confused with the Bund established by Spanknoebel) to serve the cause of German-American friendship. For his troubles Emerson obtained office space in the building which housed the German consulate general, and Kiep undertook to meet all his expenses.[5]

Another project attracted Kiep's attention in June and he forwarded details to the newly appointed ambassador to the United States, Hans Luther, who was still in the Reich. A former president of the Reichsbank, Luther had high ambitions for his new mission. It was widely rumored in Germany that his assignment to Washington was simply a convenient way to get rid of him. Luther was aware of this and was doubly anxious to produce results in the new position. Only in this way could he salvage his own power in the emerging political structure of the Reich. In the weeks before his departure for the United States, Luther was searching for promising ideas to improve relations between Berlin and Washington, and Kiep's message struck a responsive chord.

Dr. Wilbur K. Thomas, secretary of the Carl Schurz Foundation of Philadelphia, had proposed the publication of a magazine dedicated to the promotion of cordial relations between the United States and Germany. *Germany Today, An American Magazine of Goodwill* would appear ten times a year, excluding the summer months, and would seek to soften the antagonism of public opinion by concentrating on the positive accomplishments of the Third Reich. To make certain there would be a substantial audience and financial base for the enterprise, subscriptions would be tied to membership in the Schurz Foundation, in the fashion of the National Geographic Society, although nonmembers could also subscribe. The magazine would require $20,000 a year for at least the first three years. Luther recommended that the German government underwrite the venture to the extent of $10,000 annually, with the rest of the funds coming from nominal subscription fees. Existing records fail to disclose whether the ambassador's advice was accepted, but the magazine began to circulate some months later.[6]

---

5. Kiep's activities at this time are documented on serial K1052, frames K269150–162. Although he was eventually executed for plotting against the regime, Kiep seems to have served it efficiently during this period.

6. Thomas' project and Luther's report cover serial K1052, frames K269177–185. In spite of these activities Thomas assured William Dodd, the American Ambassador to Berlin, that the Foundation had ceased all propaganda in the United States. *Ambassador Dodd's Diary, 1933–1938* (New York, 1941), p. 75, entry of Jan. 26, 1934. See also Ludecke, *I Knew Hitler*, p. 576.

Before leaving the Reich, Ambassador Luther conferred at length with officials of the Propaganda Ministry to elaborate plans for propaganda in the United States. On July 6 PROMI decided to provide Kiep with $31,-000 for various projects during the last half of 1933. The Foreign Ministry, more keenly aware of the low estate to which Germany had fallen in the eyes of the American public, complained that such a pittance would be utterly insufficient, but Goebbels' office, with customary Nazi suspicion of the official foreign service, chose not to increase the allocation. As will be seen shortly, it was directing larger expenditures in the United States through other channels.

One of the major projects for which Kiep needed funds had been outlined to him by an American, Herbert Houston. Houston had succeeded in interesting the Macmillan Company in publishing a volume to be entitled *Germany Speaks.* As planned by Houston the book would have an introduction by Hitler and chapters by top-ranking Party and government officials on subjects with which they were specially concerned in the New Germany. It was thought most important that the Nazi regime provide an adequate and affirmative explanation of its views on the Jewish question. The central purpose of the work would be to "interpret the program of the present German government to the world in general and to America in particular." To make certain that the symposium was well coordinated and integrated G. S. Viereck had agreed to edit the various contributions. Work on this volume got under way in the late summer of 1933 and was to occupy the attention of these men for many months.[7]

By early August Spanknoebel had organized the *Bund der Freunde des neuen Deutschlands* and the American Fuehrer issued his initial directives, appointing his principal subordinates and proclaiming the organization's relationship to the NSDAP in the Reich. The Spanknoebel group had continued to use the former Nazi organ, *Amerika's Deutsche Post,* but difficulties with its publisher led to a crisis and Spanknoebel determined to establish a new paper for the Bund. With the financial backing of Consul General Kiep, the Bund set up a new firm, the EFDENDE Publishing Company, taking its name from the initials of the organization. On September 1, 1933, the company commenced publication of *Das Neue Deutschland,* a small weekly newspaper distributed from New York. To serve the German-Americans in the organization who had lost their knowledge of the language of the fatherland, the paper contained a special

7. Houston's outline of the project and related documents, serial K1052, frames K269162–174.

section in English, "German Outlook." Spanknoebel had already established liaison with propaganda offices in the Reich and, in exchange for intelligence and press reports on the United States, the Party's *Amt Auslandspresse* in Munich assured the Bund of ample propaganda material.

Meanwhile, developments in Germany had provided the Reich propaganda machine with a surprising and promising approach to a large part of
the American public. In spite of the fact that July had witnessed the
forced dissolution of the Catholic Center Party and the Catholic Bavarian
People's Party, as Hitler pressed forward his plan to eliminate all organized political opposition, that same month brought an unexpected agreement between the Nazi government and the Vatican. Hoping to make the
best of a bad situation, the Vatican signed a concordat with Germany
which seemed to indicate the Church's satisfaction that its interests would
not suffer unjustly in the new Reich. This afforded German propagandists
a most useful wedge to elicit sympathy among American Catholics and
other religious denominations who had been gravely worried about the
fate of their brethren under Nazi rule.

In addition to numerous and lengthy press dispatches on the subject,
Kiep sought to exploit this welcome lever still further. Operating through
Edwin Emerson he arranged for the publication of a special brochure,
entitled "Church and State in the New Germany." The pamphlet included
an English translation of the recent agreement between the Vatican and
Berlin, along with an explanatory article by a historian, Frederick F.
Schrader. In order to give the impression that the brochure was an independent American undertaking and not merely German propaganda, it
bore the imprint of Emerson's front organization, Friends of Germany.
Emerson had an initial 40,000 copies printed and mailed the pamphlet to
13,000 Catholic priests and prelates, providing two extra copies for each
parish. Kiep paid the $1,200 which the project cost, in addition to the
monthly subsidy of $500 which he had already begun to pay Colonel
Emerson. On Emerson's instructions the printer, a "loyal German and
member of the Bund," left the type standing for a second edition of
10,000 copies to be sent to the Lutheran and German Evangelical clergy in
the United States.[8]

8. Kiep's confidential memorandum on this affair, serial K1052, frames K269215–
221. Material on the founding of *Das Neue Deutschland* is found in Kiep's dispatches
of August and September 1933, serial K1052, frames K269192–206; also see the Hoffmann papers, loc. cit. Not all efforts to improve German-American relations were inspired by the Nazis. A group of United States veterans led by Congressman Edward
R. Burke of Nebraska initiated one noteworthy project. In a letter to Hitler of Sep-

While the consul general was carrying out these plans, friction began to develop in Berlin between the Foreign Ministry and PROMI over the methods of financing Kiep's propaganda activities. At the request of the Propaganda Ministry, which claimed it had no funds immediately available to meet Kiep's expenses, the Foreign Ministry had forwarded several thousand dollars to the consul. The latter office balked, however, when PROMI asked it to send Kiep an additional $15,000 in early October. Dr. Hans Dieckhoff of the Foreign Ministry frankly feared that his department would have difficulty settling accounts with the Goebbels office and that the Foreign Ministry would end up having to bear the whole expense for propaganda activities in the United States without having control over the operations. Therefore he informed PROMI that it should send funds from its own budget directly to its agents in the United States. The two ministries were to bicker repeatedly over such matters, with each being both suspicious and disdainful of the other.[9]

By the autumn of 1933 the ostentatious conduct of Heinz Spanknoebel had begun to arouse a reaction in this country. Fearful that his continued activities would do further harm to Germany's position, the Party's *Aussenpolitisches Amt* cancelled his assignment on September 23 and ordered him to hand over leadership of the Bund to Fritz Gissibl. But a number of Spanknoebel's directives, publicly announcing the Bund to be the official Nazi organization in the United States and revealing Spanknoebel's connections with the Reich, had already come to light and triggered a series of events.

The American investigative processes went swiftly into action. On October 10 Congressman Samuel Dickstein of New York, chairman of the House Committee on Immigration and Naturalization, announced his plans to conduct an investigation of Nazi agents who were thought to have entered the United States under false representations. Exaggerated

---

tember 13, 1933, he indicated that he was anxious to promote German-American amity and that he had begun a campaign to hold the 1936 convention of the American Legion in Berlin. He requested an immediate and enthusiastic invitation from the Fuehrer in order to aid his promotional work during the Chicago convention of the group in October 1933. Burke claimed that he could get at least 50,000 veterans and their friends to Berlin for 1936. The cool reception which this proposal met in Berlin was understandable. It would hardly have done to have the victorious and nationalistic American veterans parading around the capital of the defeated nation to which Hitler was preaching of its own racial and military superiority. Burke's letter was shunted to the Foreign Ministry and there is no record of any reply to it. See serial K1052, frame K269266.

9. See the file note by Dieckhoff, Oct. 4, 1933, serial K1052, frame K269222.

reports were circulating that Goebbels had sent three hundred propagandists with millions of dollars to subvert American public opinion. Ambassador Luther, acting on strict instructions, immediately saw Secretary of State Hull and denounced such claims as "pure fabrication." Meanwhile, Professor Frank Boas of Columbia publicly requested Congressman Dickstein's investigation to focus also on the activities of German exchange students at American universities. Boas cited an official order requiring German students in foreign countries to spread Hitler propaganda. An anxious Ambassador Luther noted in his report on the subject that the order described by Boas followed one printed in the official Nazi Party paper, *Voelkischer Beobachter,* on August 19, 1933.[10]

On October 26 William Phillips of the State Department formally inquired of the German embassy whether Spanknoebel was a representative of the German government as he had claimed in certain publications. Luther promptly replied in the negative, but he learned on November 6 that the Department of Justice intended to prosecute Spanknoebel as an unregistered agent of a foreign government and that a warrant had gone out for the Fuehrer's arrest. Four days later a New York grand jury indicated it would investigate the *Bund der Freunde des neuen Deutschlands.* In the meantime Spanknoebel, having been warned that action against him was imminent, had entered hiding and then secretly fled the country. Representative Dickstein announced that his committee's inquiry would commence on November 20. Reaction against the incipient Nazi activities in the United States was beginning to coalesce.

Samuel Untermeyer, a principal figure in the movement to establish the anti-German boycott, declared before an audience in Cleveland that Ambassador Luther had really come to the United States for propaganda purposes. He asserted that the Nazi Reich was spending $3,000,000 a year on propaganda abroad and that much of this sum was being funneled through the German embassy in Washington. This set off a wave of speculation in the press and a number of papers did not hesitate to attack the new German ambassador. Luther visited Secretary Hull to deny the allegations and complained bitterly about the charges being made against him in the press. He declared Untermeyer's remarks to be a serious affront. Hull expressed his regret over the incident and a State Department press release, issued to salve Luther's diplomatic dignity, indicated the govern-

10. Exchanges between the embassy in Washington and Berlin during October 1933 are filmed as serial K1052, frames K269226–265. The New York papers carried a statement by Professor Boas on October 27, 1933.

ment's concern over the attacks on the ambassador. This only provoked a renewed outburst from Untermeyer who reiterated his assertions and rebuked Hull for his readiness to accept the German ambassador's assurances.[11]

It was becoming apparent even to the most devoted Party officials that the unexpected intensity of the opposition to any and all forms of Nazi activity in the United States required another strategic retreat. During October Captain F. C. Mensing of the New York office of North German Lloyd Shipping Lines, accompanied by another Reich citizen then living in the United States, Walter Schellenberg, journeyed to Berlin to discuss the increasing anti-German sentiment in America. Mensing was chief representative of the Nazi *Auslandsorganisation* in this country, and he impressed upon his superiors the need to adopt a new policy. In conversations with Rudolph Hess and Ernst Bohle of the AO, Mensing and Schellenberg were able to gain the Party's concurrence on several points.

Henceforth only Reich citizens could be members of the Party, and Bohle, as the leader of all members abroad, would order those in the United States to cease all political activity. The Friends of the New Germany would have to take on a more American aspect and the German nationals who controlled the organization would have to surrender its leadership to an American citizen. There would, however, be no objection to Party members continuing in the Bund, provided it limited its activities to nonpolitical areas. Bohle agreed to instruct a Nazi who had been living in the United States for some time to see that these points were carried out. With these major changes decided upon, Mensing and Schellenberg informed the Foreign Ministry that Party activity in the United States would stop. The Wilhelmstrasse duly notified the American ambassador in Berlin of the ruling. The Nazis hoped that this would suffice to calm public misgivings in the United States.[12]

Events continued to compound public anxieties over Nazi activities in the United States. In the midst of the furor over Spanknoebel and the

11. This incident is adequately documented in the *New York Times,* in editions covering the period November 1–7, 1933. Untermeyer had represented the German embassy and other German interests during the First World War without a retainer, mainly, it is believed, because of his wife's ardent sympathies for the Central Powers. At that time he was a close colleague of G. S. Viereck.

12. Memorandum by A. Fuehr of the Foreign Ministry, Oct. 16, 1933, *DGFP–C,* 2, 5–8. In fact German nationals and Nazis, notably Fritz Gissibl and Walter Kappe, continued to lead the Bund. Like other orders in the future, this action by Bohle was merely a formal attempt to convince the United States that there was no Nazi complicity in the organization.

Friends, Georg Schmitt arrived in New York. Schmitt was a leader of the German veterans organization, *Stahlhelm,* which had long fought the Hitler movement but which recently had undergone the usual coordination with the Nazi regime. He had come to the United States with full powers to effect a reorganization of the *Stahlhelm* groups in this country and to integrate their operations with other German organizations. Unmindful of the effect on American public opinion, Schmitt displayed his credentials to reporters who met him at the dock. The next day he conferred with the new consul general, Dr. Johannes Borchers, who advised him that it was unnecessary to register with the State Department. Schmitt had proposed to do so in order to avoid the difficulties encountered by Spanknoebel. He also met with Fritz Gissibl, Spanknoebel's successor as *Bundesleiter,* and Baron Benno von Stulpnagel, leader of the *Stahlhelm* in the United States.

All these conferences served to create a general impression, as Borchers reported to the Foreign Ministry, that Schmitt had come to the United States to continue Spanknoebel's efforts. Ambassador Luther warned that, in the current situation, Schmitt might very well be deported. He advised the Foreign Ministry to adopt an attitude of the greatest reserve in its treatment of American sensibilities in this matter. Agents like Spanknoebel and Schmitt, he continued, simply should not come to this country. The dispatch of individuals with full powers and specific Party assignments was bound to cause highly unfavorable publicity, since, if they were discovered, their activities were thought to be subversive of American interests.

Dr. Otto H. F. Vollbehr, a confidential agent and propagandist long active for the Nazis in the United States, seconded the recommendations of the official Reich representatives. Vollbehr reported to his superior, Dr. Kurt Johannsen in Hamburg, that the Spanknoebel affair had severely damaged his efforts and that he was astonished by Schmitt's assignment. He pleaded for a more effective propaganda campaign to meet the increasingly hostile attitude in the United States, and he stressed the importance of greater secrecy in German operations.[13]

13. See Vollbehr's report to Johannsen, Nov. 8, 1933, and related Foreign Ministry documents, serial K1052, frames K269269–280. Vollbehr continued his efforts for several years, sending out "memoranda" to influential Americans and lengthy reports to Johannsen, who dutifully passed them on to PROMI, the Foreign Ministry, and other offices. His propaganda activities were seriously hampered by his own less than adequate English; e.g. he took an indication in *Who's Who* that Professor E. M. Earle was a member of the Council on Foreign Relations to mean that Earle was an interna-

The Foreign Ministry had recalled the former consul general in New York, Kiep, because of its fear that discovery of his propaganda activities would seriously compromise the entire diplomatic and consular establishment of the Reich. But the Propaganda Ministry's principal agent, Dr. Richard Sallet, remained in the United States. Sallet had been named press attaché of the German embassy over the strong opposition of the Wilhelmstrasse. In order to preserve his secret connections his position had not been made public and Germany had not informed the Department of State of his presence in an official capacity. During the summer and fall of 1933 Sallet's activities had centered on New York rather than Washington and he had been instrumental in numerous enterprises, the creation of the Bund and its paper, the Houston and Viereck book scheme, and others. The several investigations now under way made his position precarious, to say the least, and the Foreign Ministry urged his immediate recall, for his interrogation by the Dickstein committee could greatly endanger Reich interests.

PROMI was reluctant to withdraw Sallet, however, and insisted that its agent be accorded protection as a member of the embassy. Back from the Wilhelmstrasse came the reply that, in view of Sallet's involvement with Spanknoebel and other known propagandists, it would be out of the question to seek diplomatic immunity for him. The Goebbels office remained adamant and refused to order Sallet back to the Reich, although it agreed to suspend its activities temporarily and declared icily that his attachment to the embassy would not be necessary for the execution of his assignment. To emphasize its determination to maintain its agent in the United States, PROMI sent Sallet $6,000 with which he was to obtain legal counsel as to how he might best meet the dangers of the Dickstein investigation.

In order to prevent the continuation and extension of the investigations of Nazi activities, Sallet recommended in November two urgent countermeasures, which he thought would stifle the public outcry before it grew louder. He advised the Propaganda Ministry to issue a prompt invitation to a selected group of American Congressmen to visit Germany in January. There they could seek to determine the exact sources of the propaganda

---

tional lawyer (i.e. "counsel"). His reports aroused only contempt at the Foreign Ministry, where Dieckhoff noted typically in the margin of one: "A superfluous and misleading report, which can only lead to mischief." See serial K1054, frame K270273. Vollbehr's attempts to propagandize American professors who visited Germany brought him several rebukes from Ambassador Dodd; see *Ambassador Dodd's Diary, 1933–1938*, pp. 60 ff.

allegedly being sent to the United States and could draw up a list of so-called Nazi persecutions. PROMI could, of course, carefully supervise their inquiry to insure the right results to provide Germany a propaganda coup. Secondly, with a ruthlessness that the world would come to expect of Nazis, Sallet proposed that Spanknoebel, whose mission had ended in such miserable failure, should be tried promptly *by Germany.*

Ambassador Luther and the Foreign Ministry rejected both these measures, the first as "inopportune" and the second as unwise. "The name, Spanknoebel," wrote Luther, "should in my opinion be allowed to sink into oblivion, and its appearance in German publicity should henceforth be avoided."[14] The ambassador correctly estimated that Congress would authorize further investigations and that Sallet's proposals to head them off would only serve to magnify American anxieties. Finally, the Propaganda Ministry agreed to Luther's position; nevertheless, Sallet received $3,000 to carry out unspecified countermeasures against the developing wave of inquests.

While the Nazi government debated as to the best means to meet the deterioration of the German position, a New York grand jury proceeded with its efforts to unravel the history of National Socialism in that state. When a Reich citizen and Nazi named Roell refused to produce a list of the Party members in New York he was quickly prosecuted and imprisoned. Werner Haag, a prominent figure in the Bund and the American Nazi movement, complained to the Party leadership in the Reich about the lack of diplomatic support for *Reichsdeutsche* who were involved in such incidents, but the Wilhelmstrasse was taking every step it considered feasible. The Foreign Ministry praised the New York consul general, Borchers, for maintaining outward restraint while secretly providing legal and financial assistance to those under investigation. Luther delivered two strong protests to the State Department over the action against Roell. Consoling themselves in the usual fashion, Nazi diplomats and other agents blamed all their difficulties in this country on "Jewish wirepullers" such as Dickstein and Untermeyer.

Seeking to cripple Dickstein's efforts to gain Congressional approval for a full-scale inquiry in 1934, Viereck and Houston speeded up their prepa-

14. Luther's telegraphic dispatch to the Foreign Ministry, Nov. 21, 1933, serial K1053, frame K269317. This section draws largely on the exchanges between PROMI, the Wilhelmstrasse, Washington, and New York, K269310–355. In fact, after some months of personal obscurity and hardship, Spanknoebel managed to redeem himself and eventually became a general in the SS; O. John Rogge, *The Official German Report* (New York, 1961), pp. 17–21.

rations for publication of the symposium on the New Germany. Through Luther, Borchers, and their contacts in the Reich they pressed for early completion of the articles they had requested from various ministers and Party officials. Viereck was especially interested in material on the German Labor Front from its director, Dr. Robert Ley, to dispel "certain misconceptions" of the American Federation of Labor. He also made plans to publish individual articles in magazines and newspapers prior to collecting them all in a single volume. This would amplify both the circulation and the effectiveness of the project. Viereck envisaged a total of thirty-four contributions, totaling 80,000 to 85,000 words and tightly edited to produce a unified impression. Several essays were to be published in late 1933 and the book was scheduled for January 1934, timed, as Sallet's abortive recommendations had been, to coincide with the opening of Congress and the expected campaign for a major Congressional investigation.

Unexpected problems soon emerged to complicate and delay the scheme. Sallet, who had played a key role in the plan, reported to PROMI in November that the article by Ley failed to meet the criteria of being informative and developing a concrete image of the New Reich. The Propaganda Ministry, having gotten the powerful Nazi labor leader to write the piece in the first place, hesitated to tell him that it was unsatisfactory, and chose instead to order that it be used in its original form.

At the same time Nazi propaganda efforts suffered another setback. The American publishing firm of John Day and Company, after reading extracts from the proposed manuscript, had agreed to print an English edition of Hitler's speeches. On receiving the complete text, the publisher discovered that the addresses were incomplete and included only the passages which the Nazis would want published in the United States. Most notably, there was no allusion to the fate of Jews in Hitler's Germany. Day forthwith canceled the contract. "To publish such a volume would be making ourselves the instruments of Nazi propaganda rather than fulfilling our true function as publishers, which is to publish the truth and not to hide it."[15] Scrupulous publishers learned early that dealing with Nazi propagandists was a hazardous enterprise.

15. Day's cancellation of the contract was reported to the press on Nov. 19, 1933; cf. serial K1053, frame K269316. Other sources for this discussion are Viereck's letter to Luther, Oct. 17, 1933, and related documents, serial K1052, frames K269275–281; and Borchers' report to the Foreign Ministry, Nov. 18, 1933, serial K1053, frame K269313.

CHAPTER 4

Unser Amerika—Growing Frustrations

On January 3, 1934, Representative Dickstein introduced House Resolution 199 providing for the investigation of Nazi propaganda activities in the United States and related questions. Aided by his own preliminary findings and the publicity surrounding Spanknoebel and the Bund, Dickstein was able to maneuver his measure through the House with a minimum of difficulty. It was passed on March 20, with an appropriation of $10,000, later supplemented by an additional allocation of $25,000. John McCormack of Massachusetts became chairman of the special investigating committee. Operating mainly in executive session and under the exemplary chairmanship of Congressman McCormack, the committee worked through most of 1934 and submitted its report on February 15, 1935, calling attention to the budding activities of Nazi and other fascist groups in the United States and their connections with authoritarian movements in Europe.[1]

Congressional debate over creation of the McCormack Committee coincided with a number of incidents involving German ships suspected of transporting subversive literature to this country. Customs officials boarded and searched the North German Lloyd liner *Bremen,* as it arrived in New York on January 19, 1934. They discovered little besides a copy or two of *Mein Kampf.* Ambassador Luther registered a protest with the State Department over the peremptory action, but German protests were weakened when a similar search of the freighter *Este* on February 5 produced several hundred pounds of propaganda against Jews and Bolsheviks in English,

---

1. Cf. *Congressional Record,* 74th Cong., 1st Sess., Feb. 15, 1935, p. 2049; House Special Committee on Un-American Activities, *Investigation of Nazi and Other Propaganda* (Washington, 1935); August Raymond Ogden, *The Dies Committee* (Washington, 1945), p. 32. Transcripts of the executive hearings, allegedly containing many remarks slandering innocent individuals, are sealed in the Library of Congress and may be opened only by Act of Congress. However, the Germans managed to obtain copies of the more important ones and detailed reports of still others, apparently through an anonymous but cooperative member of the committee's staff, and I have made use of them. They are scattered through the files filmed as serial K1052.

Spanish, and German. E. W. Hunt, legal adviser to the German ship- ping lines, indicated to them that there was little basis for complaint since the items seized by American authorities had not been listed on the cargo manifest and United States legislation afforded liberal competence for such action. Hunt deplored this kind of incident as rendering impossible the task of Germany's friends in this country.

These events prompted the Foreign Ministry to instruct German ship- owners to take very precaution to avoid such occurrences in the future, and always to make sure that manifests included all cargo. Concomitantly, the Propaganda Ministry issued strict orders on March 22 that agencies in the Reich could no longer send propaganda in bundle form to the United States; they were henceforth to mail only individual items to precise addresses.[2]

The progress of the Dickstein resolution through the House, coupled with repeated admonitions from Luther and other diplomatic represent- atives in the United States, led the AO to take a drastic step. In order to prevent misunderstandings with the American government, *Gauleiter* Bohle issued a general order, dated February 1, 1934, forbidding Party members to belong to the *Bund der Freunde des neuen Deutschlands* or any similar organization. The order explicitly declared that the Bund was "not an organization of the NSDAP officially recognized by the Party but a purely American organization." Bohle did not make the circular public, for the Party did not wish to discourage other Bund members, but Ger- many confidentially communicated the substance of the order to the United States government through the Berlin embassy. Meanwhile, the Party was apparently still considering the possibility of maintaining a se- cret organization in America, for Ambassador Luther found it necessary to warn "urgently" against plans to reestablish local Nazi cells in this coun- try.

The Germans narrowly avoided a further complication that same month. On February 9 the Gestapo reported that Captain Mensing's role as AO representative in the United States had almost been exposed. Men- sing, it will be recalled, was attached to the North German Lloyd office in New York where he had been serving as Nazi recruiter. The Party care-

2. Cf. Hunt's letter to Christian Beck of the German shipping line's New York office, Feb. 7, 1934, serial K1053, frame K269430; PROMI order of Mar. 22, 1934, serial K1053, frame K269495; Foreign Ministry instructions to German shipowners, Mar. 14, 1934, serial K1053, frame K269442.

lessly sent the records pertaining to some five hundred members in New York to Mensing's private address, and American authorities intercepted the documents. The Nazis were barely able to prevent the exposure and prosecution of their representative and other Party members by hiring an unnamed "New York racketeer" to steal the evidence and return it to Mensing. "Had we not gotten the package back, Mensing would have landed in prison, and Dickstein would have waged a great propaganda campaign against Germany with the five hundred admissions records from New York and would have proved that official agencies of the NSDAP had an informer in America." The Gestapo demanded greater caution in communications with agents in the United States.

This incident contributed to the decision by PROMI, already mentioned, which prohibited the sending of large batches of propaganda materials to this country. On March 26 Bohle ordered Mensing and Gissibl to cease their recruiting activities, but Gissibl, a Reich citizen and Party member, retained his post as head of the Bund in spite of the AO directive of February 1. Gissibl's continued leadership of the organization and other evidence of Nazi participation in the Bund suggest that the Party never intended to enforce the instructions of February 1, but had devised them merely to placate the United States government.[3]

In yet another attempt to moderate the strong American reaction to Nazi activities, the Propaganda Ministry recalled Dr. Sallet to the Reich early in 1934, thus suspending the operations of its principal agent. This was to be only a temporary interruption and by March, even in the face of the passage of Dickstein's investigative measure, PROMI was pressing the Wilhelmstrasse to permit Sallet's immediate return to Washington as press attaché to the embassy. Only the most vigorous opposition from Ambassador Luther and Dr. Dieckhoff of the Foreign Ministry succeeded in delaying Sallet's return. The two ministries eventually reached a compromise under which Sallet worked in the Foreign Ministry to familiarize himself with official procedures and did not resume his activities in the United States until June 1934.

German desires to assuage American concern over subversive propaganda stemmed in part from Berlin's own anxiety over declining German-American trade. The 1923 commercial agreement between the two

---

3. See the exchanges between the German embassy and Berlin during early February, *DGFP–C, 2,* 467 and 492; and the report by Dr. Gotthardt of the Gestapo, serial K1053, frames K269473–476.

governments had provided for renegotiation after ten years, and trade relations now appeared uncertain. Foreign Minister von Neurath instructed Luther to seek negotiations on the matter at an early date, for Germany's balance of trade and foreign exchange holdings were increasingly serious problems. To retrieve the situation Reich economic experts hoped to bolster exports to the United States, and Germany directed its ambassador to inquire whether the State Department would be willing to receive a special trade delegation to conduct the talks. Luther dutifully made his proposals to Secretary Hull, who welcomed them, but the Secretary noted that the timing of the delegation's visit was politically inopportune. Hull's keen political sensitivity made him aware of how deeply Nazi intrigues in the United States had aroused the Congress. He feared that negotiations with Germany on commercial questions would jeopardize legislative approval of the Administration's tariff plans.[4]

On March 3, 1934, the day of Luther's conference with Hull on trade relations, the German ambassador learned to his alarm that the American Jewish Congress, the driving force behind the effective voluntary boycott of German goods, planned to hold a mock trial in Madison Square Garden. The proceedings, cosponsored by the A.F. of L. and scheduled for March 7, were to be held under the title "Civilization Against Hitlerism, a presentation of the factual record of laws and acts of the Hitler regime." Widespread publicity left no doubt that the affair would revolve around the person of the Reich Chancellor. The chairman of the American Jewish Congress even sent Luther a telegram suggesting that he provide counsel for the defense. The ambassador, of course, ignored the invitation and delivered a series of sharp warnings to the State Department, calling Hull's attention to "this impossible incident." In Berlin Foreign Minister von Neurath called in Ambassador Dodd and sternly lectured him on the serious consequences of such a meeting.

The State Department went to considerable lengths to have the trial called off but without success. Hull's genuine anguish over the affair impressed Luther, but the demonstration took place as planned. The German ambassador was sympathetic to the constitutional limitations on any federal attempt to suppress a public gathering, and he advised Berlin to ignore

4. Germany denounced the 1923 trade agreement in 1934, but it was renewed the following year by an exchange of notes, deleting the most-favored-nation clause. Cf. von Neurath's instructions to Luther, Feb. 27, 1934, and the ambassador's report of his conversations with Hull, Mar. 3, 1934, *DGFP–C, 2,* 537–39 and 551.

the incident in its statements to the press. The Reich closed the matter diplomatically by delivery of a strong protest, but the mock trial provided dramatic illustration of the anti-German currents rising in many quarters in the United States.[5]

When Neurath complained about the episode, Ambassador Dodd had responded with remonstrances of his own against Nazi propaganda, displaying a pamphlet recently sent abroad to remind all racial Germans of their alleged duty to retain their allegiance to the Reich. The Foreign Office regretted the distribution of such material, but indicated that it had no power to control it under the new regime. On March 7, 1934, the ambassador carried the issue to Hitler himself, only to be met with the Fuehrer's pretended astonishment. "Ach, that is all Jewish lies; if I find out who does that, I will put him out of the country at once." The interview was punctuated by Hitler's frequent outbursts against the Jews; he threatened darkly that if agitation over the Reich's anti-Semitic policy continued in other countries he would make an end of all Jews in Germany.

By April the much-delayed book project of Herbert Houston and G. S. Viereck was approaching completion. Viereck asked Luther to approve a draft of the volume. The perceptive ambassador frankly declared the work to be a poorly coordinated compilation and quite unsatisfactory. "In its present form, I fear that the book would not only be of no use, but might produce harmful results. It contains too many superficial attacks on critics hostile to us." He sent the draft to Germany and recommended that Sallet, who was still there, make the necessary revisions. Thus publication of the volume was again postponed. Even after Sallet had made revisions, Macmillan rejected it as unfit for release and demanded further wholesale changes. The long-planned symposium was not to appear until 1938 and then through a smaller publisher in Great Britain.[6]

April brought no relief from the succession of difficulties experienced by Nazi propagandists. After the ill-fated and overly bold efforts of Heinz Spanknoebel, his creations—the EFDENDE Publishing Company and the newspaper *Das Neue Deutschland*—collapsed immediately. They were

---

5. Cf. exchanges between Berlin and Washington, Mar. 3–8, 1934, DGFP–C, 2, 552–57, 565 f., and 574. A report of the mock trial is contained in the *New York Times,* Mar. 8, 1934. See also *Ambassador Dodd's Diary, 1933–1938,* pp. 86–89.

6. See Luther's report to the Foreign Ministry, Apr. 4, 1934, serial K1053, frame K269581. See also *Germany Speaks,* with an introduction by Joachim von Ribbentrop (London, 1938).

succeeded by the D Z Publishing Corporation and another weekly, *Deutsche Zeitung*. But the change, as one of the ranking assistants of the former U.S. Fuehrer declared, was "for strategic reasons only," intended to throw off suspicion while the group continued its propaganda work. The new journal remained under the editorship of a Nazi, Walter Kappe, although the officers and directors of the corporation were American citizens.

The establishment of *Das Neue Deutschland* and then of *Deutsche Zeitung* had left the publisher of the original Nazi organ, *Amerika's Deutsche Post,* in something of a predicament, and he saw in the formation of the McCormack Committee a possible means of recouping his losses. The publisher, Friedrich Heiss, tried to blackmail the German authorities. He paid a visit to Consul General Borchers on April 16 and threatened to sue for damages resulting from alleged promises of financial support from former Consul General Kiep and the Nazi *Ortsgruppe* in New York. Heiss claimed to have additional incriminating material regarding the Spanknoebel affair and demanded $5,000 to remain silent. Borchers, greatly alarmed that Heiss might cause dangerous complications, urged the Foreign Ministry to provide $2,500 to the D Z Publishing Corporation for the purchase of the now worthless properties of Heiss. But officials of the *Deutsche Zeitung* thought that Heiss might actually be a stooge of Dickstein and feared that attempts to buy his silence would only be taken by the committee as proof of former subversive activities. Therefore, the Nazis paid no money to Heiss, even when he renewed his threats to publish correspondence with Spanknoebel which would revive the recent cause célèbre.[7]

As the preliminary investigations of the McCormack Committee commenced in the spring of 1934, the State Department saw fit to make a formal statement to the German government regarding the extensive reports of Nazi activities in the United States. The Department called in Ambassador Luther and informed him that "any spread of the organization of the NSDAP to American soil, even in limited form, would be ill regarded by a great number of American citizens, especially in times of tension and political excitement." Luther had been reporting substantially

7. Cf. Borchers' telegraphic dispatch of Apr. 16, 1934, and replies to it, serial I1053, frames K269528–33. Heiss never carried out his threat, although he did eventually testify before the McCormack group. He added nothing to what was already known.

the same thing to Berlin for months, and this first official declaration by the Roosevelt Administration afforded the ambassador another occasion to emphasize the importance of restraint by the Party in all relations with Germans in the United States.

If exposures in the Spanknoebel case had been sensational, the disclosures before the McCormack Committee in the summer of 1934 seemed to confirm the worst apprehensions of many Americans. We have previously noted that PROMI had funneled sizable sums through channels other than the consulate general in New York. These now came to light. A number of individuals active in anti-Semitic or pro-German propaganda revealed that they had received financial support from Kiep, but the most important exposé concerned German contracts with the public relations experts Carl Dickey, Carl Byoir, and Ivy Lee.

Dickey testified that his firm, Carl Byoir and Associates, had a contract for $6,000 a month to promote tourism in the Reich. The agreement ran for eighteen months and totaled $108,000, to be paid through the German Tourist Information Bureau in New York. From this retainer G. S. Viereck was to receive $1,750 a month for editorial advice. Ivy Lee described a $50,000 annual contract, financed through I. G. Farben, to promote German trade. Dickey also testified that Kiep had paid him $4,000 to spread favorable news concerning Germany and to place articles on the Jewish question in American papers. With the assistance of Viereck, whom Kiep paid an additional monthly retainer of $500, Dickey published the *German-American Economic Bulletin* to stimulate trade with the Reich; it was mailed regularly to some 3,000 large corporations, newspapers and magazines. Much of this public relations work might have seemed innocuous were it not for Goebbels' detailed and explicit instructions of the previous September, specifying the political uses of tourist and economic propaganda.

In July 1934 Viereck testified in executive session that he had indeed been on Kiep's payroll since March 1933. Besides offering general advice on public relations and other matters, he had edited a series of pamphlets entitled *Speaking of Hitler*. These contained excerpts from American newspapers arranged so as to produce a flattering image of the new German Chancellor. In addition Viereck had received several thousand dollars to provide free transportation for American journalists assigned to Germany, hoping thereby to ingratiate himself and his German sponsors to these correspondents. Viereck denied that there was anything out of order about his activities in behalf of Germany. He vehemently disclaimed any anti-Semitism and argued that he acted purely out of pro-German, as distinguished from pro-Nazi sentiments.

> The man who founded *The Fatherland* in 1914 and continued to publish it throughout the World War needs no financial inducement to be pro-German. I was a friend of imperial Germany. I was the friend of Republican Germany. I am a friend of Adolph Hitler's Germany. . . . The son of a German father and an American mother, I always regarded it almost a consecration to interpret the land of my fathers to the land of my children.[8]

This appears to have been an honest and forthright expression of Viereck's convictions. That he was not a Nazi himself is certain, but that he was deeply impressed by the progress of the Third Reich and willing to work in its service, he himself admitted to the committee.

Byoir, Dickey, Lee, and Viereck may all have thought they were engaged in perfectly legitimate advertising programs, but the fact that the Nazi regime expected more than merely commercial publicity was clear in the reaction of Richard Sallet, who had returned to Washington as propaganda attaché in June, to the discoveries made by the House committee.

> Since the Dickstein investigation has resulted in exposing the links between German agencies and the two publicity firms, Byoir-Dickey-

---

8. Viereck released a statement containing these remarks to the Associated Press and the *New York Times;* cf. the latter, June 6, 1934. His close association with Reich agents is reflected in the many reports he filed with German authorities; see serial K1053, frames K269616–686, for reports on the congressional inquiry, to which the Nazis invariably referred as the Dickstein investigation to identify the "Jewish wire-puller" responsible for their troubles. A transcript of the executive session of June 27, 1934, at which Viereck appeared is contained in these same files, K269799 ff. Viereck had been dazzled by Hitler long before 1933. He had provided America with probably the earliest intimate glimpse of the Fuehrer ten years before the Nazis came to power. After an interview with the obscure provincial politician who was beginning to attract attention in Germany, Viereck described Hitler as a widely read, thoughtful, and self-made man, with a surprisingly mild manner for one with such aggressive opinions. Although he made clear his disapproval of Hitler's anti-Semitism, Viereck concluded with a favorable and prophetic summary:

> Hitler can probably summon more men to arms than the commander in chief of the German army. His organization compels respect. Hitler is honest. He is an idealist, however mistaken, who freely risks his life and his health for his cause. . . . If he lives, Hitler, for better or worse, is sure to make history.

Viereck wrote these striking remarks only weeks before the Beer Hall Putsch; cf. G. S. Viereck, "Hitler, The German Explosive," *American Monthly, 15* (October 1923), 15.

Viereck and Ivy Lee, their usefulness to us is almost entirely at an end. . . . The mysterious influence which these firms were supposed to exercise over the press has turned out to be an empty promise.[9]

Luther endorsed Sallet's appraisal. He pointed out that the contract with Byoir and Associates required three months notice before cancellation and urged PROMI to terminate the arrangement immediately. The Propaganda Ministry, however, felt that such precipitate action would be too obvious. It decided instead that George Schmitz, director of the German Tourist Information Bureau in the United States, should seek to reduce the size of fees paid for services under the agreement.

The boycott on German goods, sparked by the American Jewish Congress, continued to make itself felt during 1934. The campaign against trade with Germany featured an "International Trade Fair," held in New York October 22 to October 27, 1934. An organization known as the Board of Trade for German-American Commerce, Inc., was now mobilizing opposition to the boycott. This effort was under the leadership of Albert Degener and operated principally through personal contacts and correspondence with important business leaders in the United States. In addition the Board engaged in some general propaganda activities to develop goodwill for Germany.

As the year proceeded, the *Deutsche Zeitung,* still the principal outlet among pro-Nazi German-American circles, began to experience financial difficulties. The danger arose that it would soon be bankrupt. By September the D Z Publishing Corporation had an $18,000 deficit and the New York consulate general sought to relieve its distress. Borchers estimated that it would take $3,000 a month to sustain the enterprise and he tried to convince Berlin that the expenditure was necessary. Germany desperately needed the *Deutsche Zeitung,* he reported, to respond to the generally hostile American press. The paper had remained under independent control and the Nazis on its staff had moved into the background to avoid arousing suspicion, but effective direction of its policies and content had come from the original group of Spanknoebel's cohorts who dominated the Bund. Before Borchers could advance very far with his plans to bail the

---

9. Sallet's report to PROMI, Aug. 3, 1934, *DGFP-C, 3,* 1111–15; see also the exchanges between PROMI, the Foreign Ministry, and Washington, serial K1054, frames K269910–935. Sallet's dispatch of August 3 made a number of suggestions for propaganda countermeasures, two of which were later carried out in slightly altered form; viz., the establishment of an official German Library of Information and the publication of a comprehensive yearbook in English.

paper out of its financial predicament, its editor was convicted of libeling a Jewish judge and sent to prison. This ended the usefulness of the paper. Both Borchers and the Bund severed all connections with it, leaving it to an early demise. The Bund now set up yet another organ, the *Deutscher Beobachter,* its staff practically identical with that of the former paper.[10]

The congressional investigation had seriously hampered the activities of the German consulate general in New York and PROMI's chief agent, Sallet, but agencies in Germany continued to pour significant quantities of anti-Semitic and pro-Nazi propaganda into the United States. The Reich disseminated the myth of Nordic supremacy through the long-established contacts of the DAI, VDA, the *Fichtebund,* and a new agency known as *Welt-Dienst,* or World Service, which operated out of Erfurt. These organizations maintained extensive mailing lists of individual German-Americans, anti-Semitic individuals and groups, newspapers, magazines, and other media which offered promise of effective exploitation. Their efforts were handicapped not only by general antipathy for their views in this country, but by the fact that rapid assimilation had reduced their principal target, i.e., the elements among German immigrants and their descendants who retained their distinct language and culture, to almost insignificant proportions.

One of the most important measures of this decline in German separatist inclinations was the shrinking number and circulation of German-language papers in this country. There had been 750 German papers in the United States in 1904, many of them prosperous and substantial. After the war, in 1924, there remained only 225 and the figure fell off steadily with each passing year until by 1940 there would only be 118. Most of these journals were small local weeklies or even monthlies with extremely limited circulation. The trend toward extinction of the German-language press made it increasingly difficult for agencies in the Third Reich to channel their materials to large groups of Americans of German extraction. What is more, many of the remaining German papers were staunchly anti-Nazi and refused to cooperate in any fashion with the suspect propagandists of the Reich.[11]

10. Borchers' reports to Berlin of Sept. 18 and Nov. 14, 1934, serial K1054, frames K269989 ff. and K270059. Cf. also the letter from Werner Haag of the Bund and the *Deutsche Zeitung* to Rolf Hoffmann, Jan. 26, 1934, Hoffman papers, roll 27, frame 24329.

11. The decline of the German press in the United States is recorded in the annual editions of N. W. Ayer and Son's *Directory of Newspapers and Perodicals* (Philadelphia, 1880–), 1904, p. 1455; 1924, p. 1389; 1940, p. 1180. See also Carl Frederick

Typical of the activities of Nazi agencies which sought to develop contacts for their propaganda in the United States were the operations of the *Amt Auslandspresse* in Munich. Although some of the office's American correspondents were students, teachers, and similar people interested simply in obtaining information on the Nazi Party and the Third Reich, the greater number were ardent anti-Semites, would-be fascists, and genuine crackpots. Many served voluntarily as intelligence agents for the Nazi office, at least to the extent of providing materials from the American press which they believed would be helpful to Germany in its propaganda. Prominent among these informants were the successive leaders of the *Bund der Freunde des neuen Deutschlands,* but numerous other persons and organizations actively engaged in promoting fascism or anti-Semitism were in close touch with Munich. These people included Robert Edward Edmondson of New York, William Dudley Pelley of North Carolina, and Dr. Ralph Major of the University of Kansas and the fascist Crusader White Shirts.

Much of the material exchanged by persons in the United States and the Foreign Press Office would be laughable were it not so vicious. It requires no systematic analysis to state with assurance that the central theme of the myriad pamphlets, articles, magazines, speeches, press releases, etc., was violent hatred of the Jews. Perhaps the most encouraging aspect of the relationships between the Nazi agency and people in this country, from the American point of view, is the fact that the participants were such obvious racists that their influence was restricted to the few circles already disposed in their favor. A large part of the time it appears that anti-Semitic groups in the United States and the *Amt Auslandspresse* were only propagandizing each other.[12]

Wittke, *The German-language Press in America* (Lexington, Ky., 1957), pp. 260 ff. Another indication of the trend toward assimilation was instruction in German, which made only a feeble comeback in the 1920s before declining again after 1933. Cf. Bischoff, *Nazi Conquest Through German Culture,* p. 168.

12. The reader may be interested in the types of correspondents with whom the Foreign Press Office was in contact. Frequently in communication with Munich and Berlin was Colonel Charles L. T. Pichel of New York, who dispatched "secret" and "confidential" reports on developments in the United States; e.g. in a letter to Ernst Hanfstaengl, July 15, 1933: "According to the latest secret information, Franklin D. Roosevelt is to be the LAST American President, so complete has the control of our American institutions now progressed through organized Jewry." (Hoffmann papers, roll 27, frame 24538 ff.) William Sebille of New York addressed a hysterical and incoherent letter to Hitler, June 1, 1933, complaining of the "big-mouthed Jews who hang around 88th Street and 2nd Avenue," and asking the Fuehrer to put them in

Of potentially greater impact were the Foreign Press Office's relationships with newspapers and magazines in America, but here again the
effects were extremely limited. All major journals in this country gave a
cool reception to efforts to disseminate materials from the Munich agency.
There is a high probability that most of the releases from the Nazi office
were never even read by important editors to whom they were directed.
They were such transparent propaganda, familiar to anyone who has ever
held an editorial post, that no responsible journalist would ever have used
them for publication.

The items found their only fruitful market among obscure publications
of limited circulation and practically no influence. Anti-Jewish papers like
Chicago's *American Gentile* and *Pelley's Weekly* of Asheville, North
Carolina, along with the various papers of the Bund, were literally the
only outlets for the vitriolic releases from the *Haus der Presse*. Most German-language publications in the United States testified to their loyalty as
well as to their concern for honest journalism by their refusal to accept
articles supplied by the *Amt Auslandspresse* or to provide the latter agency
with free copies of their issues for its files. Its failure to gain broad access to
American public opinion did not keep the Nazi agency from continuing
and expanding its efforts throughout the thirties.

In November 1934 Theodore Hoffmann, head of the Steuben Society of
America (which had not yet assumed its pronounced anti-Nazi position
of later years), conferred with Hitler concerning the declining German
position in the United States. Hoffmann sharply criticized the Bund and
reported the common assumption in this country that the Association of
the Friends of the New Germany took its directives from Germany. The

---

chains. (frame 24626 ff.). Major Frank Pease submitted an article attacking "Judeo-
Communism" (sic), and concluding:

> Begone, Israel, thou bad dream of the centuries, thou nightmare of the ages,
> thou troglodytic atavism. Back! Back—'Behind the Urals'; back to your filthy
> nomad tents, your fly-blown Near-East marts and bagnes; back to the camel
> dung and jackals of the desert, where you have come from, where you belong, *and
> where you are going.*
> Out upon you, Israel! ... Faugh! ... Phewy! ...

(Frame 23981, undated but in a folder marked 1934.) New York regularly became
"Jew York" in the correspondence to and from the *Amt Auslandspresse,* and many
spoke of President "Rosenfeld" and the "Jew Deal." For a brief survey of American
fascist influences, which were often closely related to anti-Semitic activities, see Arthur
M. Schlesinger, Jr., *The Politics of Upheaval* (Boston, 1960), Chapter 5, "The Dream
of Fascism," pp. 69–95.

Fuehrer denied that there existed any "superior authority" which issued instructions to the Bund and claimed that it was purely an American organization, but he inquired privately of both Rudolph Hess and the Foreign Ministry whether Hoffmann's remarks were true. The Wilhelmstrasse replied that Hoffmann's views were no doubt partially due to rivalry between his organization and the Bund, but that they were probably justified in the main. Reich representatives had already adopted an attitude of restraint in view of the tactlessness and excessive zeal of some of the local groups of the Friends. To support its position the Foreign Ministry recalled the circular order of February 1, 1934, sent out under Hess's authority, which forbade Party members to belong to the Bund.

Hess, meanwhile, had asked Ernst Bohle to report on the Party's relations with the Friends of the New Germany. Bohle denied that there was now any link between the *Auslandsorganisation* and the Bund, although he thought the *Aussenpolitisches Amt* and PROMI were still maintaining ties with it. Retracing the history of the Bund, he claimed that he had opposed giving it official status as a Party agency. Obviously worried that any connection with the Bund might now prove dangerous to him personally, Bohle even asserted that he had ordered Party members out of the organization when he had first learned that some of them belonged to the Bund. This was certainly not true, for we have seen that the *Gauleiter* had explicitly approved participation of Nazis in the organization as late as October 1933 and did not order them out of it until it appeared inevitable that the House would pass the Dickstein resolution to investigate the Party's activities in the United States.

Still Bohle's support for the Bund was apparent. "I must say that the Association is the only society which has championed the New Germany actively and fearlessly." He went on to justify his reluctant acceptance of a restrained policy governing Party activity in America.

> The absolute passivity towards the USA, which has been most strictly observed by the AO, is based on my view that at present any overt efforts made in the United States on behalf of the New Germany are entirely pointless, as the opposing elements are in every respect all-powerful. It is my opinion that any intervention on our part from here would only raise dust without achieving any positive results, and it is still my view that the German-Americans should take steps of their own accord and in such a way that it would not be assumed that there was a link with the Reich. This would not be ap-

propriate in all countries of the world, but in the United States the conditions are undoubtedly different.[13]

The AO had indeed now adopted a passive policy, but only because of the growing anti-Nazi opinion in the United States and after the several investigations had begun to threaten disclosure of the Party's secret operations. It will be remembered that the Party had not ordered its representative, Mensing, and the Nazi leader of the Bund, Gissibl, to cease their recruiting activities until March 26, 1934. By November Bohle was advocating a strong and at least superficially independent German-American movement, which the Party could manipulate with impunity. He still opposed the severance of ties with the Friends of the New Germany. He thought it particularly necessary that official Reich representatives should continue to encourage the Bund by attending its more important functions. Ambassador Luther echoed this view the following month when he declared that there was no intention of breaking off contact with the Bund altogether. Diplomats and consuls would merely seek to temper their relations with the organization in such a way as to avoid unfavorable publicity.

The year ended with Nazi propaganda in the United States slowed to a trickle. The pressure of the McCormack Committee's investigation and public alarm over the menace of subversive activities had produced a number of results. Kiep, the consul general who had directed much of the early Nazi propaganda from New York, had been recalled and his successor, Borchers, had contented himself with a less active role. Sallet, the propaganda attaché, had returned to America, but he had become much more circumspect in his activities, limiting himself mainly to efforts at personal persuasian among journalistic contacts. The *Bund der Freunde des neuen Deutschlands* had grown to almost 10,000 members and continued to employ Nazi forms and to work for a unified German-American community in the service of the Reich, but an aroused American public had rendered its work a great deal more difficult and considerably less dangerous to the nation. The congressional inquiry had discredited George Sylvester Viereck and the public relations experts, Byoir, Dickey, and Lee, vir-

---

13. Bohle's report to Hess, Nov. 16, 1934, *DGFP–C, 3,* 1119; also used in this discussion are the memorandum on Hoffmann's conference with Hitler, Nov. 2, 1934, pp. 1115–16; the Foreign Ministry's reply to the Fuehrer's inquiry about the Bund, p. 1117; and the report of Ambassador Luther to the Foreign Ministry, Dec. 29, 1934, pp. 1120 ff.

tually ending their value to the Nazi propaganda machine. Goebbels' plans for exercising widespread influence on public opinion in the United States had run into unanticipated difficulties.

At the beginning of 1935, with German diplomats and other agents seeking to avoid any further bad publicity, a new threat to the Nazi cause in this country arose. The former Nazi agent, Kurt Ludecke, had undergone a change of heart, and with good reason. In 1933 Ludecke had gone to Germany to urge that the Party cancel Spanknoebel's assignment in the United States and that it cease trying to organize German-Americans. It appeared at first that Ludecke had been successful in convincing the leading Nazis of the wisdom of his proposals, until without warning he was thrown into a concentration camp, reportedly on the orders of Goering. Somehow he managed to escape eight months later and work his way back through Canada to the United States, by now a disillusioned ex-Nazi. He appeared before the McCormack Committee in October 1934 and testified at length on his former activities. His cooperation with the House investigators greatly disturbed the Nazi hierarchy and Ernst Hanfstaengl ordered a detailed report on his testimony before an executive session of the committee.

Ludecke evidently did not reveal all he knew to the Congressmen, however, for he now tried to blackmail the Party's high command by threatening to make public certain other incriminating evidence he claimed to have in his possession. He demanded $50,000 by January 21, 1935; otherwise he would publish an exposé. Ludecke's threat was a central concern of Viereck, who journeyed to Berlin in January to confer on new methods of modifying the unfavorable attitude toward the Reich which prevailed in the United States. He convinced Hanfstaengl that they must prevent Ludecke from publishing any more information that would hurt the German cause in America.

On January 17 both Viereck and Hanfstaengl appeared in something of a frenzy at the Foreign Ministry to enlist its aid. They favored paying the specified sum to keep the former Nazi silent. Dr. Dieckhoff of the Foreign Ministry argued that, on the contrary, Ludecke should be ignored. If he published "something uncomfortable" after January 21, then Berlin would release the letter in which Ludecke sought to blackmail Germany and thus discredit him. This appeared to calm Hanfstaengl and the Party took no action to satisfy Ludecke's demands. The strategy seemed to have worked, for Ludecke did not carry out his threat. He faded from the scene after leading the secession of a militant group from the Bund and forming, in conjunction with Anton Haegele, the American National Socialist League. Neither this organization nor the *Bund der Freunde des neuen Deutschlands* survived the break for long, as the movements expended their energies in internecine conflict.[14]

For a brief period early in 1935 Ambassador Luther considered the prospects rather favorable for an improvement in relations between Germany and the United States. Although American hostility toward Nazism persisted, it was tempered by the tendency of many U.S. citizens to accept the view that Germany had been treated unjustly at Versailles. By June the German ambassador thought he detected a more sober assessment of the European situation among Americans, especially after the Fuehrer's offer of May 21 to conclude nonaggression pacts with his neighbors.

The changing climate of public opinion encouraged Luther to call for another propaganda offensive. "It appears that the time has come to endeavor by means of vigorous cultural activity, to exert more influence on the shaping of American public opinion to the lasting advantage of Germany, whilst simultaneously ensuring the existence of a vigorous German-American community." He knew this would be difficult, however, after the earlier debacles. Together with the German consuls in the United States, he contended that the Reich could best exploit the opportunities that often cropped up in the cultural sphere by providing freely disposable funds to the embassy and the consulates.

To underscore the importance of his proposal Luther reminded Berlin of the decisive role of the United States in the World War and reiterated the concern he had recently expressed that American power might again oppose Germany in the event of another war. The principal question was how to protect Germany against repetition of the events of 1914–1918. In the ambassador's opinion, the embryonic American culture, still dependent on European roots, invited creative efforts to revitalize the waning Germanic idea in this country. Emphasizing that speed was imperative if the millions of German-Americans were not to lose their identity completely, Luther pointed out that political advantages would accrue auto-

14. Memorandum by Dieckhoff, Jan. 17, 1935, serial K1054, frame K270111; Hanfstaengl's order for a detailed brief on Ludecke's testimony and related materials, serial K1054, frames K270037–052. Separation of the group which became the American National Socialist League is treated in several dispatches from Borchers during early 1935, serial K1054, frames K270116–143. Two years later Ludecke published a personal narrative, but it added nothing significant to his previous testimony before the McCormack Committee; see Ludecke, *I Knew Hitler.*

matically to the Reich, given the preservation of a strong community of racial comrades in the United States.[15]

The ambassador's momentary optimism was drowned by the wave of anti-German feeling that swept America the following month. Jews, including a number of foreign nationals, had once more been victims of violence in Berlin. In protest against German anti-Semitism some Americans were calling for Washington to sever diplomatic relations with the Reich; others were proposing that U.S. athletes not participate in the 1936 Olympics, scheduled for Germany. A worried German chargé d'affaires reported from Washington that President Roosevelt was rumored to be considering either a note to the Germans or a public statement, having in mind Theodore Roosevelt's earlier break with Russia on account of the Jewish question. It was hardly a propitious time to begin a new cultural campaign among German-Americans, for the United States was almost certain to interpret such endeavors as actually or potentially subversive.

The Wilhelmstrasse was justifiably alarmed that German measures against the Jews would confound the best diplomatic efforts to smooth out political and economic relations between the two nations. While the Foreign Ministry acquiesced in the necessity for the anti-Jewish policy, it called to the attention of other Nazi agencies that, in the interests of foreign policy, "unobtrusive methods of implementing it should be chosen, such as will provide no material for anti-German agitation abroad." The Reich Minister of Economics, Hjalmar Schacht, was equally disturbed that the Party's radical treatment of the Jews would have disastrous consequences for Germany's foreign trade.

A conference between Party and government officials considered these problems on August 20, 1935, but it served only to harden the basic divergences between the two groups. To the pleas of the Foreign and Economics ministries that excesses against the Jews made their jobs impossible, the Party representatives rejoined an appeal to the superior claims of National Socialist ideology.[16] The Jews would continue to receive the special brand of "justice" dispensed by the Nazi Party.

15. Luther reported through the Foreign Office to PROMI on "German Cultural Policy in the United States," June 28, 1935, *DGFP–C, 4,* 381–89; see also his dispatches to the Foreign Office, Apr. 18 and June 18, 1935, pp. 23–27 and 316–19. Reports of the U.S. reactions to the July 15 attacks on Jews in Berlin's *Kurfuerstendamm* are in the same volume; see the dispatches from Leitner, the chargé d'affaires, July 25 and 31, 1935, pp. 474 f. and 515 f.

16. On this conference and its preliminaries see the memoranda by Roehrecke of the Foreign Office, Aug. 19 and 21, 1935, ibid., pp. 565–570.

During the rest of the year, despite the quiescence of most Nazi propagandists, opinion in the United States remained hostile to Germany. It was not improved by the lengthy trial, conviction, and execution of Bruno Hauptmann, a citizen of the Reich, for the kidnap-murder of the Lindbergh baby. Hauptmann's lawyer complained bitterly that the German consulate was not doing enough in behalf of his client, but the Foreign Ministry was satisfied with the justice of the proceedings and declined to interfere. It wished to do nothing to add fuel to the anti-German sentiments in America.

The temporary subsidence of Nazi propaganda in the United States proved insufficient to turn the tide of public opinion in favor of the Reich or even to cause the waves of positive enmity to subside. Finally, and with great reluctance, Berlin attempted to retrieve the situation by ordering all Reich citizens to withdraw from the Bund and other such organizations. The Party still did not wish to discourage the pro-Nazi elements in the organizations. Hess refused to issue the instructions publicly, but on October 11, 1935, von Neurath directed German consuls in the United States to inform all Reich citizens in their areas that they must resign from German-American groups.

The consuls were disregarded. The ardent German nationals who had dominated the Friends of the New Germany simply refused to believe that the Party meant what it said. When *Bundesleiter* Fritz Gissibl learned of the alleged order, he left immediately for the Reich to request that, if it had in fact been issued, the Party lift it at once. Ambassador Luther complained that Reich citizens were ignoring the order; they were confident that Berlin really approved of their activities. In a speech to a Bund rally in Chicago on October 17 Walter Kappe described a *New York Times* report, alleging that Hess had ordered German citizens to resign from the Bund, as "a Jewish lie by a Jewish paper." At the same time the local publications of the Bund, of which there were now three operating in New York, Philadelphia, and Chicago, all reported that there had been no such instruction.

When Gissibl arrived in Germany early in November 1935, it soon became clear to him that the Party and Foreign Ministry actually intended to enforce the ban on Reich Germans' participation in the Bund. He grudgingly reconciled himself to the order, but he still hoped to win a change in its form and timing. He reported that the Bund now had 10,000 members, of whom *60 percent were Reich nationals*. If Berlin did not modify the instructions, the movement would collapse, especially if the Party sternly enforced the order in his absence from the United States. Gissibl noted that the organization had undertaken long-term financial commitments for several houses, camps, three newspapers, and other investments. The American citizens in the group could not survive without the financial contributions of the *Reichsdeutsche.* He attempted to get the Foreign Ministry to permit those who had taken their "first papers" for United States citizenship to remain in the Bund, but he was turned down.

On November 13 representatives of PROMI, the Foreign Ministry, the *Auslandsorganisation,* and the *Buero Ribbentrop* met in conference and decided that the order definitely would stand. They allowed German citizens to remain in the Bund until the end of the year. Informed of this, Gissibl declared that he would prefer to dissolve the organization entirely and asked for enough time to carry out the necessary preparations. The conference agreed to this on the condition that if Gissibl backed out or was unable to effect the planned dissolution the Party would issue to the press an explicit order for the resignation of Reich Germans from the body. The latter action ultimately proved necessary.

On returning to the United States, Gissibl found that the German citizens in the Bund still refused to believe that Berlin actually wanted them to withdraw. The *Bundesleiter* failed in his attempt to implement the dissolution quietly, and Berlin released the aforementioned order to the Associated Press on December 27, 1935. Signed by Rudolph Hess, the directive specified that it applied to all organizations which, like the Bund, engaged in political activities, and that it covered all Reich citizens, including those with "first papers." This meant the disintegration of the *Bund der Freunde des neuen Deutschlands.*[17]

The November conference also made another provision of importance, although it was never completely carried out. All through 1934 and 1935 a series of individuals had appeared unannounced at German diplomatic, consular, and other offices in the United States and proclaimed that they were on secret missions for the Propaganda Ministry, the Gestapo, or some other Reich agency. Confusion had been rampant, with PROMI and the Gestapo usually denying that persons who claimed to be their operatives were in fact employed by them, but seldom informing the Foreign Minis-

17. Pertinent documents for this section are filmed as serial K1054, frames K270567–659; cf. especially the memorandum of the Nov. 13 conference, dated Nov. 17, 1935, frame K270623. Gissibl later became a ranking official of the DAI in Stuttgart and a member of the Reichstag; see Rogge, *The Official German Report,* pp. 16–17.

try just whom they had sent on assignments to this country. This refusal to keep the Wilhelmstrasse adequately informed was clearly related to persistent distrust of the career diplomats, almost a universal attitude among the Nazi offices. The several agencies represented at the conference on the Bund now elaborated a way to eliminate much of this chaos by channeling information on confidential agents in America through the office of Ambassador Ribbentrop. Ribbentrop, as a devoted Nazi and a member of the Foreign Ministry, would serve as coordinator. This role was an interesting token of the future foreign minister's growing power.

These developments marked the end of the first phase of Nazi activities in the United States. Ever since the autumn of 1933 and the announcement that several investigations would concentrate on the Party's operations in America, Nazi propaganda had been in retreat. Goebbels' carefully devised plans of the summer and fall of 1933 had been impossible to implement in the face of persistent public scrutiny. The Party's fondest hope, the Friends of the New Germany, had attracted so much unfavorable publicity and so damaged the German cause that Berlin finally had to dissociate itself from the organization. The major trends which were to dominate American public opinion for the next decade were already discernible and they were distinctly antagonistic to Nazi Germany. But the Reich propaganda engine had not given up its plans to exploit American public opinion. The most extensive and sinister efforts were yet to come.

CHAPTER 5

Ibero-Amerika—Planmaessig

By contrast with the United States, where prompt and vociferous public reaction placed the embryonic Nazi activities on the defensive almost from the first, Latin America's response to the advent of the Third Reich and the international dissemination of Nazi doctrines was long in coming. Although fewer Germans had immigrated to the countries of Central and South America than to the United States and Canada, German groups had tended to cluster in certain areas and to resist assimilation into the local cultures. This was particularly true in southern Brazil, south central Chile, and Argentina where German colonies had been well established for many years and had generally maintained their separate heritage. Such groups offered attractive opportunities to National Socialist preachers of German racial and cultural superiority.

Estimates of the total number of Germans in Latin America, including both Reich citizens and others of German descent, varied widely. In 1932 the VDA estimated that there were 800,000 persons of German blood in all of *Ibero-Amerika*. Four years later the *Auslandsorganisation* placed the figure at well over a million with 800,000 in Brazil, 150,000 in Argentina, 30,000 in Chile, and smaller groups scattered throughout the other countries of the region. Unlike the immigrants to the Anglo-Saxon countries of the north, many of these Germans had come in post-1900 and postwar waves, and more than 100,000 retained their German citizenship.[1] The slow assimilation of these individuals left them extremely susceptible to Nazi appeals.

Especially among the recent German immigrants, many of whom had

1. Cf. Otto Schaefer, *Sinn und Wesen des V.D.A.*, p. 5; the AO estimates are contained in a Festschrift for a 1936 conference of foreign German teachers in Stuttgart, Yivo Institute for Jewish Research, file NFI–18. See also de Jong, *Die deutsche fuenfte Kolonne*, pp. 212 ff. This chapter relies heavily on a State Department memorandum of February 1938 which surveyed "Nazi Activities in the American Republics" up to that time (cited hereafter as "Nazi Activities"). I am indebted to Dr. Bernard Noble of the Department's Historical Division for declassification of this valuable report.

suffered the physical and psychological deprivations of the world war in the homeland, the Hitler movement found a warm welcome. The determined promise of National Socialism to reassert German rights and, further, to demonstrate the superiority of the German people echoed their own inarticulate aspirations. This fact found expression in the steady growth of Nazi influence among German groups in Latin America as Hitler moved toward power in Germany, assumed it, and then began to wield it with apparent success.

The first country-wide Nazi Party outside the fatherland was that in Paraguay, where several local groups secretly formed a national Nazi movement in 1932. This development had its parallel in most other Latin American states during the next few years. There has never been an accurate and complete tabulation of the number of Party members in the Western Hemisphere, although records for such an accounting do exist. However, a precise count of a sample portion of Party membership files reveals a number of facts. There were certainly thousands and not merely hundreds of Nazis in the New World, as some have suggested, and by far the most significant numbers came from the Latin American countries with sizable German communities. Louis de Jong calculates that there must eventually have been about 1,700 Nazis in Brazil and something more than 2,000 in Argentina, although this writer's own sample check suggests that Brazil actually had the greater number and that both these figures are too low.

The growth of Nazi Party membership in this hemisphere correlates quite well with Hitler's major successes in Europe. While many individuals entered the Party in the late twenties and early thirties, the major influx occurred in the months immediately following the Fuehrer's arrival at supreme power in the Reich in 1933. The second rush to join the Party came in 1939 and 1940 when Germany's conquests were coming fast and easy, and the Reich appeared invincible. The power of revolutionary example seems always to have been highly efficacious in the weaker sister states of the Americas. Hitler's stunning successes, regardless of means, created large groups of admirers willing to adopt his methods in order to reap comparable political rewards.[2]

2. This discussion draws on a tabulation of one of thirty-four files, that for names beginning with the letter "A"; it suggested that of approximately 100,000 members of the Party abroad, i.e. of the *Auslandsorganisation,* 20% to 25% were resident in this hemisphere and the greatest percentage of those in South America. Cf. "List of NSDAP Members in Foreign Countries," Library of Congress, Manuscript Division, Accession number D.R. G1668, containers 748–767. These files are coded and, al-

The fact that German settlers had tended to retain their distinct national traditions had many favorable ramifications from the Nazi point of view. Above all, it meant that channels were still open for direct communication with the majority of *Volksgenossen* (racial comrades) in Latin America. Most important of these media were the flourishing German schools which became a prime object of Nazi infiltration. For years the VDA and DAI had cultivated friendly contacts with schools, and the coordination of these two organizations brought these relationships into the service of National Socialism. Figures on the number of German schools in Central and South America are significant.

COUNTRY	NUMBER OF SCHOOLS	ENROLLMENT
Argentina	58	7,276
Brazil	1,260	50,000 (est.)
Bolivia	3	1,068
Chile	44	4,962
Colombia	2	410
Costa Rica	1	83
Cuba	1	380
Ecuador	1	143
Guatemala	3	420
Mexico	4	967
Paraguay	31	1,169
Peru	3	337
Uruguay	6	604
Venezuela	4	316

While these statistics show that only a fraction of German immigrants and their children were involved in the activities of the schools, they do underline the fact that substantial groups, especially in the ABC countries, were still what we might call actively German, at least in a cultural sense. And the German schools were definitely on the increase. By 1936, a year after the figures given above were compiled, Chile had 62 schools, Argentina had 70, Paraguay was up to 50, and Brazil to 1,300. Well over 1,200 of the German schools in Brazil were located in the two southern states of Rio Grande do Sul and Santa Catharina. Not all of these schools fell under

though there is a key, it would require a team of several researchers to prepare an accurate and adequate tabulation. See also de Jong, *Die deutsche fuenfte Kolonne,* pp. 202–12.

Nazi domination, but it seems safe to say that most of them eventually did. It was the existence of these schools which led the *Auslandsorganisation* to comment, in a Festschrift for a 1936 convention of foreign teachers of German descent, "South America is our great hope."[3]

Most German schools had been receiving material assistance, as well as moral encouragement, from the fatherland prior to the establishment of the Third Reich. We have already mentioned that the VDA had supplied textbooks and other instructional aids. The same organization had arranged "pen pal" relationships between students in Latin American countries and the homeland. The VDA helped teachers from Germany to serve as faculty members in the "colonial" schools on an exchange basis with instructors in the German schools in the Americas. It also encouraged students from these schools to visit Germany and, although the program did not enjoy a lavish budget, it set up a system of scholarships to enable those with inadequate financial means to make study trips to the Reich. After Hitler became Chancellor, the VDA and other agencies intensified these activities and inaugurated a program of direct financial support to the schools.

United States diplomatic observers noted that German schools in Latin America consistently spent well beyond their known incomes. The embassy in Brazil reported to Washington that the principal complex of German schools in the Western Hemisphere, that in Rio Grande do Sul, derived only 60 percent of its operating revenues from tuition. In addition to the expanded budgets of the "unofficial" organizations which were assisting the German schools, the Foreign Ministry itself made specific provision to underwrite education among Germans in Latin America. The Wilhelmstrasse allocated RM 4,000,000 for this purpose in fiscal 1937. Schools also drew aid from a second fund of approximately RM 3,000,000 a year, which the Ministry designated for general cultural activities. Requests from German schools in the Americas regularly exceeded the grants from the Foreign Ministry, but it can be seen from the sums involved that the contributions were sizable.[4]

The maintenance of their distinctive national character made German

3. See the report on German schools abroad for the year 1935–36 in the papers of E. W. Bohle, National Archives, micro-copy T–120, serial 78, roll 75, frames 59023–26. Also useful for comparison is the Festschrift already mentioned, Yivo Institute, file NFI–18.

4. Memorandum regarding "The Financial Means for the Cultural Policies of the Foreign Ministry," undated but evidently 1936, Bohle papers, roll 75, frames 59003 ff. See also "Nazi Activities, p. 62.

communities in South America accessible to National Socialist propaganda in another very important respect. There were fewer German-language newspapers in Latin America than in the United States, but they were far more effective instruments with proportionately greater circulation. The prosperity of the German groups they served gave these papers greater strength and financial stability than was common among the press in the region. In Brazil the most prominent journals, the *Deutsche Zeitung* and the *Deutsche Morgen* of São Paulo, and *Neue Deutsche Zeitung* of Porto Alegre, quickly acquired a Nazi aspect. The same was true of the *Deutsche La Plata Zeitung,* the famous Argentine publication, and many other such papers. In Chile the *Westkuesten-Beobachter* served as the local voice of the *Auslandsorganisation.* There were exceptions, to be sure, notably *Deutsche Wacht,* the only German paper in Montevideo, which deplored Nazism and its anti-Semitism, as did the *Argentinisches Tageblatt* of Buenos Aires. But the Reich's influence soon became dominant among the German-language press in Central and South America.[5] These organs relied on the German news agencies, especially Transocean, as their principal sources, and ardently defended developments in the fatherland.

The Spanish and Portuguese papers of the area were, by and large, consistent in their opposition to Hitler's Germany and to National Socialism. Smaller metropolitan publications and provincial papers proved more amenable to Nazi blandishments and economic inducements. United States diplomats bemoaned the fact that through most of South America the plethora of newspapers was totally out of proportion to the literate population. This meant that many publications were shoestring operations whose financial weaknesses made it impossible for them to sustain themselves in the face of concerted economic pressure.

The Nazis generated such pressure by the simple technique which Goebbels had described in his directive of September 1933: block advertising. German merchants and sympathizers cooperated in placing their advertising en bloc in papers which proved inoffensive editorially. Favorable or at least neutral editorial policies were encouraged by the promise

5. *Deutsche Wacht* also eventually fell under Nazi control. The DAI maintained extensive archives of these German papers; a photostatic reproduction of its annotated card catalogue, prepared by the Allied military forces in 1946, is available at the Library of Congress under the title "A List of Newspapers Principally Representative of German Groups Outside Germany." The *Amt Auslandspresse* also developed widespread contacts in Latin America and supplied considerable quantities of material to these papers; cf. Hoffman papers, roll 29, frames 26361–433 and 26600–670 for examples.

of additional advertising support or, conversely, by the threat that articles antagonistic to the Third Reich would cause a mass withdrawal of advertising by German firms. Few papers were strong enough to risk the economic perils of genuine independence in their editorials and other articles. Furthermore, the weaker papers found it difficult to subscribe to the expensive news services provided by the Associated Press, United Press, Havas, Reuters, and other agencies. Many chose to accept the free services of Transocean and later of the *Deutsches Nachrichtenbuero* (DNB), just as the Propaganda Ministry had calculated. Still, German influence in the general press was limited to smaller and less powerful papers. The great and influential journals like *La Prensa* maintained a cool reserve or positive hostility toward the Nazi Reich and the movement that spawned it.[6]

In addition to German newspapers and schools, Nazi influence soon pervaded the major social organizations of the German communities in Latin America. The *Deutscher Volksbund fuer Argentinien,* the *Verband Deutscher Vereine* in Brazil, the *Deutsch-Chilenischen Bund,* and their counterparts in other countries assumed many of the forms and tenets of National Socialism. These groups were usually not very large. There were only 5,000 members of the Argentine *Volksbund,* 15,000 in the Brazilian organization, and 2,600 in the Chilean Bund. But their influence as the leading organizations of Germans in the respective countries went far beyond their numbers.

The regimentation such organizations imposed on Germans in Latin American states was strikingly illustrated by the activities of *La Cámara del Comercio Alemán,* which the Germans established in Argentina to promote trade between that country and the Reich. The auxiliary functions of this organization included fund raising for propaganda projects of the German embassy in Buenos Aires. The *Cámara* initiated the so-called Winter Relief collections in December 1933 and continued them well into the next decade, although the funds were deposited to the German embassy's account and did not go for the intended relief purposes in the homeland. The organization solicited "donations" from the commercial establishments and industrial firms which belonged to it. To augment their contributions member firms made deductions from the salaries of their ordinary employees. The companies fixed the amounts of these deductions according to a precise schedule ranging from 4 percent (for those paid less than 290 pesos a month), to 32 percent (for those with salaries of more than

6. Together with Rolf Hoffmann's files, United States diplomatic reports are useful on this point, particularly those summarized in "Nazi Activities," pp. 61–65.

2,000 pesos a month). Employees were compelled to contribute, both by social pressure and by threats to their jobs if they refused.

Although the major collections came after 1937, the organization more than doubled its receipts for this purpose during the first five years. At the same time, it was collecting funds from the sale of certificates of origin for merchandise sent to the Reich. All firms proposing to export goods to Germany now had to pay for the normally free certificates and thus to underwrite the expenses of Nazi activities in Argentina. Again, however, the sums involved were small and serve only to exemplify the operations of the German Chamber of Commerce.[7]

To emphasize the importance of the German communities in Latin America and to strengthen their ties with the Reich, Germans from the area received prominent places in the frequent celebrations staged in Germany to honor and impress foreign comrades. This was notably the case at the annual Festival of Foreign Germans which the DAI held in Stuttgart and the yearly congresses of the *Auslandsorganisation* in that same city.

In early 1937 the Chief of the AO in Uruguay, Felix Schmidt, toured the large German settlements in the Rio de la Plata region to survey the progress of Germany's campaign to win over her racial comrades. Aided by Gerhard Huttula, a well-known film director, Schmidt produced a short motion picture portraying the rejuvenation of Germans in Argentina through the influence of National Socialism. The film, entitled *Lejos del País de los Antepasados* (Far from the Land of the Ancestors), circulated through the German settlements in Latin America as an indication of the universal comradeship of *Volksgenosse* with each other and with the fatherland. The Fifth Congress of the AO later that year featured the film as convincing evidence of the Party's conquest of foreign Germandom. Short films of this type became a standard item in the Nazi propaganda arsenal. Along with documentaries and feature films from Germany they received frequent performances at German schools and at meetings of German cultural organizations in Latin America.[8]

---

7. Cf. Cámara de diputados, Comisión Investigadora de Actividades Antiargentinas, *Informes* (Buenos Aires, 1941 and cited hereafter as *Argentine Reports*), number 2, Sept. 5, 1941, pp. 14–20. Also see de Jong, *Die deutsche fuenfte Kolonne,* p. 212. Testimony before the Argentine investigating committee left no doubt that contributions were involuntary. To supplement the operations of the German Chamber of Commerce, Berlin's Association of Chemical Industries established *La Oficina de Fomento del Comercio Alemán en la Argentina,* which carried on much the same sort of work.

8. *Argentine Reports,* number 1, Aug. 29, 1941, p. 14.

Nazi cultural organizations in the Reich often decorated leading members of German settlements in Central and South America for their contributions to Germandom. For this purpose Dr. Stroelin of the *Deutsches Ausland-Institut* established a series of three special awards in recognition of the work of foreign Germans. The DAI created other honors and decorations for non-German Latin Americans and judiciously bestowed them on individuals who seemed likely to serve the fatherland's interests. Germany usually broadcast via shortwave the ceremonies at which these awards were made, occasionally transmitting to *Ibero-Amerika* in Spanish and Portuguese, as well as in German. Berlin lost no opportunity to cultivate both Germans and non-Germans who might prove valuable to the Nazi cause in Latin America.

Joseph Goebbels had a particular interest in broadcast propaganda, and shortwave transmissions from Germany to audiences in Latin America and elsewhere increased steadily during the nineteen-thirties. With the construction of several new transmitters in 1934 the Reich began broadcasting four hours daily to South America. The next year special radio propaganda to Central America more than doubled the daily total and by late 1939 Germany was beaming over sixteen hours of programs each day to the region as a whole. A good deal of this material was adapted directly from domestic German broadcasts, since Goebbels, with practically no personal knowledge of the distinctive interests and vulnerabilities of foreign listeners, seldom practiced his theoretical policy of tailoring propaganda to the varying traits of different communities. To the Propaganda Minister the main thing was the "essentially authoritarian" nature of radio as a mass medium, which he contrasted with the "liberal" character of the press. Radio was more easily managed under his system of centralized control, and he sought to apply it to advantage at home and abroad. English, Spanish, and Portuguese broadcasts to the Western Hemisphere attempted to inform and entertain, but also to indoctrinate and instruct members of the *Auslandsorganisation* and other Germans living in the area.[9]

Germany's immediate interest in Latin America was economic. The expanding Reich industry required raw materials which the region could supply and Germany could also hope to profit from the growing Latin American market. The Hitler regime gave prompt attention to the pros-

9. Broadcasts to the United States rose from two hours a day in 1933 to almost twelve hours daily in 1939. See Z. A. B. Zeman, *Nazi Propaganda* (London, 1964), pp. 50, 54–75, 113.

pects for increased trade with the area. German trade with all the countries in Central and South America had reached an all-time high in 1930, when Germany had imported RM 959,000,000 worth of goods from the region and had exported to it products valued at RM 745,000,000. With the depression the total volume of this trade had plummeted to half those figures before it began to rise again after 1933.

In hopes of stimulating the recovery, a German trade delegation toured South America in the fall of 1934, visiting every country on the continent except Paraguay and Bolivia. This was the first such delegation to visit the region in the history of German economic relations with Latin America and reflected the importance which the Third Reich attached to the area. The trade group, including representatives of the Foreign Ministry, the Economics Ministry, the Food and Agriculture Ministry, and the Reichsbank, had broad competence to conclude agreements on long-term commercial relations. German diplomatic missions in the various countries had worked for months to lay the groundwork for the delegation's visit. Operating on instructions from Berlin, they had informed the governments to which they were accredited that, in return for "reasonable concessions," the Reich was "prepared to guarantee to the South American countries fixed and possibly even increased quotas in supplying the German market with such raw materials and colonial produce as may be involved."[10] This was the first of many efforts to entice the Latin American republics into closer economic ties with Hitler's Germany.

The delegation prolonged its negotiations in Latin America from July 1934 through January 1935, spending a considerable amount of time in each country and dealing in detail with problems connected with the marketing of its products. At the same time the members of the trade mission had occasion to contact and gain the goodwill of influential German commercial circles. Although its efforts were unproductive in several countries, the delegation was successful in the most important states. It concluded separate agreements on foreign exchange transactions with Argentina, Brazil, Chile, and Uruguay.

Typical of Nazi commercial agreements, they were designed to alleviate the pressures on international exchange by a system of barter arrangements under which each party delivered goods to the other in return for cumu-

10. Instructions to missions in South America, June 23, 1934, *DGFP–C, 3,* 74–77. Another indication of the priority attention being given to Latin America by the Reich was the elevation to embassy status, late in 1934, of German legations in Buenos Aires, Rio de Janeiro, Santiago de Chile, and Mexico City.

lative bank balances in the currency of the receiving country. These balances could then be used to purchase products in that country. The effect of such provisions was to eliminate virtually all possibility of multilateral trade and to restrict the commercial flow between the two signatories to bilateral channels. In other words, proceeds from one of the Latin American countries' sales to Germany were only good for purchases in the Reich and could not be internationalized to buy much-needed products, for example, from Great Britain or the United States. This made it possible for Germany to expand her exports to the region in exact proportion to the increase in her imports from it.

Germany's trade inroads in Latin America became a genuine concern for the United States, and Washington felt obliged to make representations to all countries which entered into barter arrangements with Berlin. The State Department scrupulously avoided any hint of reprisals, however, and carefully tried to maintain in every respect the Good Neighbor Policy. The United States specified in each case that its interest was to see that previous agreements between it and the respective country were not infringed, and to exercise its influence wherever possible in behalf of liberal international trade policies.

The Latin American states, realizing the value of their trade relations with the United States, had generally followed the practice of keeping Washington informed of the progress of their negotiations with Germany. One of the rare complaints by the United States came late in 1934 when the Chilean state railroads canceled a contract with the Pullman Corporation in favor of a new offer of locomotives from the Reich. For a moment the United States was disturbed that its trade agreements with Chile had been violated by discrimination against American firms, but it quickly softened its representations to Chile when it learned that the German sale was due mainly to the Nazi government's subsidization of the locomotive industry, estimated at some 60 percent for all sales abroad.[11] Governmental support facilitated the efforts of German enterprises to undercut their competitors in Latin America.

Although German trade continued to rise after 1933, several South American countries were soon disillusioned by their trade arrangements with the Reich. In Colombia, for instance, where a small but prosperous and highly influential German trading community existed at Barranquilla, sympathy among business circles progressively turned against Ger-

11. Cf. the dispatches between Washington and Santiago concerning the German sale of locomotives to Chile, FR, 4 (1935), 394 f.

many during 1935. Technical arrangements for trade with the Reich were inordinately complicated, and the German commercial attaché in Bogotá had offended many businessmen by his tactless and aggressive behavior. By September the United States minister to Colombia reported that friction over the exchange system and other disagreements had led to virtual suspension of trade between that country and Germany.[12]

The key nation in German trade plans throughout the nineteen-thirties was Brazil. That country's government soon learned of the shortcomings of barter trade with the controlled economy of Nazi Germany. During 1936 Brazil became increasingly dissatisfied with her commercial treaty with Germany, feeling properly that the Reich was exploiting her. For example, the Nazis now funneled goods which Brazil had formerly bought from Germany, such as aniline dyes and coal, through Holland and Switzerland, so that Brazil could not make its customary purchases from the Reich with its accumulated balances in "compensatory marks." Instead the Brazilians had to use the balances to buy other German products that they would normally have bought elsewhere or not at all. This forced more German goods onto the Brazilian market, especially heavy machinery and cars, but not the products which the South American country needed or wanted.

After unsuccessful attempts to revise the agreement, Brazil decided to terminate the treaty by July 31, 1936. Officials in Rio de Janeiro were determined "to buy from the Germans what we want from them, not what they want to sell us and to sell them what we want them to take not what we could sell elsewhere anyhow."[13] Such incidents point up the antagonisms Germany provoked in her endeavor to gain a greater share of Latin American trade on her own terms.

In addition to official efforts to penetrate the region's economy, unofficial German agencies were extremely active in seeking to influence economic developments in the area. Perhaps the most effective commercial propaganda for the New Germany came from an organization known as the *Aufklaerungs-Ausschuss Hamburg-Bremen*. This "enlightenment committee" operated through a network of several hundred confidential agents in Latin America and, unlike German news bureaus, made certain that its

12. See the dispatches between Secretary of State Hull and the American minister in Colombia, ibid., pp. 442–48.

13. Quoted in a dispatch from the United States embassy in Brazil to Secretary Hull, Apr. 24, 1936, *FR*, 5 (1936), 249; also see the other reports during June 1936, pp. 266–72. The Brazilian position, one notes, sounded rather like an echo of the German formula for exploitation to which Rio was objecting.

activity was "fully camouflaged." While it cooperated in the general cultural propaganda of the Reich, its principal purpose was to expand the
German economic foothold.

The committee dated back to 1923 and had steadily expanded its contacts and operations in the New World. After the advent of the Hitler
regime, the organization became an affiliate of the Propaganda Ministry
and lost its private character. By 1937 it was disseminating several hundred thousand brochures, pamphlets, articles, and similar items through
Latin America each year. Its most substantial efforts were two periodicals,
Revista Alemana in Spanish and *A Nova Alemanha* in Portuguese, which
it dispatched to all prominent business offices and firms in the area. These
magazines aimed to establish close rapport with powerful commercial interests in Central and South America.[14]

German chemical and pharmaceutical firms had long done business in
Latin America and enjoyed enormous prestige among the scientific and
medical circles there. The respected German scientific journals and special
publications which the chemical industry distributed in the area bolstered
and expanded this influence. One of the most important links with these
scientific groups was the *Revista Médica Ibero-Americana,* a quarterly
subsidized by the chemical and pharmaceutical firms. Georg Thieme had
published this review in Leipzig since 1928. Like most other such enterprises it underwent "coordination" by the Nazi government and received
official support in its work. The review served to spread word of German
scientific accomplishments among a small but highly important segment
of the Latin American population. Besides helping to stimulate business
for a specialized German industry, it was a valuable vehicle in developing
generally favorable attitudes toward the Reich among doctors and other
scientific personnel.[15]

Most of the activities of Nazi Germany and its agents aroused little
opposition in Latin America during the early and mid-thirties. This was
primarily due to the relative caution shown in their efforts to organize and
control the local German communities. From 1933 to 1937 German
groups seldom displayed in public portraits of Hitler, swastika flags and

14. Cf. "Der Aufklaerungs-Ausschuss Hamburg-Bremen und seine besonderen
Eigenheiten," a report dated Dec. 22, 1938, and covering the committee's history and
activities, Yivo Institute, File G–PA–7. The committee was directed by Dr. Kurt
Johannsen, who also controlled thirteen affiliated propaganda, press, and photo services,
including the *Ibero-Amerika Verlag* in Hamburg.

15. Information on this matter comes from the DAI archives, container 279, Library of Congress, Manuscript Division.

Nazi insignia, or the other paraphernalia of the New Reich. Nazi operatives among them satisfied both their penchant for conspiracy and the exigencies of the situation by avoiding offensive public demonstrations until the organizational work among the Germans in Latin American countries was sufficiently far advanced. It was not until March 14, 1937, that German communities in Argentina, Brazil, and elsewhere openly celebrated the Day of the German People. Thereafter the evidence of Nazi influence and control among such groups began to emerge more clearly.

That same year the Argentine school inspector reported that Nazification had progressed rapidly in German schools throughout the Argentine. Growing Nazi strength in the region made Berlin more confident that public displays of the local groups' affection for the fatherland would be useful. Already Ernst Wilhelm Bohle had declared the success of the AO's mission:

> The Foreign Organization of the National Socialist Party, realizing that there can be no greater sin than to renounce willingly one's German blood, aims to retain the German individual whether poor or rich, young or old, in whatever part of the world he may be. *Today we can state with pride and with joy that our Party comrades have conquered foreign Germandom for the Reich.*[16]

Although developments in Latin America were generally *planmaessig,* the Party still experienced difficulties. The Reich diplomatic and consular officials proved reluctant partners to the Party's aggressive recruitment and organizational policies. The *Amt Auslandspresse* complained repeatedly that consuls and diplomats in Central and South America were unsympathetic to its activities. Party officials often charged members of the foreign service with infidelity to the Hitler regime's *Weltanschauung.*

16. Bohle's speech to the AO Congress in Nuremberg, Sept. 11, 1936, quoted in *The German Reich and Americans of German Origin* (New York, 1938), p. 26. The emphasis is my own. In 1934 Rudolf Hess had set forth in remarkably explicit terms the Nazi view on this subject. Speaking in Berlin to a Conference of German Chambers of Commerce Abroad, he said:

> You know as well as I do that the one great mistake of the former regime was in not keeping up the ties of blood which connect the Germans in their home country with the Germans abroad; in not having kept these ties alive and in not having used Germandom abroad politically, for the mutual benefit of both of the sections of Germandom.

Quoted in ibid., p. 22.

Serious conflicts between the Party and state representatives abroad continued throughout the period, the former working actively to insure the Nazification of German communities in Latin America and the latter desperately seeking to restrain the Party from activities which would jeopardize good relations with the governments of the countries involved.

Nor was this the only point of friction in the Reich's foreign operations. There were frequent disputes between the AO and other agencies coordinated by it. For example, Hildegard Pack, the Buenos Aires representative of the German Academy of Munich, had been dismissed in 1935 because of her continued opposition to the aggressive local Party leaders and the AO itself. Even Dr. Haushofer was not always on the best terms with the Party hierarchy. There is no doubt that he retained his position as long as he did only because of his close connection with Hess.[17]

By 1938 it was apparent to United States diplomats in Latin America that Nazi influence among Germans in the region had become predominant. Apprehensive about the inherent dangers of such a development, the State Department prepared a detailed study of Nazi activities in the other American republics. In almost every country Bohle's assertion that the AO had conquered foreign Germandom seemed to be confirmed. In no state, however, did United States diplomats detect significant general influence by the Nazis on the local government's policies. Argentina was the only country that retained a German military mission and sent many of its officers to study in the service schools of the Reich. United States missions offered reassuring appraisals of the situation, noting only that close observation of future developments was in order. This complacency was soon to vanish.[18]

Nazi plans were moving according to schedule. Without having aroused

17. The friction in Nazi operations in Latin America will require our attention again. These few general remarks draw on a broad range of documentation. Regarding the Pack case, see the *Deutsche Akademie* files, National Archives, micro-copy T-82, roll 10, folder 809. Haushofer's recurrent disagreements with Bohle and other Party functionaries are revealed in Haushofer's personal papers, National Archives, micro-copy T-253, roll 49, frames 1503571 ff. Antagonism between the *Amt Auslandspresse* and diplomats in Latin America is repeatedly apparent in the Hoffmann papers; see especially Hoffmann's report to PROMI, Jan. 15, 1934, roll 27, frames 24068–75. Difficulties in distributing Nazi literature in Brazil, due mainly to the costs of importing printed materials and the duties on them, led Hoffmann to propose the establishment of a special publishing house there under von Cossel, the Party leader in the country. His recommendations were defeated by stout resistance from the consular officials in Brazil and from domestic German publishers, who foresaw a great loss of profits.

18. Cf. "Nazi Activities," pp. 49–72.

serious opposition in the Latin American countries, and even without having unduly disturbed the United States, the Reich had carried out its conquest of Germandom in the region. As Hitler had described it to Hermann Rauschning in 1933 and 1934, phase one of his scheme for the New World was progressing quite satisfactorily.[19] The timing was perfect, for the Nazi regime had been able to secure a strong hold on Germans in Central and South America before it began the adventures in Europe which were bound to create difficulties in its relations with the American Hemisphere.

But the combination of increasing belligerence by the Reich in the Old World and the open demonstration of affection for National Socialism and the New Germany in the New World were to bring a reaction the Hitlerites had not correctly anticipated. The Nazi assumption that a tightly unified and coordinated Germandom in Latin America could exercise a major restraining influence on the governments in the area ultimately proved ill-founded. The early months of 1938 marked the end of Latin America's passive attitude toward National Socialism and the beginning of the movement which would result in a united hemispheric front to meet the threat of fascist subversion. By this time, however, the roots of the Nazi cancer had struck deeply and were not to be easily excised. One can only speculate as to where and how the rapidly diffusing malignancy might have erupted, had Hitlerism survived as the dominant force in Europe. The tardiness and initial hesitancy of the Western Hemisphere's response to Nazi penetration had opened the door to potential catastrophe.

19. Hermann Rauschning, *The Voice of Destruction* (New York, 1940), pp. 61–70. See below, Chapter 11 for an extended discussion of the available evidence on Hitler's personal attitude toward the Western Hemisphere.

CHAPTER 6

Unser Amerika—The Latter Phase

At the beginning of 1936 the fortunes of Nazi Germany were at low ebb in the United States. Withdrawal of Reich citizens from the *Bund der Freunde des neuen Deutschlands* reduced that organization to less than half its original strength. On the advice of Consul General Borchers the Party recalled the former leaders of the Bund, Fritz Gissibl and Walter Kappe, in order to avoid further incidents. The first effort to promote a vigorous National Socialist movement in the United States had failed miserably.

Nevertheless American citizens whom the Friends of the New Germany had indoctrinated were determined to start anew. Gissibl and Kappe had appointed Fritz Kuhn, an American of German extraction, to assume the leadership of the movement. Kuhn was to prove a mixed blessing to the Nazi cause, but his prompt and energetic action to save the Bund brought new hope to the Party hierarchy. The new American Fuehrer and his associates were agreed that it would be necessary to change the name of the organization and at the same time to reunite the splinter groups which had developed. For this purpose Kuhn called a special convention for March 1936 in Buffalo, New York. Members of the Friends who were United States citizens and other German-Americans attended the meeting and formed the *Amerika-Deutscher Volksbund,* which was to become the largest and most influential of all pro-Nazi organizations in this country.[1]

The nature of the new association soon became clear. Kuhn's basic instructions to local units declared unequivocally that "the *Amerika-Deut-*

---

1. See Foreign Ministry files, K1052, frames 27666–713, for materials on the formation of the Bund; see also Bischoff, *Nazi Conquest,* pp. 174 ff. The most confidential Bund files were destroyed on Kuhn's orders when he learned that a House committee planned to investigate the organization. A large group of Bund papers was eventually deposited by the Justice Department in the U.S. National Archives, but they add little to the voluminous documentary information published in 1940 and 1941 by the House Un-American Activities Committee in its sixteen volumes of hearings and series of annual reports.

scher Volksbund is conducted upon the Fuehrer principle. Consequently there are no elections nor majority decisions."[2]

Wary of public reaction after the experiences of the first Bund, Kuhn made provision for keeping the existence of local cells secret and for pseudonymous or anonymous individual memberships He further specified that Aryan blood was a prerequisite for membership in the organization. Appropriate uniforms were the standard garb for official meetings at any level, along with armbands and insignia which incorporated both American and German emblems. The swastika received a place next to the American flag, and German anthems, including on occasion the Nazi *Horst Wessel Lied,* rang out more often than the Star-Spangled Banner.

The Bund employed both German and English, although the former language tended to predominate, being used in the organization's directives, its various organs, and at most meetings insofar as possible. Commanders of the various groups concluded every meeting by leading members in the Nazi salute and reciting the motto: "To a free, Gentile-ruled United States and to our fighting Movement of awakened Aryan Americans, a three-fold, rousing 'Free America! Free America! Free America!' " In these and other respects, it would have been difficult to imagine a more accurate adaptation of the Party's forms to the United States.

In spite of its largely indigenous membership, the obvious similarities of the new organization to the Nazi movement and to its own admitted predecessor, the Friends of the New Germany, kindled renewed concern among other American citizens. Even more than its forerunner, the German-American Bund sought to gain control over whole families of Americans of German descent. It devoted much attention to youth. The association formed an auxiliary group to parallel the Hitler Youth. Under the direction of Theodor Dinkelacker, this body elaborated a comprehensive program for children of Bund members. The group worked to insure that German-American children retained their language and distinctive culture, and to instruct them in the militant practices of the new Reich. The Bund maintained several camps for youth training and other activities, the largest being Camp Siegfried on Long Island and Camp Nordland, near Andover, New Jersey. In St. Louis, where 100,000 German-Americans lived and made up one-eighth of the city's population, Bund members

2. "Basic Instructions for Unit and Branch Directorates," House Special Committee on Un-American Activities, *Investigation of Un-American Propaganda Activities in the United States* (Washington, 1940–1941 and cited hereafter as *HR Investigation*), Appendix, part 4, pp. 1490–1505.

organized programs in the public schools for summer study of the German language. When authorities discovered that Nazi doctrines formed an important part of the course, they immediately abolished this project.[3]

Exact records of the organization's membership were destroyed, but it is known that the Bund grew rapidly. By 1937 the Justice Department estimated that 6,500 persons belonged to the group. Kuhn later claimed 25,-000 members and 100,000 "sympathizers," but he was notoriously unreliable and these figures are probably too high. At any rate the sudden proliferation of the association brought it quickly to public attention.

Since it employed the appurtenances of a Nazi organization, the general conclusion was that the Bund received its directions ultimately from the Reich. This was not strictly true, but the Bund readily adapted itself to the will of the Nazi Party without the need of specific instructions. Shortly after the founding of the Bund, Kuhn led a delegation to Berlin for the 1936 Olympics, where he was received briefly by Hitler. This is the only known meeting between Kuhn and the Fuehrer and there is no evidence that Hitler attached any special significance to it, although Kuhn subsequently claimed to his storm troopers that he had made a secret arrangement directly with the Chancellor.

Kuhn also asserted that he had obtained power over the German ambassador and consular establishment in the United States. This was certainly not the case. The Bund hierarchy did, however, establish extensive contacts with important offices in the Reich and proved quite receptive to any suggestions from them. This was especially true of the Propaganda Ministry, the *Amt Auslandspresse,* VDA, and similar bureaus. The VDA cooperated in instructional activities among the Bund youth and arranged for them to make study trips to the fatherland. For PROMI and other propaganda agencies the Bund performed intelligence work and assisted in disseminating Nazi literature in the United States.[4]

To serve as official organs of the Bund Kuhn set up newspapers in principal cities. The major outlet was the *Deutscher Weckruf und Beobachter,* published in New York. Publications bearing similar titles and serving identical functions appeared in Philadelphia, Chicago, and Los Angeles. An affiliated organization, the DKV or German Consumers League, carried on the fight against the voluntary boycott on trade with Germany. Reich citizens continued as members of the latter organization and thus maintained their close cooperation with the new Bund. Beginning in 1937

3. Ibid., pp. 1451–56.
4. Ibid., pp. 1465–89.

the *Volksbund* published an annual yearbook which declared forthrightly that the "supreme task" of the organization was to "defend the old Fatherland against agitation and slander."

> We stand here as the heralds of the Third Reich, as preachers of the German world-viewpoint of National Socialism which had displayed before the eyes of the world the incomparable German miracle, the miracle of National Socialism.[5]

In Kuhn and the other members of the German-American Bund Hitler had found willing allies who required little prompting.

The German-American *Yearbook* seems to have been the outgrowth of Dr. Sallet's previously mentioned recommendation to PROMI in August 1935. Another of his proposals for propaganda in the United States had also borne fruit. In May 1936 the Reich established an official German Library of Information as part of the consulate general in New York. Directed by Heinz Beller, the Library of Information published and distributed a wide variety of materials, usually in English and directed to the general public. It coordinated its operations closely with the Party's *Amt Auslandspresse* in Munich and the German Tourist Information Bureau in New York. To insure saturation of at least part of the American public, these and other agencies followed the practice of swapping mailing lists. Thus an individual who inquired of the Tourist Bureau for information on a possible trip to Europe would soon be receiving materials of quite a different character from the Library, the *Fichtebund,* or the World Service.

The extent of the Library's activities is difficult to assess, for all the pertinent records have not come to light, but Beller's successor as director, Matthias Schmitz, admitted to Congressional investigators in 1940 that the agency had spent $350,000 during that year. Until September 1939, the Library remained a part of the consulate and made no separate accounting of its expenditures. A safe assumption is that at least several hundred thousand dollars were channeled through this office in the five years of its existence. Most of its operations were by direct mail and its mailing list totaled some 100,000 names.[6]

The German Tourist Information Office had functioned in America since 1920 and maintained offices in Chicago and San Francisco in addition

---

5. German-American Bund, *Yearbook* (New York, 1937), p. 5. Kuhn also controlled the DKV, which did a brisk trade in uniforms, armbands, insignia, and related equipment needed by Bund members.

6. *HR Investigation,* Appendix, part 2, pp. 1045–54.

to its headquarters in New York. After 1933 the annual budget of the agency rose to an average of $200,000—an astronomical figure in the years before television advertising—as the "promotion of tourism" assumed new importance. Goebbels' instructions had left no doubt as to the strategic role of this agency. The Tourist Information Office applied itself diligently to the task of encouraging a more favorable political attitude toward the Reich. Its director, Dr. Ernst Schmitz, prepared and distributed a weekly newsletter, *News Flashes From Germany,* along with a variety of other items. The office's mailing list contained more than 125,000 names, and the agency remained in touch with people who long since had concluded any business they may have had with it. Both the Tourist Information Office and the Library of Information made heavy use of lectures for schools, clubs, and other organizations, accompanying their presentations with films and lantern slides showing the remarkable progress of the Reich under National Socialism.[7]

The resurgence of a race-conscious German-American movement during 1936 and 1937 stimulated new fears that dangerous Nazi influences were percolating through some quarters of American society. In January 1937 Representative Dickstein sought House approval for a new investigation. On June 21 Martin Dies of Texas introduced a similar resolution with a request for $100,000 to carry out a thorough study of subversive influences.

While the House debated Dies' resolution, continued pro-Nazi agitation by the German-American Bund led the State Department to make representations to the Reich. On October 2, 1937, Prentiss Gilbert, the American chargé d'affaires in Berlin, called on State Secretary Ernst von Weizsaecker at the Foreign Ministry and delivered a formal complaint over Nazi subversive activity in the United States. Gilbert stressed particularly

7. Ibid., pp. 1060–63. Rolf Hoffmann of the *Amt Auslandspresse* worked closely with Beller and the German Library of Information. He also began a new project in November 1937 when he moved to different headquarters and began publishing a little green news sheet called *News From Germany.* Hoffmann tried to present the weekly newsletter as the work of a private individual who was "altogether dependent upon honorary translation and occasional articles which are usually contributions of friends." The crude nature of this item earned it no respect and, although the publication continued to be circulated to thousands of individuals and newspapers in this country until 1941, the influence it attained was nil. After war broke out in September 1939 *News From Germany* had to be sent via Siberia and invariably arrived weeks and even months after the events to which it referred had been driven from the public consciousness by new developments. Though Hoffmann had much faith in the merit of his work, it became a genuine farce. See Hoffmann papers, rolls 25 and 26.

American concern over Nazi connections with the Bund and emphasized the bad effect such activities among German-Americans were having on public opinion at large. Weizsaecker reminded Gilbert of the earlier order for Reich citizens to withdraw from organizations like the Bund and denied that there now existed any link whatsoever between the Nazi Party and German-American "clubs." He insisted that the Bund was purely an American organization.

Although Weizsaecker denied any connection between Reich agencies and the Bund, he knew that in fact ties had been maintained. The *Volksdeutsche Mittelstelle* had used the Bund to arrange certain details on foreign exchange remittances from both Reich citizens and American citizens of German descent. The Bund had also processed various application forms and other materials being sent to and from "ethnic Germans" in the United States. After Gilbert's protest to the Wilhelmstrasse the use of the Bund by Reich agencies for official purposes was forbidden, since the Foreign Ministry wished at all costs to avoid a recurrence of the friction with Washington that had followed the Spanknoebel affair.

Discussions at the Foreign Ministry recalled that similar difficulties had arisen between the United States and Italy during the early twenties, when Rome attempted to organize local Fascist units in a number of American cities. Washington had demanded the recall of several Italian consuls before Italy gave up her efforts in this direction and turned to less offensive cultural activities among Italian-Americans through the Dante Alighieri Society. After the conflict caused by the activities of the Friends of the New Germany, the Foreign Ministry now decided to adopt a reserved attitude toward the German-American Bund, although it hoped to duplicate Italy's success in the cultural sphere by lending assistance to another organization, to be called the Immanuel Kant Society. The Foreign Ministry felt that a society should be formed for strictly cultural activities among German-Americans and that the Reich's cooperation in it would provide adequate moral support for the Pro-Nazi activists of the Bund.[8]

In May 1937 Dr. Hans Heinrich Dieckhoff, one of the leading Foreign Ministry authorities on the United States, replaced Hans Luther as ambassador to Washington. As the brother-in-law of Joachim von Ribbentrop, Dieckhoff presumably enjoyed greater access than his predecessor to the inner circles in Berlin. After observing the steady deterioration of the German position in America, largely because of the blatant imitation of

8. Memorandum by Freytag of the Foreign Ministry, Oct. 11, 1937, *DGFP–D, 1,* 635–38.

Nazi forms and practices by the Bund, he prepared a lengthy dispatch under an extended title: "Relations between the United States and Germany
and the German-American element. Are we in a position to exert political
influence on the German-Americans? The German-American Bund." This
was a most acute analysis of the situation and, for a Nazi diplomat, an
amazingly frank report.

Dieckhoff first called attention to the fact that relations between the two
countries had actually worsened during 1937. Many Americans feared that
Berlin was seeking to export Nazism and that the Bund was its Trojan
horse in this country. The ambassador warned that the German element in
the United States was numerically much weaker than commonly assumed
in the Reich. Of the total population of 130 million, perhaps twelve to
thirteen million were of German descent, but most of them were completely anglicized. At most there could be four or five million who still
spoke, read, and wrote German and these were never unified. Political,
denominational, geographical, and other divisions made it impossible for
this group to attain political power commensurate with its numbers. The
advent of the Third Reich had even accentuated these cleavages.

> The figures on German-Americans in Chicago are significant.
> There 700,000 are of German descent, in the broadest sense; of these
> about 40,000 are members of clubs of a definitely German character
> (athletic clubs, choral societies, German regional societies, etc.); of
> these, in turn, only 450 are in the German-American Bund, the
> only really politically minded organization which energetically stands
> up for Germany! In brief, 700,000, 40,000, 450! These figures hold
> good for most of the other sections of the country, and I feel that they
> speak volumes. Things being as they are, any attempt to urge or
> force any pro-German political activity on the German-Americans
> would not lead to unification; on the contrary, it would rather inten-
> sify the existing differences.[9]

On the basis of these considerations Dieckhoff argued vigorously against
Party plans to form native assault troops for the "crucial moment," brand-
ing such "conspiratorial child's play" as utterly senseless in the United
States. Any sort of political contact between the Reich and German-
Americans, he warned, could only endanger legitimate endeavors of racial
comrades in this country.

9. Dieckhoff to the Foreign Ministry, Jan. 7, 1938, ibid., pp. 664–78. Joachim Remak offers a balanced view of Dieckhoff in "Hitlers Amerikapolitik," *Aussenpolitik*,
6 (February 1955), 706–14.

While the envoy had warm praise for the spirit of the German-American Bund and its fight for Nazi ideals, he contended that the group's methods consistently produced results opposite to those it sought. "Instead of arousing sympathetic understanding of the German cause among the masses, they engender antagonism. Moreover, the Bund's methods are likely to cause difficulties and discord between the United States and Germany." In the face of the hostile American attitude toward authoritarian states and ideologies, Dieckhoff proposed a policy of absolute restraint toward the Bund. Most importantly, there should be no political contact between authorities in the Reich and the organization. The Bund should in no case continue to be used for official German purposes. Furthermore, Berlin must impress the association with the need to assume a more truly American character, notably by designing its own flag instead of using the emblem of the Third Reich. The Bund leaders should cease stressing their allegedly intimate liaison with prominent Nazis in Germany, for this only had negative effects in the United States. Only in the last resort should the German government openly disavow the Bund, but that possible necessity was at least recognized.

Dieckhoff's detailed report led to a high-level meeting in Berlin on January 26, 1938, at which the Foreign Ministry and the AO concurred in his appraisal. Ernst Bohle, who had recently moved into the Wilhelmstrasse as State Secretary, while retaining his position as chief of the Party's Foreign Organization, reluctantly agreed to release another statement to the press reminding Reich nationals that they could not participate in purely American organizations like the Bund.

Berlin's readiness to appease American sensibilities at this time may well have been related to the inner tensions then brewing in the Nazi regime. Through the first quarter of 1938 a series of significant communications were exchanged between the Foreign Ministry and the embassy in Washington regarding the attitude which the United States would be likely to take in the event of war in Europe. Dieckhoff unhesitatingly replied to an inquiry from Berlin that the United States government could take the nation into a conflict more quickly than in the last war and that he thought America would intervene if Great Britain became involved.

The Foreign Ministry's concern with the matter no doubt stemmed from Hitler's secret announcement of his war plans the previous November. Action against Austria and Czechoslovakia might come at any moment and Foreign Minister von Neurath, a cautious man and one of the few old-line civil servants still surviving from the Weimar cabinet, was obviously exploring the prospects for keeping the United States out of any new European conflict. It is quite possible that the January press release concerning the prohibition on Reich German membership in the Bund was part of a precautionary campaign to ward off American intervention.[10]

Congress resumed deliberations on the Dies resolution in early 1938 and approved the new investigation, with an appropriation of $25,000, in May. Dies himself became chairman of the committee appointed to conduct the inquiry. Passage of the Dies proposal came in the midst of continued public clamor over the Nazi Bund. Ambassador Dieckhoff complained repeatedly to Berlin that Reich agencies had not yet severed their connections with the organization. In February 1938 Fritz Kuhn had gone to Berlin and returned claiming that both Goering and Goebbels had given him a warm reception. He further informed Bund members that the Party had issued elaborate instructions for Bund activities in the United States. The *Bundesleiter* assured his associates that he was in the closest and most cordial contact with the *Volksdeutsche Mittelstelle.*

Dieckhoff anxiously wired Berlin to find out if Kuhn's statements were true. The ambassador noted that the German-American situation was already difficult enough without complications from the Bund "whose leading personalities again and again secretly point out or hint that they are in closest contact with the Reich Government and even receive instructions from it." Agitation over Nazi subversion in the United States compounded German concern over trade with this country, which had suffered yet another sharp decline during 1937.[11]

10. See the exchanges between Berlin and Washington, Jan. 26 to Mar. 30, 1938, *DGFP–D, 4,* 685–97. This was a critical period for the Nazi regime. A few weeks prior to the crisis over Austria, the German government underwent a drastic shakeup. On February 4, 1938, Hitler removed von Neurath, Hjalmar Schacht, and Generals Blomberg and Fritsch from their positions because of their apparent reluctance to implement his plans for aggression. Neurath's dismissal was an interesting maneuver. He was "elevated" to the presidency of a so-called Secret Cabinet Council to advise the Fuehrer on foreign policy. This Council was nothing but a myth and never convened. Ribbentrop's appointment as Foreign Minister meant that dedicated Nazis controlled all German foreign operations for the first time. Otto Dietrich, *12 Jahre mit Hitler* (Munich, 1955), pp. 49 ff., reviews this episode. Schacht, in anticipation of some such chain of events, had hinted to the American ambassador the previous December that he might emigrate to the United States and take a banking position; *Ambassador Dodd's Diary, 1933–38,* p. 436.

11. Dieckhoff's dispatch to Berlin, June 2, 1938, *DGFP–D, 1,* 454 ff. After a six-month investigation the Foreign Ministry informed the embassy in Washington that Kuhn had not been received by Goering and Goebbels and that Berlin had urged the removal of all Reich citizens who remained in the Bund. "The natural conclusion is that Herr Kuhn has—as already on other occasions—consciously deviated from the truth in order to strengthen his position with his adherents." See ibid., 4, 650; Dieckhoff's report to Weizsaecker, Nov. 8, 1938, p. 638; and a memorandum by a Foreign Ministry econo-

Tension between Germany and the United States increased in 1938, as Hitler annexed Austria and then concentrated pressure on Czechoslovakia. The momentary relief which came in the wake of the Munich agreement ended abruptly when widespread anti-Jewish pogroms, abetted by the Nazi government, broke out all over the Reich in November. President Roosevelt gave a firm indication of this country's attitude toward these events by withdrawing Ambassador Wilson from Berlin on November 14. Germany in turn ordered Dieckhoff back to the Foreign Ministry. Neither man was ever to return to his post.

The Wilhelmstrasse recognized that American public opinion was solidly behind Roosevelt. There was growing disaffection even among previously friendly German-Americans and newspapers. The *New Yorker Staatszeitung,* which had tended to be noncommittal on Hitler's Germany in the past, now moved into the camp of active opponents of Reich policy. To add to the diplomatic crisis between Berlin and Washington several sabotage trials involving Germans were pending in the United States. Litigation of the "Black Tom Dock" and "Kingsland" cases, which centered around German military espionage in New Jersey prior to American entry into the First World War, was still under way. In New York four Germans, including one woman, were tried for conspiracy to steal United States military secrets and were sentenced to prison on December 2, 1938. A month later two other Germans were convicted of espionage and of photographing military fortifications in the Panama Canal Zone. Relations between the two countries had taken a critical turn from which there would be no recovery.[12]

Upon his arrival back in Berlin Dieckhoff urged the immediate repatriation of all *Reichsdeutschen* presently residing in the United States; he estimated that there were 150,000 to 200,000 German citizens in America. If some of them proved unwilling to return, the ambassador advised that pressure be applied through the withdrawal of their passports. Since Nazi racial policies encompassed all those of German blood, Dieckhoff also gave consideration to seeking the return of German-Americans to the

---

mist on the effects of a possible rupture with the United States, Nov. 18, 1938, pp. 641–43.

12. The various espionage trials are covered extensively in the *New York Times* during October 1938 to January 1939. See also the memorandum by Woermann of the Foreign Ministry, Nov. 22, 1938, *DGFP–D, 4,* 644–48. The Foreign Ministry weighed a possible break with the United States and anticipated serious repercussions in Latin America, where Roosevelt's policy and the Pan-American movement were winning strong friends for America.

fatherland, but he abandoned the idea because he realized that the United States government was unlikely to concur. That the Foreign Ministry considered such a plan affords a revealing insight into Nazi thinking and underlines the seriousness of the breach which had developed between Germany and the United States by late 1938.[13]

Meanwhile the State Department had come into possession of a circular from a certain Dr. Rettig, director of the German Student Exchange Agency in New York, which required German students in the United States to prepare political reports on the prevailing attitudes of various colleges and universities at which they were enrolled. Other documents also suggested that the Reich was making use of German exchange students to disseminate Nazi doctrines and to gather intelligence. The Department called in the German chargé d'affaires, Hans Thomsen, and demanded that the Student Exchange Agency be closed. Thomsen, apprehensive lest another public clamor be aroused, made no effort to defend Rettig or the agency and warily inquired if the incriminating information was to be made public. The Department said that its information was confidential and would remain so, provided Germany abolished the office. The Nazi chargé d'affaires readily agreed and the agency was eliminated in January 1939.[14]

The same month Captain Fritz Wiedemann, Hitler's commanding officer in the First World War, arrived in the United States to assume his duties as consul general in San Francisco. Wiedemann had served as adjutant to the Fuehrer since 1935 and it was generally thought that he had come to America on special assignment to promote the Nazi movement and related propaganda. Wiedemann did engage in limited propaganda activities, lectures, and the like, but there is no evidence that he had a special commission, if such indeed were necessary, for these tasks. His chief interest turned out to be promoting Nazism and the Reich through personal association with members of high society. The career diplomats

13. Memorandum by Dieckhoff, Dec. 16, 1938, ibid., pp. 652–54. Dieckhoff prepared this paper in response to an inquiry from Goering who had heard that German workers in the United States were being fired to provide jobs for refugees from the Reich.

14. Memorandum by James D. Dunn of the State Department, Jan. 9, 1939, FR, 2 (1939), 600–02. Thomsen had come to the United States in 1936 after serving as an official in the Reich Chancellery. With Dieckhoff's recall he was to remain the Reich's principal diplomatic representative until Pearl Harbor, proving himself a shrewd protagonist for Nazi Germany. His work in this post much impressed Hitler, who planned to hold him "for a post of exceptional difficulty" after the war.

in the foreign service were quite suspicious of the former adjutant, and Ernst von Weizsaecker rebuked Wiedemann for his contacts with William Randolph Hearst and Herbert Hoover.[15]

The first report of the Dies Committee went to the House on January 3, 1939, urging that its preliminary studies warranted a fuller investigation. The House concurred and overwhelmingly approved the continuation of the investigation with a larger appropriation of $100,000. Two weeks after the House extended the committee, the German-American Bund staged its largest demonstration to date. The organization had always held four annual celebrations, honoring United States Independence Day, the day of the founding of the Third Reich, Hitler's birthday, and George Washington's birthday. The latter event was the occasion for a gigantic rally in Madison Square Garden on February 20. More than 20,000 people attended, although not all of them were Bundists, to witness a strange demonstration of perverted American patriotism and transplanted Nazi racism.

As a concession to American traditions, the speakers addressed the crowd in English, although even *Bundesleiter* Kuhn had an inadequate command of the language. But the substance of the proceedings, featuring the swastika and other Nazi symbols equally with American emblems, was dominated by the political philosophy of the Third Reich. Brawls erupted in the hall between Kuhn's storm troopers and hecklers. The uniformed Bund members looked for all the world like a miniature version of the famed Nuremberg rallies of the National Socialist Party. Kuhn and other speakers left no doubt of their virulent anti-Semitism and fiercely attacked "the Jewish-Communist" influence which allegedly governed the United States. This massive gathering of the Bund touched off a new wave of public apprehension and Consul General Borchers reported to Berlin that the function had done no service to the German cause in the United States.[16]

There was an important aftermath to the February Bund rally. On May 26 Kuhn was arrested on charges of embezzlement and misuse of the organization's funds, including the receipts from the demonstration in Madison Square Garden. Thomas Dewey, the young federal attorney in New York, conducted a vigorous and successful prosecution.

15. Dispatches between Wiedemann and Weizsaecker, *DGFP–D*, 4, 887 and 6, 140–42 and 443–44.

16. See Borcher's dispatch to Berlin, Feb. 27, 1939, *DGFP–D*, 4, 675–78. See also Ogden, *The Dies Committee*, pp. 46–62.

Meanwhile the Dies investigation uncovered connections between a number of American fascists and anti-Semites and offices in Germany. George E. Deatherage, the head of the white supremacy group known as the Knights of the White Camellia, and General George Van Horn Moseley, who publicly advocated violent army action to eliminate Communists from the federal government, had long been in communication with a number of agencies in the Reich and were cooperating in the spread of anti-Jewish and authoritarian propaganda in this country. The F.B.I. produced compromising documents and correspondence connecting Deatherage, Moseley, and their associates with the Nazi Party and various other German offices.

These disclosures brought the strongest instructions yet to German agencies concerned with racial affairs. The *Volksdeutsche Mittelstelle* explicitly directed that ties with American fascists be severed and added "that there may be no correspondence between Reich offices concerned with *Volksdeutschen* affairs and the German-American Bund, if the connection between the Bund and an official German institution is recognizable or even deducible."[17]

This order evoked strong opposition from the *Kameradschaft USA,* an organization of German citizens who had been active in the Nazi movement in the United States before their repatriation. Fritz Gissibl, who was now attached to the DAI as director of the *Kameradschaft,* argued vehemently that the Reich must support the Bund, morally and financially. The organization had sent a secret agent to the United States for eight months during 1938 and 1939 to work out plans for cooperation with the Bund. The agent was highly impressed by Kuhn's Nazi sympathies and leadership of the Bund, even in the face of the pending legal action against him. The agent's confidential report on the Bund echoed Gissibl's own thoughts: "The Bund, in my opinion, constitutes the only organization to which it serves Germany to lend moral support. If it does not receive financial assistance as well, it will be ruined by the many court proceedings (at present five cases have been instituted)."[18] Reluctance to abandon the Bund persisted, even when the association's usefulness seemed definitely at an end.

17. The *Volksdeutsche Mittelstelle* order of July 15, 1939, is filmed with the records of the *Kameradschaft USA,* U.S. National Archives, micro-copy T–81, roll 145, frame 0183244. On Deatherage and Moseley, see their testimony before the Dies Committee, *HR Investigation,* 5, 3455–3703.

18. Cf. *Bericht ueber den Amerika-deutschen Volksbund,* Aug. 1, 1939, *Kameradschaft USA* files, roll 145, frame 0183228–30.

Other German enterprises were also encountering problems. In the fall of 1938 Dr. Manfred Zapp had come to New York to take over the Transocean news agency's operations in the United States and to coordinate its activities throughout the hemisphere. His efforts met with little success in this country, for TO afforded slight competition to the established American press services. But Zapp increased the agency's transmissions to South America and the Far East, providing these areas with a growing volume of unfavorable dispatches on events and policies in the United States. In April 1939, during a conversation with a Swedish reporter who mentioned that his coverage of the United States was usually favorable, the chief of Transocean's Washington bureau confided:

> My instructions are entirely different. We send news to South America, Germany and some of our stuff goes to the Far East, and for us it is a matter of policy to damage the prestige of the United States as best we can. We work all our stuff that way and don't send anything else unless it cannot be avoided from the point of view of news value.[19]

While seeking to undermine the United States elsewhere in the hemisphere, TO continued its attempts to gain a foothold in the North American press.

Since there appeared little likelihood that Transocean would prove an effective force in this country, the German embassy began more frequently to employ alternative outlets. Thomsen, the chargé d'affaires, had long followed the practice of circulating in the United States copies of the speeches of Hitler and other leading Nazi spokesmen. He distributed 200,-000 copies of the Fuehrer's address of April 28, 1939, in which Hitler scoffed at reports of German aggressive intentions both in Europe and in the Western Hemisphere. Further to allay American fears, Thomsen ordered a translation of the decision of the Argentine Court of Appeals in the so-called Patagonia Affair, which he then sent to American journalists and newspapers. The Argentine court had found insufficient evidence to convict the number two Nazi in that country, Alfred Mueller, on charges that he had masterminded a plot to seize Patagonia and then surrender it to Germany for annexation. The outcome of the case seemed to strengthen German disclaimers of any territorial ambitions in the New World and the

---

19. Statement of Eric T. Winberg of *Dagens Nyheter* (Stockholm), Sept. 17, 1940, *HR Investigation*, Appendix, part 2, exhibit 132, p. 1250.

German embassy in Washington made certain that the point was not lost on the press in this country.[20]

Thomsen reported to Berlin, however, that there was only a slender possibility of expanding propaganda in the United States. To improve the present system he recommended that the German Library of Information be detached from the consulate general in New York and given a more adequate staff. A competent German editor should then take over the Library and turn out a regular English information service dealing with current political problems from the German point of view. The operation should remain technically subordinate to the embassy, while appearing outwardly as an independent endeavor. The Germans implemented these proposals several weeks later.

As war approached in Europe during the summer of 1939, German propaganda in the United States turned to the task of justifying the Third Reich's actions and demonstrating that responsibility for the conflict lay elsewhere. An important step in this direction was the distribution of 120,-000 copies of Hitler's correspondence with French Premier Daladier, in which the Fuehrer repeatedly professed Germany's peaceful intentions. Thomsen carried out this operation in August, working anonymously through the German Library of Information.

Immediately after the outbreak of war, Hitler confirmed the role of the German embassy as the controlling force behind Nazi propaganda in the United States. A bitter struggle had been under way between Ribbentrop and Goebbels since 1938 for control of propaganda abroad. The two men even set up rival press clubs in Berlin to compete for the favors of foreign journalists.

Otto Dietrich, the Reich Press Chief, has described the fierce battle between the two ministers:

> One day at headquarters Ribbentrop persuaded Hitler to transfer to him in writing [authority over] all propaganda intended for foreign consumption; Reich Propaganda Minister Goebbels knew nothing at all about this. On the morning of the next day movers, sent by the Foreign Office, appeared at Goebbels' Ministry and his various offices in Berlin to haul away the physical apparatus used for

20. Thomsen's dispatch to Berlin, July 24, 1939, *DGFP–D, 4,* 967–68. The Mueller case arose over certain documents which Germany claimed to be forgeries. Recalling Goebbels' plan to leak false documents to the press, one wonders whether the incident was staged for the precise purpose of calming the fears of many people in this hemisphere and discrediting the advocates of preparedness. See below, Chapter 8.

foreign propaganda. Goebbels' officials barricaded themselves in their rooms, and the Propaganda Minister himself promptly telephoned to Hitler for help. Hitler, who had actually signed the order in question, had Goebbels come over by plane. He ordered Goebbels and Ribbentrop to sit down together in a compartment of his special train and not to leave it until they had come to terms on the matter. Three hours later both men emerged red-faced and informed Hitler—as might have been expected—that an agreement was impossible. Furious, Hitler withdrew and dictated a compromise decision which largely annulled his [previous] written order. In practice, however, Ribbentrop never adhered to this latter decision. Holding a facsimile of the first, rescinded order, he challenged the Propaganda Minister's jurisdiction in the Reich and in all German missions abroad until the end of the war.[21]

The latter directive, dated September 8, 1939, provided sufficient basis for the continued power struggle. It specified that foreign propaganda would henceforth be governed by the general policy and guidelines of the Foreign Minister but disseminated mainly through the Propaganda Ministry. This belated effort to bring some order into the chaos of Nazi activities abroad was prompted in part by prolonged disputes between Party and Reich representatives in Latin America. Although the persistent bickering of Goebbels and Ribbentrop robbed the Fuehrer's decision of much of its vigor, it did have the effect of making the German embassy the focal point of subsequent propaganda endeavors in the United States.

Thomsen quickly outlined the embassy's strategy. Germany must direct all efforts toward exploiting the isolationist sentiment of an important segment of the American population. The chargé d'affaires warned sharply against any further sabotage activity in the United States. It would only serve to undermine the isolationists. Radio and press services from the Reich should also bear in mind the urgent need to make the isolationist position credible and therefore must avoid any harsh attacks on the United States. On September 24, 1939, a dispatch from Thomsen considered in detail the approach to be taken in Nazi efforts to insure American neutrality. He cautioned that there must be no appearance of support for the isolationists in the current debate on the arms embargo, for this would only backfire on Germany. Utmost care was imperative in all propa-

21. Dietrich, *12 Jahre mit Hitler*, pp. 129–30; see also Thomsen's report to the Foreign Ministry, Aug. 30, 1939, *DGFP–D*, 7, 436.

ganda activities, because the American people were much more hostile to Germany than they had been in 1917.

Thomsen listed several themes which he considered most effective for Nazi propaganda:

1. The senseless and useless loss of lives and wealth which the United States had sustained in the war of 1914–1918.

2. The vast burden of public debt due to American participation in the last conflict.

3. The economic disintegration suffered by the United States and the world after the previous war.

4. The role of the munitions industry as war profiteer.

5. Britain's "cynical" role as a debtor.

6. British chicanery regarding American trade and shipping during both the last and the current wars.

7. British double-dealing in 1916 (her concealment of the secret treaties with her allies).

8. The negative result of the "lying slogan," "Make the world safe for democracy."

9. America's refusal to ratify the Versailles Treaty, thereby conceding the justice of the German cause.

In exploiting these and other themes, Thomsen again stressed that Germany should in no way become involved in the arms debate in the Congress, for "all the effective arguments will be advanced by the isolationists themselves." Anti-British propaganda must not be too crude and should focus principally on arguments from American sources, of which there was an ample supply in isolationist literature, e.g. "England expects every American to do his duty."[22]

Through the fall of 1939 every available instrument of Nazi propaganda broadcast these themes. Thomsen reported with satisfaction that, while the Transocean service still enjoyed only marginal success, editors at least used TO dispatches to check on reports from American sources. He was especially pleased that the *New Yorker Staatszeitung*, the leading

---

22. Thomsen's dispatches of Sept. 18 and 24, 1939, *DGFP–D, 8,* 89–91 and 127–29. The last reference is to the isolationist volume by Quincy Howe, *England Expects Every American to do His Duty* (New York, 1937).

German paper in the United States and one whose anti-Nazi policies had caused it to be banned for a time in the Reich, had now begun to employ Transocean material to present the German viewpoint.

Meanwhile the German Library of Information had developed into a veritable institute of propaganda. As soon as the war broke out, the Library had sent out thousands of copies of a German White Book setting forth the Reich's position on the Polish crisis. In addition it distributed several addresses by Hitler and Ribbentrop to hundreds of thousands of people in this country. To counteract the de facto press boycott of German news agencies, the Library began to publish a weekly news letter, *Facts in Review,* with the editorial assistance of George Sylvester Viereck. Initially this weekly publication went to a selected group of 20,000 influential citizens, Congressmen, educators, journalists, and others. In a similar vein Manfred Zapp inaugurated a special program under which Transocean mailed its dispatches directly to private individuals.

> Both through the Library of Information and the office of the German Railways in New York, which works with hundreds of travel bureaus distributed over the whole continent, German films and propaganda materials are circulated. Since the outbreak of the war, the regular advertising matter of the German Railways Office has been given a decidedly political tinge.[23]

An embassy press office, in close collaboration with German consular officials throughout the country, directed all these activities. Simultaneously Thomsen was studying the possible purchase of newspapers, periodicals, radio stations, and other media, but he found no worthwhile opportunities in this respect. The chargé d'affaires emphasized the importance of cultivating American journalists both through the embassy and through contacts with correspondents in Germany. Thomsen reported that he was seeking to induce suitable American writers to visit Germany and claimed credit for the fact that "the distinguished feature writer, L. Stoddard, is at present reporting in Germany for the North American Newspaper Alliance, which supplies a hundred influential American, British, and Latin American papers."

23. Thomsen to Berlin, Nov. 21, 1939, ibid., pp. 432–34. See also *HR Investigation,* Appendix, part 2, pp. 1046–53. Viereck had grown more cautious in his dealings with Nazi propagandists. His contract with the Library, for which he received $500 a month, explicitly stated that the relationship could be terminated in the event of a break between the United States and Germany, and that he would undertake no assignment which would conflict with his duties as an American citizen.

The previous April another pro-Nazi organization had come into exist-ence under the leadership of Dr. Frederic Ernest Ferdinand Auhagen. Known as the American Fellowship Forum, it was a front organization de-voted to keeping the United States from intervening against Germany in any European conflict. Auhagen, a former Columbia University faculty member, had also hoped to turn the organization into a money-making arrangement for himself. He was still a German citizen and had been on the payroll of Kurt Johannsen and the *Aufklaerung-Ausschuss* of Ham-burg since 1938. Although the by-laws of the Forum limited alien mem-bership to 10 percent of the total, Auhagen and other Reich nationals actually controlled the organization.

With the assistance of that ubiquitous factotum, George Sylvester Viereck, Auhagen launched a magazine entitled *Today's Challenge*. There was little response to the publication, however, and the Forum had to give it up after the third issue in December 1939. It was succeeded by a more modest weekly news letter, *Forum's Observer,* which soon suffered a simi-lar fate. The Forum's membership was never more than a few hundred and the organization collapsed early in 1940.[24]

In December 1939 the trial of Fritz Kuhn ended in his conviction on charges of grand larceny and fraud in connection with his embezzlement of Bund funds. He and an associate, James Wheeler-Hill, were sentenced to prison. The *Deutscher Weckruf und Beobachter* and other Bund papers tried to picture Kuhn as the victim of anti-German persecution and even described him as the first German-American prisoner of war, but the at-tempt was half-hearted and farcical. With the disclosure of the *Bundes-leiter's* criminal conduct and the public revelations concerning the organi-zation made before the Dies committee, the Bund quickly withered, most of its followers painfully disillusioned.

24. Viereck actually contributed little to the organization and eventually sued it for $5,000, although he settled out of court for $150. Ibid., pp. 1063–1110. Another prominent figure in the Forum was Dr. Ferdinand A. Kertess, a naturalized American who engaged in a variety of intrigues on behalf of the Nazis. Most important was a scheme which he devised to retain the position of German chemical firms in supplying the Latin American market. To do this he made large purchases from Du Pont for delivery to German customers elsewhere in the hemisphere, pending the conclusion of hostilities and the resumption of deliveries from the Reich. Kertess also laid plans, in cooperation with other Nazi operatives, for a reorganization of German and Ger-man-American industry in the United States after the war and its coordination by an official Reich ministry. See the documents on Kertess' activities printed in ibid., pp. 1101–05.

The German diplomatic corps had anticipated such a development and it had maintained absolute restraint during Kuhn's trial. Consul General Borchers reported with relief that the press had not implicated official German agencies in the course of the proceedings against Kuhn. He expressed the opinion of most of his colleagues when he added that "Kuhn, who would not take any advice, made one gross tactical error after another to the detriment of German interests."[25]

Although the German embassy had obtained nominal control over propaganda, there remained serious problems in coordinating Reich agents in this country. Thomsen learned with alarm that his urgent recommendation against sabotage activity in the United States was being ignored. Early in 1940 he discovered that a German-American and a German citizen in New York were preparing plans for sabotage in several Atlantic ports. The chargé d'affaires ordered them to desist until further notice. He hastily contacted Berlin and informed the Foreign Ministry of his action. "Since our foreign policy aims at keeping America out of the war under all circumstances, it is my opinion that all such attempts must be prohibited."

Weizsaecker replied from the Wilhelmstrasse that Thomsen's action had been entirely correct. The two men involved, identified only as von Hausberger and Walter, had claimed that they acted on instructions from *Abwehr,* the German military intelligence office, but Weizsaecker informed Thomsen that they had no connection with the German military. In fact, however, and evidently unknown to Weizsaecker, an *Abwehr* agent had left Buenos Aires for New York in December 1939 to gather intelligence on American aircraft plants and arms shipments to the Allies. He "was not to make his presence known to the German diplomatic representation in the United States." Another agent left Buenos Aires a month later to rendezvous with Fritz von Hausberger at Weehawken, New Jersey. The High Command of the German *Wehrmacht* chose to keep the Foreign Ministry in the dark as to its activities in the United States, probably because it knew that the Wilhelmstrasse would oppose them as likely to cause conflict with American authorities.[26]

Friction between the Foreign Ministry and the military continued to arise over the question of saboteurs in the United States. Thomsen was con-

25. Borchers to Berlin, Dec. 8, 1939, *DGFP–D, 8,* 504–06.

26. Thomsen's urgent wire to Weizsaecker, Jan. 25, 1940, ibid., pp. 700–01; also n. 4, p. 701, recording the substance of other unprinted documents pertaining to this incident.

vinced that massive espionage was already underway through a regular organization when he complained again to Berlin in May 1940:

> If my chief task is to prevent by all the means at my disposal the entry of the United States into the war, and to cultivate the few valuable contacts we still have here, it is practically being sabotaged by the activities of the agents of the *Wehrmacht*. . . . These activities are the surest way of bringing America into action on the side of our enemies and of destroying the last vestiges of sympathy for Germany. I cannot discern any political or military advantage in it.[27]

Sabotage activity remained a thorn in Thomsen's side as he initiated the most ambitious Nazi propaganda campaign of all, the effort to ensure United States neutrality by defeating Franklin Delano Roosevelt in the presidential election of 1940.

27. Thomsen to Berlin, May 22, 1940, ibid., 9, 410–12.

CHAPTER 7

Ibero-Amerika—Authoritarian Eddies
and the Democratic Mainstream

Like an ominous German U-boat, Nazi influence in Latin America broke the surface in 1937. Until that year the Party had carried on its activity among Germans in the region with relative discretion and had attracted only moderate attention. Observers now suddenly realized that the many German groups and organizations in the Latin American countries had proved easy prey to the radical philosophy of the new Reich. In country after country Germans began to stage mass celebrations in honor of the founding of the Reich, Hitler's birthday, the Day of the German people, and other festivities symbolic of their ties with the fatherland. The swastika, Nazi uniforms, insignia, and other Party forms appeared increasingly at the public functions of the German immigrants. It was no longer a secret that, as Ernst Wilhelm Bohle had boasted in 1936, the Party had "conquered foreign Germandom for the Reich."

A major Nazi goal during 1937 was to enlist the support of the principal South American countries for the Anti-Comintern Pact which Germany had recently concluded with Japan and Italy. Berlin hoped to generalize the Pact and believed that adherence of the ABC countries would attract their neighbors into a broad anti-Soviet front in Latin America. This failed to materialize, and by late in the year the German Foreign Ministry was forced to recognize that Latin American countries were unlikely to subscribe formally to the agreement.

Developments in Rio de Janeiro were especially disappointing. In spite of the authoritarian tendencies of Brazil's President Getulio Vargas, who set aside the constitution and began to rule by decree in November 1937, the Wilhelmstrasse doubted that Brazil would align herself with Germany. Nazi leaders in Brazil had begun to think that the Vargas coup actually made it probable that democratic institutions would remain in existence for some time. Herbert Kuehne, reporting to the *Haus der Presse* in Munich, asserted that the Party would delay overt action to seize power in the country until it was certain of success. "Is it not better to postpone the great moment until everything is well prepared?"[1]

Having virtually abandoned efforts to bring the Latin American countries into the Anti-Comintern camp, the German government was surprised in December 1937 when the Brazilian Minister of Justice and Internal Affairs, Dr. Francisco de Silva Campos, approached German Ambassador Karl Ritter with a view to gaining the Reich's assistance in organizing an anti-Communist exhibition. The minister reported that Vargas was personally interested in the matter and inquired further if confidential, permanent liaison could be established between Brazil and the Anti-Comintern Bureau. The Nazis were elated. Within a month the materials for the proposed exhibition were on their way to Brazil, and Berlin informed Ritter that he should issue a warm invitation to Brazilian police officials to send representatives to the Anti-Comintern Bureau.[2]

The momentary promise of amity faded as swiftly as it had appeared. In February 1938 the Vargas regime began a strong campaign against the NSDAP organization in Brazil and many of its individual adherents. German schools and cultural and social organizations also felt the pressure. Ritter sharply protested the arrest of Ernst Dorsch, the leading Nazi of Rio Grande do Sul. In a stormy interview with the President the German ambassador even tried to cow the Brazilian by adopting a distinctly threatening tone, but Vargas sternly rebuffed him, and Ritter immediately became more moderate.

The Nazi envoy reported to Berlin that Vargas was not really anti-German, but that he was obsessed with the idea of forging a homogeneous Brazilian race with a uniform language and culture. Therefore he was highly displeased by the retention of German traits among the one million *Volksdeutschen* of the country's three southern states. Germany now received a taste of its own medicine as the Vargas regime, with greater subtlety, less inhumanity, and incomparably more justification than the Nazi

1. Reports to Rolf Hoffmann, Oct. 10 and Nov. 10, 1937, Hoffmann papers, roll 29, frames 26600–656. See also *FR*, 5 (1937), 312–16 for United States dispatches dealing with Vargas' coup. Vargas justified his action to the United States as necessary to put a brake on the growth of the native fascist movement. The United States press emphasized the fascist nature of Vargas' own action and intimated that he had secret ties with the Axis, but Secretary Hull decried such statements in an off-the-record news conference. Hull did order American consuls and diplomats to report on any detectable Nazi or other fascist influence in Brazil.

2. Memorandum by an official of the Foreign Ministry, Nov. 30, 1937, *DGFP–D*, 5, 815; Ritter to Berlin, Dec. 23, 1937, pp. 816–19; also n. 7, p. 819, reporting Berlin's reply of Jan. 24, 1938.

Reich, intensified its campaign to insure national unity in Brazil. Ritter shrewdly foresaw that the Brazilian attitude was unlikely to change and that Vargas would probably be "permanently opposed to everything German and all German activities."[3]

In an attempt to overcome Brazilian hostility to "cultural activities" among her immigrants, Germany sought to coordinate Latin American policy with Rome, for the Italians were also anxious to devise means whereby they could continue the pursuit of their aims in Brazil. During a trip to Rome in late May, Hitler himself took up the subject of harmonizing cultural policies between the two fascist powers. Mussolini and his associates proved evasive. They clearly did not wish to jeopardize their own relative success in this sphere by affiliating too closely with the less adroit Germans. Since cooperation could not be worked out at the top level, Weizsaecker directed the German missions in Argentina, Brazil, and Chile to investigate the manner of Italy's activities in their respective countries for possible duplication by the Nazis.[4]

Meanwhile the major Nazi organ in the Rio de la Plata region had run into serious financial difficulties. The German chargé d'affaires in Buenos Aires urgently wired the Propaganda Ministry on January 9, 1938, that the *Deutsche La Plata Zeitung* was on the verge of bankruptcy. He asked PROMI to provide RM 25,000 at once to relieve the paper's distress. Berlin promptly dispatched these funds, and PROMI, the Foreign Ministry, and the AO continued discussions on the situation well into February. Their studies revealed that a sustained effort in behalf of the paper would be necessary for at least the next two years. On February 21 the AO submitted a report stressing the journal's crucial importance to Nazi groups in Argentina, Uruguay, and Paraguay. It was vital to keep the *Deutsche La Plata Zeitung* in operation, and the German government determined to spare no effort in this direction.[5]

The functioning of the Party machine in Brazil had already undergone some modification, but May 1938 brought a fundamental change in the

3. See "Cooperation of the Government of the United States in Checking Nazi Activities in Brazil," *FR*, 5 (1938), 408–20; Ritter to Berlin, Mar. 30, 1938, *DGFP–D*, 5, 824–27. On April 28 Brazil banned all foreign political organizations and the Minister of Justice inaugurated a system of tight supervision and censorship of all foreign-language papers, cultural and educational societies, and other groups.

4. Memorandum by Weizsaecker, May 16, 1938, and Weizsaecker's dispatch to Buenos Aires, Rio de Janeiro, and Santiago de Chile, May 21, 1938, ibid., pp. 841 and 852 ff.

5. Chargé d'affaires in Argentina to the Foreign Ministry, Jan. 9, 1938, ibid., pp. 819 ff.; nn. 5 and 6, p. 819, recording the substance of other pertinent documents.

German position in that country. The European fascist movements had inspired the formation in 1932 of an authoritarian Brazilian party, the Integralists, headed by one Plinio Salgado. The group had supported Vargas' abrogation of the constitution and his assumption of dictatorial powers, but Integralist leaders were obviously disappointed that they did not receive a prominent role in the new scheme of things. Smoldering discontent and bitterness toward Vargas personally led the party to attempt a coup d'état during the night of May 10, 1938. Integralist forces attacked the presidential palace and other key centers in Rio de Janeiro, hoping to assassinate the President and thereby to eliminate organized opposition to their revolution. Vargas himself aided in the defense of the palace and the revolt disintegrated within a matter of hours.

This abortive undertaking had widespread repercussions on the German position throughout Latin America. The press and some official quarters in Brazil and elsewhere held the German embassy and local Nazis responsible. Nazi involvement in the plot was undoubted by the Brazilian government, which took stern action against German communities and associations. Argentina, Chile, Guatemala, and other states initiated preventive measures to control their German colonies and to guarantee that fascist elements did not attempt similar uprisings. Anti-Nazi literature, which had previously been scarcely a trickle in the region, now became a flood and gushed forth in several languages.

In April the Vargas regime had banned all foreign political organizations and given them thirty days to liquidate their property. The Nazi Party, adopting a practice it would employ many times in Latin America, had hoped to continue under the guise of a purely native organization. Now Vargas decreed an absolute prohibition on the National Socialist Party in Brazil. In São Paulo the government arrested and peremptorily imprisoned many Nazis and ordered a large number of Reich citizens suspected of involvement in the affair to leave the country.

Did the Nazis actually participate in the attempted coup d'état? The question remains tantalizing and, on the basis of present evidence, unanswerable. Foreign Minister Ribbentrop himself was uncertain at the time and directed the German embassy in Rio de Janeiro to determine "whether, as a result of bungling and mistakes on the part of persons of German origin or of other German elements, the reproaches leveled and measures taken against us are in any way justified."[6] Ambassador Ritter

6. Weizsaecker to Ritter, including inquiry from Ribbentrop, May 16, 1938, ibid., p. 842; Ritter's dispatches to Berlin on the uprising and the ensuing crisis, May 12,

replied that there had been such "bungling" up to the beginning of 1937, but that he was unaware of any German complicity in the latest revolt. He consistently denied any prior knowledge of the uprising and blamed the anti-German agitation which followed it on Jewish manipulators and North American propaganda. His plea of innocence in the affair may, of course, have stemmed from recognition that in the Nazi scheme of things failure was too costly to admit. But after an extended diplomatic crisis between Berlin and Rio de Janeiro, on May 21 the Brazilian government issued a communiqué declaring that it had no evidence that *German nationals or firms* had lent support to the insurrection. The statement was deliberately and obviously ambiguous, leaving open the possibility that local Nazis of German extraction had been involved. It is also possible that Getulio Vargas, like many political manipulators before and since, had raised the issue of foreign support for the rebels as a means of strengthening his hand against domestic opponents.

On balance it seems improbable that either local Germans or Reich nationals played important roles in the plot. But, as leading advocates of authoritarian political solutions, the Nazis reaped much of the public antagonism generated by the Integralist revolt. Ironically, the unsuccessful fascist insurrection by the Nazi Party's ideological associates in Brazil marked a decisive turn in Germany's fortunes in Latin America. The tarnish that was beginning to dull the Reich's reputation in the area would not rub off.

As the German position in Brazil rapidly deteriorated, another crisis was brewing for the Nazis in Argentina. After the annexation of Austria in March, Hitler decided to conduct a referendum among all Germans to ratify his actions. At the same time, he scheduled elections for the rubber-stamp Reichstag. The Fuehrer called on Germans abroad, as well as those in the fatherland, to take part in the voting and on April 10, 1938, German nationals registered at many Reich missions and consulates abroad.

13, and 18, 1938, pp. 837–43; memorandum by Weizsaecker, May 18, 1938, pp. 843–45. United States reports on the situation are in *FR*, 5 (1938), 408–20. Typical of the tidal wave of anti-Nazi books, pamphlets, and articles which followed the May revolt in Brazil are Ernesto Giudici, *Hitler Conquista America* (Buenos Aires, 1938); León de Vivero, *Avance del Imperialismo Fascista en el Peru* (Mexico City, 1938); Samuel G. Inman, *Democracy Versus the Totalitarian State in Latin America* (Philadelphia, 1938); Carleton Beals, *The Coming Struggle For Latin America* (Philadelphia, 1938); and "Totalitarian Inroads in Latin America," *Foreign Affairs*, 17 (October 1938), 78–89. These and dozens of other publications expressed deep-seated anxiety over Nazi infiltration.

The conspicuous nature of the registration, along with the participation of Argentine citizens of German descent, aroused a furor in Argentina, where the moderate left-wing government of President Roberto M. Ortiz had recently succeeded the semi-fascist dictatorship of Generals José Francisco Uriburu and Agustín P. Justo.

On orders from the new Foreign Minister, Dr. José Maria Cantilo, and in the wake of the right-wing revolt in Brazil, the Argentine ambassador in Berlin, Labangle, conferred with State Secretary Weizsaecker on May 18 and delivered a sharp complaint over the previous month's registration of Germans in Argentina. He bluntly termed the "plebiscite undertaken on Argentine sovereign territory" an intolerable incident. The next day Ambassador Labangle called on Weizsaecker again for a more elaborate discussion of the disturbing conduct of Germans in his country, with their militant meetings, marches, and all the accoutrements of the alien National Socialist ideology. The German diplomat returned only a stolid silence when the ambassador warned that measures similar to those instituted in Brazil were imminent in Argentina.[7]

The crises in Argentina and Brazil and the sudden emergence of anti-German sentiment among their Latin American neighbors necessitated a shift of tactics by the Party, although the basic Nazi strategy and the goal of a unified Germandom remained unaltered. The preceding year, when Ernst Bohle had been named State Secretary in the Foreign Ministry and thus acquired additional authority over all members of the Reich foreign service, he had attempted to tighten the Party's security provisions and to prevent unfortunate episodes with local authorities in the Western Hemisphere. Secret orders circulated to Party members had specified that propaganda materials, equipment, and other items would henceforth be provided through diplomatic channels. Bohle directed Party leaders in the various countries (who were known as *Hoheitstraeger* or "bearers of sovereignty," a bit of Nazi jargon commonly used in the fatherland) to re-

7. Cf. the memoranda by Weizsaecker, May 18 and 19, 1938, *DGFP–D, 5,* 845–47. The German ambassador to Argentina, von Thermann, reported on May 18 that anti-German sentiment had swept the country. He himself was highly annoyed over the tactless behavior of local Nazis; e.g. in Misiones the Nazi *Ortsgruppenleiter* was arrested for setting up a sign on the local colony's school reading "National Socialist German School." Thermann noted that Nazi interference with the assimilation of *Volksdeutschen* would inevitably cause trouble with the Argentine government. To insure amicable relations, he proposed a new organization exclusively for German nationals and for purely cultural objectives. His suggestion met a frigid reception in Party circles. Thermann to Berlin, ibid., pp. 848–52.

strict their communications with headquarters and with each other to the minimum necessary. Confidential correspondence and comparable materials were to be sent by special couriers on German ships. The Party hoped in this manner to avoid arousing suspicion.

These measures had proved insufficient and in May 1938 Bohle was obliged to direct additional steps to protect the Party's operations.

> The situation requires the following measures in support of the work of the AO: First, avoidance of any open activity, and concentration of forces on internal indoctrination. Second, separation from *Volksdeutschen;* dismissal of *Volksdeutschen* and persons with double nationality from the Party, the German Labor Front, and their formations; separation of German nationals from *Volksdeutsche* organizations with political objectives. Third, preparation for the establishment of organizations for German nationals led from within by the Party. . . . Submit statutes of organization to Berlin.[8]

For the moment it appeared that the Party would have to retreat, but Bohle soon decided not to implement this directive in full. The risk of losing control of the *Volksdeutschen* in Latin America was too great and the AO chose to ignore the distinctions between ethnic Germans of Reich and foreign citizenship.

In Brazil, the focus of Nazi concern at this time, there occurred a transparent shift of Party leadership into the German embassy itself. On May 22, 1938 Hans Menning von Cossel, the Party's *Landesgruppenleiter* for Brazil, flew to Berlin for extensive conferences with Bohle, Hess, Ribbentrop, and other Foreign Ministry officials. Early in July von Cossel returned to Rio de Janeiro as cultural attaché of the embassy and resumed his direction of the Party organization, which was now operating underground.

In the meantime, tension between the Brazilian government and the German ambassador increased, with one incident leading to another. Ritter had refused an invitation to attend a ball in honor of the visiting Chilean Foreign Minister and announced that he would not participate in such affairs until the Vargas administration released the German nationals it had imprisoned after the May 10 uprising. The erratic and impetuous Nazi diplomat went further, informing the Brazilian government that its ambassador in Berlin would not receive any invitations to diplomatic func-

---

8. See Bohle's circular orders of May 3, 1937, June 12, 1937, and July 22, 1937, Bohle files, National Archives, micro-copy T–120, serial 72, roll 66, frames 51658–68. Cf. also his circular order of May 18, 1938, *DGFP–D, 5,* 843.

tions until the Reich's demands were met. Ritter declared that his social boycott and the ostracism of the Brazilian ambassador to Germany would continue so long as Brazil prohibited the NSDAP.

But Ritter was acting entirely on his own initiative and Berlin hastily repudiated his statements. Weizsaecker sternly reprimanded the German ambassador and ordered him to retract his remarks. Thus humbled from above, Ritter notified the Brazilian Foreign Ministry that his self-proclaimed social boycott did not exist after all and that Moniz de Aragão, Brazil's ambassador to Berlin, would still be included in the diplomatic activities of the German capital.[9]

The Germans had hardly smoothed over this affair when a more serious incident arose. In June the Brazilian state police arrested a close associate of von Cossel, a certain Herr Kopp, and discovered in his possession a number of incriminating files. Kopp, secretary of the *Federacão 25 de Julho,* a Nazi front organization for *Volksdeutschen,* had been associated with the Integralist plot of the preceding month. Among his papers were a detailed plan for a new fascist uprising with the cooperation of the German colonies in the three southern states, and a secret document outlining a new Nazi organization, the "German-Brazilian Youth Ring," and containing a number of provocative provisions, e.g. "The principle is recognized that German-Brazilians and Germans must stand and work together since they share a common destiny." Kopp, a Brazilian citizen, had drawn up these plans with another Nazi, Neubert, who was a German national.

To enlist the sympathy and assistance of *Volksdeutschen,* the two conspirators had privately claimed that their schemes had the approval of the German embassy, although Ritter later disclaimed any complicity. Kopp died during his interrogation, reportedly by his own hand, but perhaps as a result of torture. His principal accomplice, Neubert, sought and received embassy asylum even though Ritter laid most of the responsibility for the fiasco at his feet. Another important Nazi and Reich citizen, Barwich, who was the local Transocean representative, also obtained sanctuary at the embassy. He admitted that he too had prior information on the attempted revolution in May. So deeply compromised was the embassy that Ritter did

9. Ritter's reports to Berlin, May 25 and June 27, 1938, ibid., pp. 853–54 and n. 5, p. 854; p. 859 and n. 3; also cf. United States Ambassador Caffery's dispatch to Secretary Hull, May 22, 1938, FR, 5 (1938), 416. Before von Cossel's departure he and Ritter called on the chief of police in Rio Grande do Sul, where Cossel had been active, to obtain a formal statement that no charge was pending against him. They did not wish to take the chance that Brazil might deny him permission to return to the country.

not even register the customary protest over Brazilian persecution of Germans.

Although the Brazilian authorities released relatively little information, the discovery of Kopp's treason led to an intensification of police efforts to root out all vestiges of Nazi activity. Ritter's position became increasingly difficult. In September he returned to Germany to attend the annual Party rally and the conference of the *Auslandsorganisation.* At that time the Brazilian ambassador called at the Foreign Ministry to suggest that it would be "very desirable if a way could be found so that Ambassador Ritter did not return" to his post. When the Foreign Ministry refused to take the hint and act on this basis, the Brazilian envoy declared that Ritter was persona non grata. Germany, in retaliation, demanded the recall of de Aragão and relations between the two countries entered their coolest phase yet.

This development gravely disturbed the Reich's economic experts, who feared that political differences might interfere with economic relations with Brazil. "From an economic point of view," one declared in 1938, "Brazil was for us by far the most important country in South America." The Nazi economy especially needed Brazilian cotton for the Sudeten textile industries which Germany had just taken over.[10]

Although Brazil and Argentina were the main areas in which the activities of local Germans and the Reich missions provoked diplomatic crises, apprehensiveness over Nazi subversion increased markedly throughout Latin America during 1938. In Peru, for example, the German minister reported that opinion had turned distinctly unfavorable to Germany, even though the regime of General Oscar Benavides shared many of the characteristics of Hitler's and there were too few *Volksdeutsche* to cause strife. Like most people in Latin America, the Peruvians found the accomplishments of the Reich very impressive, but they were no longer sure of Berlin's peaceful intentions. "It must unfortunately be said that along with the Catholic elements just about all the intelligentsia and many businessmen are also now arrayed against us."[11] Similar themes pervaded the dispatches of practically every German legation in Central and South America.

The perceptible trend of Latin American opinion toward hostility to Germany and suspicion of German residents in the countries of the West-

---

10. Ritter to the Foreign Ministry, June 29, 1938, *DGFP–D,* 5, 860–63. The quotation is from a memorandum by Clodius of the Foreign Ministry's Economic Policy Department, Oct. 4, 1938 (a week after Munich), ibid., pp. 874 f.

11. Minister Schmitt to Berlin, June 4, 1938, ibid., pp. 854–57.

ern Hemisphere necessitated a conference among the top Nazi diplomats in South America. The meeting took place in Montevideo on July 28 and 29, 1938, with the ambassadors to the ABC countries and the minister to Uruguay in attendance. The consultations resulted in an important analysis of the general political situation in South America and a call for clarification of Reich policy—a call which reflected the lack of adequate information among German diplomats in the area.

> The present anti-foreign and particularly anti-German attitude of most of the South American countries is not a transitory phenomenon produced by isolated occurrences. On the contrary, German policy must reckon with it for a long time to come, at least for a matter of years. Considering this situation, Germany must clearly realize what goals she has in South America. Does she wish to confine herself to economic and cultural problems? Or does she wish to go further than this and pursue aims of power or combat North America politically from South America? In South America and particularly in Brazil the view is held at present—even in authoritative political circles—that Germany is pursuing her own aims of power in South America. It is considered necessary that Germany clearly repudiate such intentions . . . and confine herself to economic and cultural aims. If German policy is thus restricted to economic and cultural aims there is promise of success, particularly in the economic field.[12]

The traditional diplomats in the German foreign service, dedicated to maintaining proper and satisfactory relations with the governments to which they were accredited, found the aggressive conduct of the local Party agents, oriented toward eventual seizure of power in the various countries, an impossible hindrance to their tasks. They warned that an attempt would probably be made at the coming Pan-American Conference in Lima to crush the Party organization all over the continent.

With these points in mind, the dean of the German diplomatic corps in South America, Edmund von Thermann, argued that there must be a complete organizational separation of German nationals from racial Germans who were citizens of the local countries. Leadership of the *Volksdeutschen*

---

12. Memorandum by von Thermann on the Montevideo Conference, August 2, 1938, ibid., pp. 863–68. A few of Thermann's proposals on propaganda, discussed below, did bring action. Transocean began expanded service within the hemisphere late in 1938 and the official PROMI agency, DNB, opened its first office in Argentina in September 1938.

should be their own and not that provided by the Party. He urged that Bohle's May directive for establishing separate organizations for Reich citizens should now be carried out. Above all, the Party must cease its manifest opposition to the policies of assimilation which the South American states had adopted. Local Nazis should no longer use Party forms and paraphernalia in public. Companion organizations like the German Labor Front and the Women's Organization would have to become completely nonpolitical, if they were to survive. Wherever the Party continued to function, the chief of the diplomatic mission ought to have greater authority over its leaders and activities, for "in critical times such as now exist in South America, the decisive responsibility of the representative of the Reich must be assured."

In the important matter of propaganda, Thermann complained that materials presently being supplied from Germany were simply not suited to the individuality of the Latin American audiences and that they were more often harmful than helpful to German interests. Propaganda must appear in the dominant local tongue, rather than German, he insisted, and the Reich should no longer send any materials in German to Brazil, at least not until the situation there improved. The ambassador added that the previous methods of influencing the South American press were totally inadequate. Pressure exerted by placing or withdrawing advertisements did not suffice to develop a favorable press, for the method was simply inoperable with the truly influential papers. He concluded that the only suitable technique would be to gain financial control over a large daily newspaper in each key city.

As for the operations of the Transocean News Agency, important publications now ignored most of its items. If Transocean hoped to increase its audience in the region, the agency would have to supplement its transmissions between Germany and South America by comparable coverage within Latin America and between North America and the southern continent. Up to the present time most of the propaganda activities had fallen within the domain of the Party; now Thermann called for the subordination of press and propaganda work to the various diplomatic missions.

Needless to say, the position of the foreign service representatives differed radically from that of the more influential Party leaders and Thermann faced formidable opposition to his plans, especially to his recommendation that the *Volksdeutsche* provide their own leadership. In August Ernst Bohle sent a special emissary, Dr. Schomaker of his staff, to confer with von Thermann and the Nazi *Landesgruppenleiter* in Buenos

Aires. The divergent views of the ambassador and the two Party officials became apparent at once. The *Auslandsorganisation* adamantly declared that it would be impracticable to attempt a separation of *Reichsdeutschen* and *Volksdeutschen* in the schools, "the nucleus of German cultural policy in Argentina."

Schomaker also began to water down Bohle's order regarding the creation of separate organizations for German nationals. Von Thermann vehemently argued for the immediate establishment of a *Reichsdeutsche Gemeinschaft* (RDG), but he could not get the approval of either the *Landesgruppenleiter* or the *Gauleiter's* personal representative. They referred the dispute to Berlin where Richard Zeissig, chief of the Ibero-American section of the AO, decided against the formation of the RDG.

Bohle himself met with the ambassadors to the ABC countries and the minister to Uruguay when they came to Germany for the annual Party rally in September 1938. The AO chief decided that his earlier directives would only apply to the separation of *Volksdeutschen* and German nationals within the Party and its direct affiliates. Reich citizens and Nazis should remain in the various *volksdeutschen* organizations and guarantee the Party's control over the entire German communities in the several countries. The Party had no intention of abandoning its goals of unifying all Germandom and of wielding its racial comrades as a political instrument for the benefit of themselves and the fatherland.[13]

The Munich crisis of September 1938 engendered new enmity for Germany through most of Latin America, and the Wilhelmstrasse again had cause to worry. German missions reported that Transocean and other media were ineffective weapons against the Associated Press, United Press, and Havas, especially in moments of tension. In December the Eighth Pan-American Conference convened in Lima and proceeded to deliver a barrage of declarations, proposals, resolutions, and other actions, many of which were directed against the recognized danger that Nazi racial doctrines and authoritarian ideology might subvert American governments and principles. Hemispheric opposition to the European totalitarian movements crystallized in the Lima pronouncements and the twenty-one republics took steps to improve the consultative procedures which they had already created for defense of their peace, security, and territorial integrity.

The Germans had foreseen the developments at the Lima Conference and fully realized the significance of the growing solidarity among the

13. Memorandum by an AO official, Sept. 24, 1938, ibid., pp. 869–72 and n. 5; Bohle's directive to Thermann, October 13, 1938, p. 875 f.

American states. Although he took some consolation from Argentina's resistance to most proposals for coordinated action, the Reich minister in Peru, Noebel, had to sum up his report on the conference by observing that "the important resolutions adopted by the conference are directed against us: the Declaration of Lima, the Declaration of American Principles, the resolutions denying minority character to foreign ethnic groups and opposing political activities by foreigners."[14]

Despite the Lima declarations, the aftermath of Munich was not wholly unfavorable to the Reich. The maxim, "nothing succeeds like success," received additional confirmation as a thaw began to develop in Brazilian-German relations. Lacking documents from the Brazilian archives, one can only speculate as to Vargas' motives in seeking to improve relations with Berlin. The Brazilian President may only have been hedging against the possibility of Germany's eventual success in dominating Europe. At any rate there were a number of indications that the Vargas regime was becoming more hospitable to the Reich.

The turning point came in February 1939, when the Brazilian chargé d'affaires in Berlin inquired at the German Foreign Ministry regarding arrangements for President Vargas' son to attend the University of Berlin. No difficulties developed and young Vargas studied there for six months. After this initial approach a period of quiet negotiations ensued and full diplomatic relations were restored on June 1, 1939.[15] To avoid renewed controversy over Ritter, Ribbentrop named another loyal Nazi, Curt Pruefer, as ambassador to Rio de Janeiro.

---

14. Noebel's report to Berlin, Dec. 28, 1938, ibid., pp. 885–86, and dispatches from other missions during September, October, and November, dealing with the reaction to the Munich settlement in Latin America, pp. 876–85. On the Lima Conference see *FR,* 5 (1938), 1–85. Cf. also Samuel Flagg Bemis, *The Latin American Policy of the United States* (New York, 1943), pp. 356–61; Langer and Gleason, *The Challenge to Isolation,* pp. 41–43. Cordell Hull described his feelings at the time of the Lima Conference:

> To me the danger to the Western Hemisphere was real and imminent. It was not limited to the possibility of a military invasion. It was more acute in its indirect form of propaganda, penetration, organizing political parties, buying some adherents, and blackmailing others. We had seen the method employed with great success in Austria and in the Sudetenland. The same technique was obvious in Latin America.

Cordell Hull, *Memoirs* (New York, 1948), *1,* 602.

15. Memorandum by Freytag of the Foreign Ministry, Feb. 27, 1939, *DGFP-D,* 5, 889–92 and n. 2, p. 893; dispatch from German embassy in Brazil, Jan. 2, 1939, pp. 886–89.

Although relations with Brazil began to show a slight improvement, 1938 had marked a decisive reversal for Germany in Latin America. The hemispheric unity achieved at Lima was genuine, at least in the common recognition of the need for precautions against Nazi infiltration. On May 15, 1939, an executive decree banned the Party in Argentina and ordered the dissolution of its affiliated agencies, the German Labor Front, Women's Organization, and other groups. Nine days later Guatemala, the crux of German policy in Central America, announced a similar prohibition. Other governments also threatened action against the Nazis.

In spite of determined efforts by German diplomats to smooth over dissension with the Latin American regimes, the Party's persistent activity among German immigrants continued to raise obstacles to the success of Reich foreign policy in the area. Seeking to harmonize the roles of the Party and the missions, and to stave off further political disasters in Latin America, Ribbentrop decided in April 1939 to have a major conference with all the heads of missions and the *Hoheitstraeger* in Ibero-America, together with top officials of the *Auslandsorganisation* and the *Volksdeutsche Mittelstelle*. This crucial assembly did not convene, however, until June, by which time the Foreign Minister himself could not attend, owing to his crowded schedule in the weeks prior to the Nazi attack on Poland. State Secretary Weizsaecker presided for the Foreign Minister.

Weizsaecker opened the conference with an attempt to make the participants recognize that "the representatives of the Foreign Ministry and the *Auslandsorganisation* had come together as comrades pursuing entirely identical interests," but the fundamental conflict between the diplomatic corps and the Party chiefs was evident from the start.

Ambassador von Thermann led the way in an emphatic statement of the diplomats' position. He demanded that each Reich representative be given the right to full and prior information of all Party plans, as well as authority to give directives to the *Hoheitstraeger*. Thermann put his finger on the basic antagonism between the Party's campaign to galvanize the local German communities into common action and the Latin American states' efforts to assimilate their immigrants. With the ban on the Party in several countries, Thermann warned against its continued existence as a camouflaged organization. All representatives of the many German agencies operating in the various countries should be supervised by the missions and firmly subordinated to the chief diplomat, reporting to their headquarters in the Reich only through diplomatic channels.

Although Chile had not yet prohibited the Party, the ambassador to

Santiago, von Schoen, strongly seconded von Thermann, noting that the government there would almost certainly follow the Argentine lead. He added that a necessary precaution was the concentration under mission control of all press activity, which had heretofore been in the hands of the local Party. For this purpose the missions should have press advisers with competent knowledge of the local language.

Other diplomats recommended increased use of provincial radio stations in the different countries. Until now the AO itself had sponsored "The German Hour" in dozens of cities, but other means ought to be devised to support these broadcasts. The members of the foreign service wholeheartedly endorsed continued propaganda, but they opposed the Party's direction of future campaigns. In countries where the governments had proscribed the Party, the diplomats urged that it acquiesce in the local legislation, for covert activities were bound to do serious harm to German interests.

Gauleiter Bohle abruptly rejected the diplomats' arguments, leaving no doubt that, even if the Party were banned throughout Latin America, it would continue to function.

> The Party could in no way depart from its contention that every drop of Germanic blood abroad must be preserved; it was therefore fighting against the attempts at assimilation in the Latin American countries.

> Germans abroad must not only become National Socialists; they must remain so. In an emergency it was the duty of the Party to place a disciplined German community abroad at the disposal of the Head of the Mission. It was to the credit of the *Auslandsorganisation* that the Reich today could rely on its German community abroad with far more certainty than in 1914.[16]

It would not be permissible for the mission chiefs to issue directives to the Party, since this contradicted the Nazi principle that the State could give no orders to the Party. Bohle refused to surrender control over press, propaganda, and radio work until the mission demonstrated that it could perform these tasks as well as the Party. The purpose of the conference, declared the *Gauleiter*, was to devise means to keep the Party active in the face of the expected prohibitions on the organization in the Americas. To-

16. Bohle's remarks of June 12, 1939 are translated in *DGFP–D*, 6, 705. The principal source for this discussion is the material on the conference in Bohle's papers National Archives, micro-copy T–120, serial 72, roll 66, frames 51568–84.

ward this end, Bohle proposed the inclusion of an AO representative on the staff of each mission as an "expert on the local German community."

The primacy of the Party in the Nazi scheme of government rendered the diplomats' opposition to these provisions futile. Accordingly, Weizsaecker concluded the meeting with the servile insipidity he usually displayed in the presence of prominent Party functionaries like Bohle. He added to the burdens of his subordinate foreign service officers by announcing Ribbentrop's decision to hold the mission chiefs "fully responsible for all happenings in foreign policy, not only connected with their own work but also with that of the AO. Good cooperation with the Party representatives meant a relief from this responsibility but did not mean a release from it."

The Party's wishes prevailed. In the countries where prohibitions on the organization were in effect, the Nazis continued to function underground. Hans von Cossel, cultural attaché at the German embassy in Brazil, retained control of the local Party and the front organizations behind which it now operated. The *Landesgruppe* in Argentina simply changed its name to the *Federación de Círculos Alemanes de Beneficencia y Cultura,* retaining the same quarters, the same employees, and the same members. The German Labor Front in Argentina became *La Unión de Gremios.* Initiates even continued to pledge loyalty to the Reichsfuehrer, Adolf Hitler. Though driven under cover, the Party did not succumb to the local prohibitions.[17]

Relations between the Party and the Reich diplomats showed no improvement during the summer of 1939. In August Berlin further complicated the awkward and uncomfortable position of the mission chiefs. A secret directive required them somehow to reach an understanding with the local *Hoheitstraeger* so that the wishes of the diplomatic corps would

---

17. *Argentine Investigation,* report number 1 (Aug. 29, 1941), pp. 5–34. Quite apart from the Nazi Party activities, a topic which gravely concerned the United States Department of State and military leaders was German control of airlines in several countries, notably Colombia, from which they feared bombing raids on the Panama Canal might come in the event of conflict with the Reich. From 1938 to 1941 the United States sought and achieved the gradual removal of this potential threat. The problem is discussed in William A. M. Burden, *The Struggle for Airways in Latin America* (New York, 1943); Langer and Gleason, *The Challenge to Isolation,* pp. 134 ff. and 274 f.; Stetson Conn and Byron Fairchild, *The Framework of Hemisphere Defense* (Washington, 1960), pp. 238–48. One should point out that there were only forty-odd aircraft involved, and those generally of ancient vintage, but the substance of American anxiety was no less real. A successful raid by very few aircraft might have been able to render the Canal inoperable at some critical period.

prevail in any controversy. Ribbentrop ordered the heads of missions to meet in a top-secret conference, "which the AO should not attend," whose purpose would be to work out practical measures to assure priority of foreign policy considerations in all German activities in Latin America. As a contribution to this end, official Reich representatives must keep Party officials well informed on all matters within their province.

But, demanded the Foreign Minister, "the quasi-official functions still being discharged by the Party (for instance in the sphere of the press, propaganda, repatriation, and economic questions) must, according to local circumstances, be handed over to the competent Reich Missions in the quickest and most suitable manner." Weizsaecker, studying the Foreign Minister's order and no doubt aware of the complex triangular power struggle being waged among Ribbentrop, Hess, and Goebbels, as well as between official and Party representatives in the field, commented tersely, "Situation tense." This was certainly true, particularly in view of the impending invasion of Poland and the need to guarantee effective political action to keep Latin America neutral.[18]

With the outbreak of the war, as we have seen, Hitler lent greater authority over propaganda to Reich missions by his decision to allow Ribbentrop to control policy for propaganda abroad. Coordination between the Party and German envoys to Latin America was still imperfect, but this was a decided improvement in the Reich's foreign operations. Nazi psychological warfare now grew more intensive.

18. Memorandum by Hencke of Ribbentrop's personal staff, Aug. 17, 1939, *DGFP–D*, 7, 111–12. Also see above, Chapter 6, pp. 94–95 and n. 21 on Ribbentrop's fight for authority in foreign countries. The controversies in Latin America seem to have played a key part in stimulating the Foreign Minister's bitter struggle on this point, although his own megalomania was no doubt more important.

CHAPTER 8

Argentina: The Axis Artery to the Americas

As war began in Europe, the American nations sent their foreign ministers to Panama to seek means of safeguarding the security of the Western Hemisphere. For several weeks before the delegates assembled on September 23, 1939, Germany directed its diplomatic and propaganda efforts toward influencing the course of events at the Panama Conference.

After the Panamanian government refused the Reich's request for permission to send a German observer to the conference, the Germans adopted more diffuse tactics. Berlin instructed all missions in Latin America to make representations to their host governments and to press for absolute neutrality. As one might have expected, the Reich strongly supported Argentine insistence that trade in foodstuffs to the belligerents not be cut off. In addition the Franco regime in Spain employed its diplomatic influence in behalf of the Nazi campaign for neutrality of the American republics. But these obstructionist tactics had little effect on developments at the conference where the common interest of the American states produced a strong and unified hemispheric front.

Berlin sought to make the best of the situation by generally ignoring the conference and by observing a calculated reserve in evaluating its results. Argentina's continued independent action, however, did not pass unnoticed. The traditional antipathy of the Argentines for North American leadership led the totalitarian powers to focus their propaganda and diplomatic pressure on Argentina, thinking thus to control the "decisive factor" in Latin America. In the following months the German embassy in Buenos Aires became the pivot of the Nazi propaganda campaign throughout the southern continent.[1]

Even though the Party had been banned in Argentina, Nazi activities

1. On Nazi efforts to influence the developments at the Panama Conference, see dispatches from United States legations in various Latin American republics, *FR*, 5 (1939), 28–29 and 55 ff.; also cf. memorandum by an official of the Foreign Ministry in Berlin, Sept. 17, 1939, *DGFP–D*, 8, 86–88; Foreign Ministry to German embassy in Spain, Oct. 17, 1939, p. 304, a dispatch which records the decision to concentrate on Argentina.

had continued and actually expanded in recent months. One indication of this was the fact that almost 65,000 persons, substantially more than in previous years, took part in the Nazi winter relief campaign during 1939–1940, the collections from which were diverted to support the Party's work in the country. Since the financing of Nazi activities now had to be managed covertly, the embassy assumed responsibility for the bulk of the budgetary operations. The embassy's expenditures quadrupled after 1938, rising to 3,146,400 pesos in 1939 and to 5,983,100 pesos the following year.

Although it is impossible to detail the precise manner in which the Nazis spent these funds, it is certain that they were not related to proper diplomatic functions. The German embassy's expenditures soared to five times those of the British legation and almost twenty times those of the United States embassy. The staff of the German embassy increased 65 percent and was now several times as large as those of the English or American missions. The Germans could scarcely justify these astonishing increases on grounds of economic interest in Argentina; e.g., the Reich's capital investment in the country amounted to less than 36,000,000 pesos as compared to British and U.S. holdings of 5,400,000,000 and 1,771,-000,000 pesos respectively.

The German embassy did not keep records of its expenditures for fear of discovery, but careful investigation by members of the Argentine legislature established that millions of pesos went for propaganda and other political activities. Within a single year the embassy paid sums totaling more than 2,000,000 pesos in checks made out "payable to the bearer," a convenient technique to conceal the purposes for which the money went.

Following the embassy's lead, the Transocean agency, DNB, the German Railways Bureau, and other offices actively engaged in pro-Nazi propaganda avoided the customary business accounts in order to obscure the scope of their operations. The Argentine investigators determined that Transocean was spending at least 250,000 pesos a year by 1939 within Argentina alone. Berlin provided all its funds, since it had operated at a deficit for years. The official DNB office also spent several hundred thousand pesos during the months immediately after war erupted in the Old World.[2]

2. In the winter of 1939 the campaign for *Winterhilfswerke* brought in 1,147,546 pesos in Argentina and in 1940 it increased to 1,337,723 pesos. These funds never left the country and are another measure of the scale of Nazi activities in Argentina. *Argentine Investigation,* report number 2 (Sept. 5, 1941), p. 22; also see 36–51 for details on embassy expenditures. Cf. also report number 3 (Sept. 17, 1941), pp. 5–25.

Nor were these activities limited to Argentina. The Transocean bureau in Buenos Aires was the headquarters for all Latin America and regularly transmitted dispatches to other countries in the area for free distribution by branch offices. Perhaps most impressive was the enormous quantity of printed matter which the embassy sent to other nations in the region. During 1940 the Germans mailed from Buenos Aires more than one and a quarter million items, for which the embassy paid postal fees of 112,071 pesos.

Even these figures do not reveal accurately the whole amount of material involved, for each package could contain thousands of propaganda leaflets, posters, etc. A better indication is the weight of the mail sent out from the embassy. In one month more than 9,668,000 pounds of mail went to other countries in Latin America, mainly to Chile, Colombia, Mexico, and Paraguay. And these figures include only bundles or packages, not individual pieces or letters. These amazing sums shed considerable light on the central role played by the German embassy in Argentina in the Nazi propaganda campaign after 1939.[3]

Great quantities of the sort of propaganda materials which the Reich was distributing at this time have survived. A succinct summary of their nature and contents is afforded by the directives which Ribbentrop issued after he gained authority to set propaganda policy. One of them sets forth the five principal themes around which Nazi propaganda was to revolve in Latin America.

1. Central America is completely under Roosevelt's domination.

2. The cowardly and corrupt government of the Central American states have sold their lands to North American capitalism.

3. The United States of North America is seeking to subjugate South America.

4. A war with Europe would be South America's ruin.

5. North America can never absorb South America's products in the long run. On the other hand, the New Europe is the natural and best market for South America.

In short German propaganda was to exploit fears of "Yankee imperialism" and to play up the economic advantages of South American cooperation with the Reich.[4]

3. Ibid., pp. 25–44 and 53–115.
4. Ribbentrop's directives were later collected and printed in a strictly confidential

The Foreign Ministry permitted and even encouraged variations on these themes, so long as the materials accorded with the general tenor of the directive. For use against the United States in Latin America and elsewhere, Dr. Karl Megerle, the journalist who served as Ribbentrop's propaganda specialist, developed an elaborate file of materials portraying the United States in an adverse light. His tactics included the heavy use of American self-criticism through the translation and dissemination of excerpts from books and articles published in the United States.

Under Megerle's direction, Dr. Karl Heinrich Frahne of the *Deutsches Institut fuer Aussenpolitische Forschung* prepared additional themes and drafts of pamphlets, news releases, and articles dealing with a large variety of subjects in ways designed to injure United States prestige. Among the favorite topics were "The Treatment of the Negro in the United States of America"; "Interference of the United States in the Affairs of Ibero-American Republics"; "The Findings of the American Committee to Investigate Munitions Manufacturers" (i.e. the Nye Committee); "The Seizure of Texas, California, Arizona, and New Mexico by the United States"; "The Treatment of German Citizens and Americans of German Blood in the United States During the (First) World War" (intended to show that American persecution of Germans during 1914–1918 was fully as bad as Nazi outrages against the Jews); and "Race Hatred and Lynch Justice in the United States." Frahne employed these and many other polemics to disparage the United States.

To emphasize U.S. hypocrisy Megerle's office was especially fond of using critical works written by Americans. The Nazis frequently cited and quoted Charles Callan Tansill's *The Purchase of the Danish West Indies* to demonstrate that Washington had in fact forced Denmark to sell the islands. The Nye Committee investigations and the publications they inspired afforded a storehouse of incriminating material for Reich propagandists.

Works of isolationists, pacifists, and revisionist historians of the First

---

handbook for the use of the foreign service. A copy of this invaluable volume is available at the Library of Congress; see *Standardthesen und Richtlinien fuer die Deutsche Auslandspropaganda* (marked "For Official Use Only" and with a covering letter by Karl Megerle, the propaganda expert on the Foreign Minister's staff), directive number 14, p. 10. For examples of the Nazi propaganda materials being distributed in Latin America after 1939, see "German War Propaganda for Latin America," Library of Congress, Prints and Photographs Division, file 7666. By this time the Germans were using ever greater volumes of propaganda in Spanish and Portuguese, and they appear to have received Franco's liberal assistance in its distribution in Ibero-America.

World War lent themselves readily to German efforts to shift the onus to the United States for many of the vicious consequences of that conflict. Foreign Ministry propaganda releases made frequent reference to H. C. Peterson, *Propaganda For War: The Campaign Against American Neutrality, 1914–1917;* Edwin Borchard, *Neutrality For the United States;* Harry Elmer Barnes, *The Origins of the World War;* John Kenneth Turner, *Shall It Be Again?;* Hubert Herring, *And So To War;* and Charles Tansill, *America Goes to War.* The Germans even honored the latter volume by a translation and publication in Stuttgart in 1939. These were the types of works on which Nazi publicists drew to convince their own people and others of Germany's innocence, past and present, and of the large measure of American responsibility for existing evils.[5]

The period of the twilight war in Europe had also seen a lull in the intensity of German activity in Latin America, but the spring of 1940 brought a new propaganda offensive in conjunction with Hitler's onslaught against Western Europe. Even before the German forces rolled westward, another cause célèbre had agitated Argentine public opinion against the Reich. In March the anti-Nazi newspaper *Argentinisches Tageblatt* uncovered an alleged report to the Reich's Colonial Policy Office which described Nazi plans for the collection of secret intelligence in preparation for German annexation of Patagonia. As a result of the discovery of this document, the Argentine police arrested Alfred Mueller, deputy *Landesgruppenleiter* of the Nazis and one of the authors of the reputed conspiracy. Because of the scanty evidence, Mueller obtained his release in May, but the matter occupied the Argentine courts well into the summer before it was finally dismissed. The extended legal proceedings prolonged the nationalistic furor in the Argentine press.

The Patagonian affair stimulated a new wave of alarm over the dangers of the *Quinta Columna,* the fifth column, throughout the hemisphere. Mueller's release and the ultimate dismissal of the case, although German propagandists sought to exploit them fully, made little impression on the millions of people who were highly perturbed by the possibility that a Henlein or Seyss-Inquart might deliver their countries over to the terrors

5. This discussion is based on Megerle's own file, laconically entitled *Gegen Amerika, 1939–1941,* Library of Congress, Manuscript Division, accession number 11,522. See also Phillip E. Jacob's excellent analysis of Nazi propaganda themes during this period, "The Theory and Strategy of Nazi Shortwave Propaganda," in *Propaganda by Short-Wave* (Princeton, 1942), pp. 80–91.

of Nazi rule. Recalling Goebbels' original instructions of 1933, one conjectures whether the Nazis actually planted the false documents regarding Patagonia in the hope that a public demonstration of their spurious nature would allay fears of Nazi subversion in the American republics. If this was an instance of the PROMI technique of leaking false information, it misfired badly.[6]

Coupled with the brutal blitzkrieg of 1940 in Europe, the Patagonian incident and concern over virulent Nazi propaganda in Latin America induced a shift of the Argentine government toward opposition to the Reich. Ambassador von Thermann reported to Berlin on May 3 that Argentina's neutrality policy was no longer strictly impartial, but was rather sympathetic to the Allies. The Argentine Foreign Minister warned von Thermann to tone down the overly vigorous German propaganda, stressing the provocative articles carried by the newspaper *El Pampero* and numerous pamphlets and posters distributed from the embassy itself. Thermann denied outright that the Reich was subsidizing *El Pampero,* although the embassy had actually been financing the journal's operations since its inception at the beginning of the war. The ambassador defended the many pamphlets and press releases which he was sending out as a just measure to combat Allied propaganda, in view of the de facto press boycott on German news. In turn Thermann complained of the defamatory campaign being waged against the German element in Argentina, asserting that the group was loyal and not a fifth column.

To support his counterattack on the fifth-column scare, the German ambassador called for an official declaration by an authoritative personage in the Reich, rejecting as "infamous calumny" all reports of Nazi designs on the Western Hemisphere and saying that Germany only demanded the return of her former colonies, not new conquests in Latin America. The Reich missions in Rio de Janeiro, Lima, and Santiago echoed this request as the most likely means for pacifying the outcry. At the same time, the Foreign Ministry sought to halt the deterioration of the German position in Latin America by preventing any sabotage on the South American mainland and avoiding belligerent naval activity within the three hundred mile security zone proclaimed at the Panama Conference. The German High

6. On the Patagonia affair, see *La Prensa* and the *New York Times,* Apr. 1, 1940, and May 7, 1940. See also *DGFP–D,* 9, n. 1, p. 293. From the rash of publications which the case provoked two may be mentioned, José Bernal de León, *La Quinta Columna en al Continente Americano* (Mexico City, n.d. but evidently 1940) and Alfredo Schlesinger, *El Arma Secreta: La Quinta Columna* (Guatemala, 1940).

Command (OKW) agreed to the Wilhelmstrasse's request that it abstain from such activities.[7]

The sinking of an Argentine merchant ship, the S.S. *Uruguay,* by a German submarine on May 27, 1940, added fuel to Argentine fury. Noisy demonstrations took place before German clubs in Buenos Aires and the offices of the *Deutsche La Plata Zeitung.* Although it was soon known in Berlin that a Nazi U-boat was responsible, Ribbentrop ordered Thermann to call at the Argentine Foreign Ministry and indicate his astonishment at the agitation against the Reich. The ambassador dutifully delivered a strong protest over the outbreak and, on instructions from his superior, expressed suspicion that the enemies of Germany had sunk the vessel in order to undermine German-Argentine relations. He demanded stronger action by the Argentine government to quell the anti-German clamor. Meanwhile the German embassy was circulating statements to the press insinuating that English and American manipulators were behind the campaign against the Reich.

Nevertheless, the Reich's position in Argentina remained on the decline. On June 8, a week after his confrontation with the Argentine Foreign Minister regarding the demonstrations in Buenos Aires, von Thermann summed up the situation in a lengthy dispatch. Noting the decisive economic influence of England and the cultural leadership of France in the country, he pointed out that Germany had few effective means at its disposal with which to oppose the Allies. The Reich's purchases had only amounted to a fraction of what the British bought from Argentina and they had ceased entirely since the outbreak of war. There were cliques with pronounced pro-German sympathies among medical and scientific circles and a number of Germanophile officers in the army and navy, but the latter group was losing its influence as the Minister of War gradually eased them out of service.

In the sphere of press policy, only two major pro-Nazi outlets continued to function: *Deutsche La Plata Zeitung,* whose general influence increased but little after it introduced a *Pagina Castelana* for the Spanish-speaking public; and the evening paper, *El Pampero.* Nazi films and radio broad-

7. Thermann's reports to Berlin of May 3, 7, and 18, 1940, *DGFP–D,* 9, 278, 292–93, and 371; also see Foreign Ministry's note to the Foreign Department of OKW, May 22, 1940, p. 414, and the OKW reply of June 18, 1940, p. 616. The Nazi military chiefs would have welcomed such a security zone had it been effective and respected by the British. It would have enabled them to conserve their inferior naval forces for concentrated attrition within a smaller area and provided their vessels sanctuary within the vast reaches of the Western Hemisphere's neutralized waters.

casts so far had achieved no noticeable effect and efforts to circulate White Books justifying the German struggle had produced hardly any impact on a public which was not keen on such literature.

The political influence of German elements in the population had been virtually wiped out by the uproar over the fifth-column menace. German enterprises which were large and powerful before the war now had to exercise the greatest restraint or accept the penalty of being blacklisted by the American nations. Even the *Deutsche La Plata Zeitung* and *El Pampero* were in jeopardy. It was increasingly difficult to obtain the necessary newsprint for them, since the English and Canadians controlled the sources of pulp. There had recently been a danger that *El Pampero* would lose its printing facilities, but Thermann was determined to continue its publication at all costs, even if it were necessary to print it on the premises of the *Deutsche La Plata Zeitung*. The ambassador dolefully reported to the Wilhelmstrasse that there was meager prospect of improvement in the situation.[8]

Still the Reich would not give up its efforts. In response to suggestions from von Thermann, Berlin sought to ensure at least neutrality for Argentina by promise of material gain. The German embassy received permission to enter into negotiations for advance purchases from Argentina in amounts up to 3,000,000 Reichsmarks. While delivery could not be made until after the war ended, the Germans hoped thus to reinforce the Argentine government's neutralist inclinations. In addition, the Foreign Ministry provided half a million pesos to the embassy to aid in winning over influential persons who would be interested in doing business with Germany after the conclusion of hostilities, and who would throw their influence into the neutralist camp. To bolster Nazi propaganda among those who read little, the Germans bought a radio station in Montevideo to serve the entire Rio de la Plata region and allocated funds to keep it in operation.

Another maneuver was of considerable importance. The repeated requests from German diplomats in this hemisphere for a public affirmation that the Reich had no political goals in the Americas finally bore fruit. In June Hitler reportedly granted an interview to Karl von Wiegand of the Hearst newspapers in the United States and the Nazi propaganda machine saw that it was reprinted in every country of the New World.

In fact, according to later testimony by Paul Karl Schmidt, director of

8. See Ribbentrop's note to Weizsaecker with instructions for von Thermann, June 1, 1940, ibid., pp. 483–95 and n. 8, p. 495; Thermann's dispatch to the Foreign Ministry, June 8, 1940, pp. 529–32.

the German Foreign Ministry's News Service and Press Department, the so-called interview was completely stage-managed. The *Deutsches Nach-richtenbuero* (DNB), the news agency operating under the Propaganda Ministry's auspices, conceived the operation and prepared the questions. Hans Dieckhoff and his associates on the Foreign Ministry's America Committee drafted a set of proposed answers and, after being checked and altered by Hitler, the prefabricated package was supplied to Wiegand.[9]

As he had done in his speech of April 28, 1939, when he had denied aggressive intentions toward any nation, the Fuehrer scoffed at reports that Germany cherished aims in South America. He claimed that it would be militarily impossible to invade this hemisphere. Hitler clearly fashioned his remarks to calm the anxieties of the American peoples and to weaken the position of the groups who were leading the campaign for hemispheric preparedness. The Fuehrer's facile assurances seemed but empty words to those who had observed his callous disregard for similar guarantees in Europe.

There was one state in Latin America where German optimism was waxing in the summer of 1940. The blitzkrieg in Western Europe triggered a number of disturbing responses in Brazil. Even in Rio de Janeiro the German residents began to talk openly of what would take place there later on. With Italy's entry into the war the Brazilian government felt compelled to be more circumspect than ever toward the Axis, for Italian immigrants to Brazil were outnumbered only by the Portuguese.

In talks with American Ambassador Caffery, Foreign Minister Aranha stressed that Brazil could not risk interruption in the flow of essential arms from Germany, unless the United States was prepared to supply weapons on comparable terms. Aranha added that dependence on German armaments would make it natural for Brazil to rely on military instructors from the Reich. Caffery reported further that Krupp, the German industrial empire with which Brazil had previously contracted for artillery and anti-aircraft guns, was seeking to conclude arrangements to build a major steel plant in the country, offering attractive financial enticements.[10] It

9. The *New York Journal American* published Hitler's interview on June 14, 1940. See also the memorandum by Freytag of the Foreign Ministry summarizing these developments, June 18, 1940, *DGFP-D*, 9, 614–16. O. John Rogge, *The Official German Report*, pp. 233–37, records the substance of Schmidt's history of the "Interview." Hitler's repeated promises to respect the Monroe Doctrine, provided a similar doctrine were acknowledged for Europe, reflected a desire to exploit such an arrangement as cover for his aggressions in the Old World. See Lothar Gruchmann, *Nationalsozialistische Grossraumordnung: Die Konstruktion einer "deutschen Monroe-Doktrin"* (Stuttgart, 1962), pp. 155–66.

10. See Caffery's reports of May through July, *FR*, 5 (1940), 43–51.

seemed likely that the prospective German domination of Europe might well pave the way for a vast expansion of Nazi economic activity in South America.

Sharing the widespread expectation that the fall of Great Britain was imminent, Getulio Vargas began to hint at a new willingness to accommodate the Reich in trade relations. In an address in early June, the Brazilian strongman scorned "the sterile demagogy of political democracy" and suggested that virile peoples remove the debris of old ideas.[11] Although his terms were quite general, the essence of his statements struck a familiar chord, unmistakably akin to the views of Europe's totalitarian leaders.

On June 21, the Brazilian President invited German Ambassador Pruefer to a private audience at which he put out feelers on what Germany had to offer. After reporting to Berlin on this auspicious conference, Pruefer received instructions to present a statement to Vargas pointing out the fact that the German market had now swelled from sixty-five million to ninety million people. Positive cooperation on economic matters would therefore assure Brazil a larger market than any other country could offer, especially when one took into consideration the economies "associated" with the New Order. The Reich was prepared even now to enter into general written agreements for a favorable development of economic relations.

After he had offered these incentives to Vargas, Pruefer informed Berlin that Brazil was planning a shift away from dependence on North America and toward trade with Germany and Europe after the fall of England. The eager German ambassador may have exaggerated this tendency, but it seems more than likely, particularly since Vargas had initiated the exchanges, that the Brazilian President was considering a move in this direction. He was certainly interested in exploring possible arrangements, for more than half of Brazil's trade in recent years had been with Europe.

Emphasis on potential economic gain for the several Latin American countries became the central theme of German diplomacy and propaganda during July. Ribbentrop instructed all missions to underline the advantages of trade with the enlarged Reich as both supplier and purchaser. The principal goal of these endeavors was to thwart the United States plan to form a hemispheric cartel to assure Latin American countries a market for their products and a source for their vital imports. Germany knew that the United States would press for some such arrangement at the Havana Con-

---

11. For the repercussions of the Vargas speech see the exchanges between Caffery and the State Department, ibid., pp. 615–26.

ference of Foreign Ministers, which had been moved up from October to July because of the unexpected collapse of France and the other states of Western Europe, and the consequent danger that their colonies in this hemisphere might attract the war to the New World.

The Reich recognized that the proposed cartel would undermine its economic relations with *Ibero-Amerika* and did its utmost to promote opposition to the scheme. In the days leading up to the Havana meeting, Nazi missions in Latin America made repeated and firm representations on the subject to the local governments. They disseminated press releases, posters, and other assorted propaganda, arguing vehemently that the cartel would cost Latin America its political independence and make the region economically subservient to the United States. At the same time they sought to demonstrate to the public in some detail the virtues of trade with the Reich.[12]

To Berlin's chagrin the prospects which had momentarily flared in Brazil sputtered out. By July 5 Pruefer was less excited about the likelihood of Vargas' active cooperation, for the Brazilians had submitted no concrete proposals and the German ambassador considered it possible that they would not offer any. If Rio would not be specific, Berlin would, hoping to secure Brazil's resistance to North American leadership at Havana by providing Vargas an "impressive proposal" to bolster his attitude. On July 10 Ribbentrop directed Pruefer to present a detailed and gigantic offer. In the first year after the end of the war, Germany declared its willingness to double the pre-war level of transactions between the two states, including among individual commodities a steel mill and Krupp armaments. Total trade would approximate RM 300,000,000 during that first year.

In spite of the attractiveness of the offer, Vargas coyly delayed his reply until long after the Havana Conference, although he did oppose the United States proposals for a cartel. His reasons were not difficult to surmise, as indeed the German ambassador himself reported in August. First of all, the anticipated early conquest of the British Isles had not occurred and it began to appear that stubborn British endurance might extend the

12. See Pruefer's dispatch to Berlin, June 21, 1940, *DGFP–D*, 9, 649 and n. 4; Ambassador Ritter (in Berlin) to Pruefer, June 27, 1940, ibid., 10, 41; and Pruefer to the Foreign Ministry, July 1, 1940, pp. 100–01; circular by Ribbentrop to all missions in Latin America, July 2, 1940, p. 103; memorandum by an official of the Foreign Ministry's Economic Policy Department, July 16, 1940, pp. 229–31. These Nazi activities are also the subject of a number of United States diplomatic reports; see "Attempts by the German Government to Obstruct Co-operation on Neutrality Measures Among the American Republics," *FR, 1* (1940), 787–809.

conflict many months or even years. This turn of events presented several obstacles for the German proposal to Brazil. Vargas had no desire to alienate the British or the North Americans by premature affiliation with Germany.

Furthermore, with the British fleet still controlling the seas, the immediacy of the German proposition was eliminated and the possibility of implementing such an agreement removed to the indefinite future, with a corresponding reduction in its value. Even more important, although he had been unwilling to endorse the cartel plans of the United States, Vargas did count on new proposals from Washington and wished to retain his freedom of action in that case. Thus, even in Brazil, where the Reich's opportunity for an economic foothold seemed most promising, Nazi inducements proved insufficient.[13]

The summer of 1940 brought the rapid and almost unanimous coalescence of the American nations. They had been moving in this direction ever since the 1938 Lima Conference and had taken additional steps to create a united front at the Panama meeting of foreign ministers. The Nazi military successes in Europe reverberated throughout the Western Hemisphere and stimulated joint action by the American nations to meet what they perceived as a common danger.

In June 1940 an investigating committee of the Uruguayan Parliament announced that it had uncovered evidence of a Nazi plan to seize control of that country and use the rich Uruguayan basin as the nucleus of a German agricultural colony in South America. Quick action by the Uruguayan government, with strong public support from the United States minister, staved off the revolutionary efforts of local Nazis. On July 7 Argentine officials reported the discovery of a Nazi plot for an insurrection in that country and less than two weeks later the Chilean Nazis actually attempted to overthrow the popular front regime in Santiago.[14]

As in the 1938 Integralist revolt in Brazil, the character and degree of German involvement in these incidents remain uncertain. The records of the German Foreign Ministry throw little light on the matter, and one is inclined to believe that the Reich missions in the several countries were not

13. The Brazilian-German clearing agreement of June 6, 1936, had been discontinued by Brazil on December 12, 1939. See Pruefer to the Foreign Ministry, July 5, 1940, *DGFP–D, 10,* 131–32; Director of the Economic Policy Department to Pruefer, July 10, 1940, pp. 177–78; Pruefer to the Foreign Ministry, Aug. 7, 1940, p. 426.

14. Cf. Hugo Fernandez Artucio, *The Nazi Underground in South America* (New York, 1942), pp. 28–113, for a detailed discussion of the Uruguayan incident. On the developments in Chile and Argentina, see Langer and Gleason, *The Challenge to Isolation,* pp. 610–15 and 689 ff.

directly responsible for the affairs. This is not surprising since the most intimate and vital ties to local German communities were through Party channels and cultural organizations. If any of the reported conspiracies was directed from the Reich, it would presumably have been handled by these latter mechanisms. Lacking evidence to confirm or disprove participation by Reich agents, the most plausible speculation seems to be that the episodes were local endeavors of Nazis stimulated by German victories and hoping to emulate the movement in the fatherland. It can hardly be doubted, however, that Berlin would have welcomed the success of the frustrated coups d'état. Whether domestically or internationally planned, Nazi seizure of power in a Latin American state would have provided the Reich with an ideological ally and potential counterweight to U.S. influence in the hemisphere.

The abortive intrigues of 1940 gave vivid emphasis to the dangers posed by the continued existence of Nazi groups in the New World. Combined with the catastrophic collapse of France, these events helped to produce the united front which the American republics formed at Havana and maintained, with but a single major exception, for the next five years. Meeting in the Cuban capital from July 21 to 30, the foreign ministers of the Western Hemisphere reaffirmed support for the "no-transfer" principle of the Monroe Doctrine and elaborated means to enforce it.[15] An Act of Havana provided for protective occupation and administration of any colonial possession in the New World which might be threatened with transfer from one non-American power to another. An important indication of the close cooperation which now came to characterize inter-American relations was the Act's provision for its unilateral implementation by any of the American republics, should an emergency arise.

Another resolution declared the intention of the twenty-one governments to consider an act of aggression against any one of them an attack on them all, and to consult on measures for common defense. This was no time for petty bickering or suspicions, and the family of American nations wisely perceived their mutual interest in collective action. There would still be ominous eddies, but by the summer of 1940 the Nazi cause was in retreat in the New World and the American republics faced with growing confidence the ordeal which was to come.

15. John A. Logan, Jr., provides a thorough account of inter-American activities during this period in *No Transfer: An American Security Principle* (New Haven, 1961), pp. 277–385. The circumstances surrounding the Havana Conference, and the results, occupy the latter pages of Bemis, *Latin American Policy,* pp. 367 ff.

CHAPTER 9

The Nazi Campaign to Defeat Roosevelt in 1940

The most intensive of all Nazi propaganda efforts in the United States began to take shape in 1939. Even before the European war erupted in September, the fascist powers had begun discussions concerning the pronounced hostility of President Roosevelt toward the totalitarian states. The necessity of altering the American attitude became an important factor in their plans to establish the New Order in Europe. Could it be done by the propaganda devices which Hitler's cohorts had been working to perfect?

Visiting Rome a few weeks after the Munich Conference, Ribbentrop commented to his Italian hosts that "the last crisis has revealed the power of the isolationists" in the United States.[1] "Jewish propaganda," as he phrased it, held sway only in the eastern part of the country; other, more important sections seemed less inclined to intervene and more receptive to arguments in favor of preventing U.S. involvement in foreign problems.

Additional conversations on the matter took place in the early summer of 1939 when Count Ciano, the Italian Foreign Minister, conferred with Spain's Generalissimo Franco at San Sebastian. High on the informal agenda was the problem of Roosevelt's antipathy for the authoritarian regimes in Madrid, Rome, and Berlin. In recounting the substance of the talks later to Eberhard von Stohrer, the German ambassador to Spain, the Spanish Caudillo declared that

> he had told Count Ciano, and wished to tell me as well, that he thought vigorous propaganda against Roosevelt urgently necessary to prevent him from being reelected President. According to reliable information which he had, influence should be brought to bear on the Vatican, which had great influence over the American Catholics, who were opponents of Roosevelt's policy of intervention and thus of his war policy. By reasoning that Roosevelt's reelection would endanger

---

1. Saul Friedlaender, *Hitler et les États-Unis, 1939–1941* (Geneva, 1963), p. 19.

world peace, strong feeling against him could be engendered through the Vatican and American Catholics.[2]

Franco's proposal struck a responsive chord in Berlin, although the German plan of attack was different. As Hitler prepared and launched his war in Europe, the principal task of Nazi activity in the United States became to defeat Roosevelt in the 1940 presidential election and thereby, so the Germans believed, to insure U.S. neutrality toward the totalitarian subjugation of the Old World.

The first important step in this direction came in March 1940 when the Germans published in Europe a group of documents they had captured in the Polish campaign. These papers, selected from Polish diplomatic correspondence, purported to show grave responsibility on the part of President Roosevelt and his ambassadors in Warsaw, Paris, and London for the outbreak of war. They included a number of reports that responsible American officials had urged Poland, Britain, and France to be intractable in their relations with Germany, and that the United States, by definite promises of assistance to the Allies, had encouraged them to make war on the Reich. (The Nazis had manufactured several incidents to make it appear that Poland had actually attacked Germany; to this myth, Nazi propaganda consistently clung.)

In its instructions to the German press on March 29, PROMI emphasized the Reich's fundamental purpose in releasing the documents:

> the intention in publication of these documents is to reinforce the position of the American isolationists and to place Roosevelt in an impossible situation, especially concerning his current candidacy for the presidency. However, it is not at all necessary that we ourselves bring out Roosevelt's responsibility; his enemies in America will take care of that.[3]

Publication of these materials caused great commotion in the United States, attracting widespread comment in the press and on radio. At his news conference on March 29, the President felt obliged to make a state-

2. Stohrer's memorandum on his conversation with Franco, July 16, 1939, *DGFP–D, 6,* 929. A later report by Bergen, the German ambassador to the Vatican, made clear that the Holy See would have nothing to do with any attempt to get U.S. Catholics as a group to support an isolationist policy. Bergen to Berlin, Sept. 26, 1939, *DGFP–D, 8,* 145.

3. Friedlaender, *Hitler et les États-Unis,* p. 76, quoting records of the PROMI press conference, Mar. 29, 1940, *Bundesarchiv,* Koblenz.

ment on a reported dispatch from the Polish ambassador in Washington, Count Jerzy Potocki, in which the United States Ambassador to Paris, William Bullitt, was said to have expressed American readiness to support the Allies in a possible war against Germany. Roosevelt dismissed the reports as completely false and described publication of the documents as a transparent propaganda maneuver by the Nazis. The same day Secretary of State Cordell Hull told reporters, "The statements alleged have not represented in any way at any time the thought or policy of the American Government."[4]

Nevertheless, excerpts and summaries of the documents gained heavy newspaper and radio coverage in the United States, frequently under banner headlines. As Hans Thomsen, the German chargé d'affaires in Washington, gleefully informed Berlin, journalists and radio commentators had to go into details of the contents and scope of the documents before they could adequately register the denials by Roosevelt and Hull, along with the disclaimers issued by Bullitt and Potocki. "Thus the widest publicity is achieved in America and public opinion is informed. In spite of all attempts at denial the average American is so fully aware of Roosevelt's interventionist policy that he is quite prepared to take for granted the accuracy of the statements contained in the documents."[5] Some observers recognized that the date of publication was designed to influence the forthcoming presidential election and criticized the Reich for inadmissible interference in American domestic politics, but Thomsen thought the documents would remain a useful weapon in the campaign to defeat Roosevelt.

Realizing that the documents could be most effectively exploited by their release in the United States, the Reich decided to issue them in this country. The Nazis originally intended to distribute photostatic reproductions of the originals through the embassy itself. Thomsen, however, was apprehensive that publication of the papers in the United States might bring sharp action against German agencies here. He was particularly afraid to identify the embassy with propaganda activities which would pro-

---

4. For Roosevelt's and Hull's remarks, see the *New York Times,* Mar. 30, 1940. Whether or not Bullitt ever made the alleged statements remains unclear. He may well have done so, perhaps calculating that a firm stand by Poland, Britain, and France, based partly on an expectation of U.S. assistance, would deter Germany from further aggression. Or, on similar grounds, Potocki may have exaggerated the likelihood of American support, hoping to encourage his superiors to resist Nazi pressure. Both men denied the accuracy of the published reports of their discussions.

5. See Thomsen's dispatches to Berlin, Mar. 29 and 30, 1940, *DGFP–D,* 9, 43–49.

vide the Roosevelt Administration with an excuse for stern reprisals, possibly including severance of diplomatic relations with Germany.

On the advice of the chargé d'affaires, Berlin agreed to a change of plans; the Germans would seek an American publisher for the documents. Thomsen noted that extreme discretion was required to conceal the embassy's part in the matter. By April 20 he had received copies of the materials and, working through a confidential agent, he completed arrangements with an American firm "closely connected with the Republican opposition" to print 3,000 copies, for which the embassy would make an initial contribution of $3,000. Gunther Altenburg, director of the Foreign Minister's Information Department, promptly replied to Thomsen that 3,000 copies would be utterly insufficient. If necessary to obtain a much larger printing, he directed the embassy to finance the distribution of free copies. On May 2 Ribbentrop himself telegraphed the chargé d'affaires that the limited arrangements he had proposed were completely unsatisfactory. Thomsen revised his scheme.

Manfred Zapp, the Transocean representative in New York, who was serving as Thomsen's confidential intermediary, resumed negotiations with the prospective publisher, Howell and Soskin of New York. William Soskin, senior partner in the firm, had inquired of the German embassy early in April whether his company might publish the documents. He remained a willing accomplice in the enterprise, although he later claimed he was ignorant of Zapp's connection with the embassy. Thomsen reported that "unusually high fees" had induced C. Hartley Grattan, well known for his revisionist writings on the First World War, to provide a suitable introduction to the little volume.[6] By early May the company had begun printing a gigantic edition of the papers as a special brochure, encouraged by a guarantee of sales up to 100,000 copies.

Since the publishers hesitated to circulate such enormous quantities on their own responsibility, the embassy arranged for other organizations to accept large numbers of the books from Howell and Soskin and to distribute them on their own. In order to gain the assistance of the agents and leaders of these organizations, whose names the German records do not

---

6. Though critical of Roosevelt, Grattan's foreword pointed out the partisan character of all such "color books": "By selecting a few documents which place American officials in an extremely bad light and failing to place them in anything like a full context, the Germans have made them appear to mean more than they really do." *The German White Paper* (New York, 1940), p. 10. Photostatic reproductions of some of the original documents appear in the German edition, Auswaertiges Amt, *Polnische Dokumente zur Vorgeschichte des Krieges* (Berlin, 1940).

disclose, Thomsen guaranteed to protect them against possible counter-measures by American authorities. His confidential agents assured the collaborators that the embassy would indemnify them for any loss or damage sustained as a result of their cooperation and, if necessary, would pay their travel and other expenses for a stay in Germany for the duration of the war.

Armed with this proposal, the embassy's secret representatives journeyed throughout the country to enlist the aid of individuals and groups either friendly to the Reich or hostile to Roosevelt. As a final precaution to camouflage the embassy's involvement in the affair, Thomsen had the Foreign Ministry instruct a German publishing house to dispatch a telegram to Dr. Zapp, conveying the impression that he was the private representative of the German publisher and that he had conducted all negotiations with the American firm on a purely commercial and unofficial basis.

The German Library of Information mailed out large numbers of the volume, as did the Norristown Press, the Pennsylvania concern which had printed the work for Howell and Soskin. Many people who unexpectedly received the German White Paper wrote tart letters to the publisher complaining that the documents were plainly Nazi propaganda and saying that they had notified federal officials of the suspicious manner in which free copies were distributed. Grattan registered his objections on the same matter and informed the publisher of his regret that he had ever become involved with the project. By contrast, a few readers like Harry Elmer Barnes, who had recently been associated with the American Fellowship Forum, wrote Howell and Soskin commending the publication and volunteering to help promote it.[7]

The Germans recognized as their most promising allies in the campaign to defeat Roosevelt the isolationist opponents of the administration, and the embassy did its best to strengthen these domestic forces. The lightning victories of the Germans in Western Europe had profound repercussions in the United States, where public apathy was rapidly dissolv-

---

7. Barnes' letter to the publisher also had warm praise ("the best book of the decade on the fundamentals of the world situation") for Lawrence Dennis' *The Dynamics of War and Revolution,* in which the well-known fascist forecast an authoritarian overthrow of the U.S. republic. This discussion draws on Thomsen's dispatches of Mar. 31 and May 4, 1940, *DGFP–D, 9,* 57 f. and 281 f.; and the replies from Berlin of Apr. 26 and May 2, 1940, pp. 225 f. and p. 225 n. See also *HR Investigation,* Appendix, part 2, section 9, pp. 1054–59, for Soskin's rather incomplete version of how the documents came to be printed; and Rogge, *The Official German Report,* pp. 229–31.

ing into a state of acute alarm for the security of the Western Hemisphere. Thomsen informed Berlin that there were now fewer isolationists even in the Republican Party and he echoed the demand of his colleagues in Latin America for an effort by the Reich to pacify American fears.

Hitler made such an attempt, as we have already mentioned, in his staged interview with the Hearst correspondent, Karl von Wiegand, which the *New York Journal-American* carried on June 14, 1940. To amplify the impact of this propitious statement, Thomsen had 100,000 copies of the Fuehrer's interview printed and circulated through the German Library of Information. Congressman Jacob Thorkelson of Montana, whom the embassy considered one of the more cooperative isolationists, agreed to insert the item in the *Congressional Record,* where it appeared on June 22.[8]

To bolster the isolationist position further, Thomsen mapped out a whirlwind campaign to be executed in connection with the Republican National Convention which was to open in Philadelphia on June 24. The embassy's press attaché had established close liaison with "a prominent Republican Congressman" (whose name is still unknown) who was willing to carry out the embassy's plan. With the assistance of $3,000 from the Germans, he invited fifty isolationist Congressmen to Philadelphia. Their function was to bring pressure to bear on delegates to the convention to assure adoption of an isolationist policy pronouncement in the Party platform.

As a counter to the recent "Stop Hitler Now" advertisements which the pro-Allies committee headed by William A. White had published, the same Representative agreed to form a small ad hoc committee of Republicans. During the convention this group sponsored a full-page appeal to "Keep America Out of War!" This appeared in the *New York Times* and other leading dailies on June 25, well calculated to influence the proceedings of the convention. While precise accounting is impossible, since the embassy destroyed all records of such expenditures in order to avoid detection, it seems probable that the Germans advanced at least half of the

8. See Thomsen's reports on this subject to the Foreign Ministry, especially that of June 27, 1940, regarding Thorkelson's cooperation, U.S. National Archives, Foreign Affairs Branch, serial 4515H, container 2276. For an indication of the growing concern of public opinion in the United States during this period, cf. Hadley Cantril, "America Faces the War: A Study in Public Opinion," *Public Opinion Quarterly, 4,* (September 1940), 396–410. On September 17, 1939, a Gallup poll reported that 82% of the American people confidently expected the Allies to win; by the end of that month, however, a Gallup survey indicated that 63% feared the Nazis would attack the United States if Hitler were successful in Europe; cf. ibid., (March 1940), pp. 101–02.

sixty to eighty thousand dollars spent for this purpose. It is certain, and ought to be recorded, that most of the Republicans involved in the undertaking were unaware of the source of these sizable contributions.[9]

The German chargé d'affaires also initiated "literary countermeasures" to turn the emerging tide of sympathy for the Allies. Still working behind the scenes, he managed to conclude arrangements with the literary agency of William C. Lengel to promote isolationist books and articles. Ribbentrop personally approved the expenditure of $20,000 to encourage five projects which Lengel had described.

1. Theodore Dreiser was thought prepared to produce a volume warning against intervention.

2. S. F. Porter, the female journalist, had already submitted a number of articles to the agency depicting the economic consequences of any intervention from the housewife's point of view.

3. George Creel, the publicist who had been America's propaganda chief under Wilson, was to write a series of articles and perhaps a book debunking the fifth-column menace and jingoism.

4. Burton Rascoe was planning to compile a list of arguments based on postwar experiences against any form of American involvement, and to publish the product in book form.

5. Kathleen Norris, the popular novelist, would do a series of articles or a book entitled *War Crazy*, setting forth her pacifistic views and denouncing Roosevelt's foreign policy.

Thomsen thought the latter project was especially promising, since the Norris articles could be placed in popular magazines with the largest circulation. These works would be the more valuable because of their indigenous origin, for "none of the authors knows who is behind the publisher's offer."[10] However, at least one of the writers became suspicious of the backers of the Lengel projects. Miss Porter managed to cancel her contract with the agent, although she did complete a book on the subject

9. Thomsen's dispatch of June 12, 1940, summarized these events, *DGFP–D*, 9, 550 ff.

10. Thomsen's report to Berlin of June 13, 1940, ibid., pp. 558–59; and memorandum by a member of Ribbentrop's staff, June 16, 1940, p. 585. Not all of these undertakings reached print in time to influence the election, but a number did appear as contributions to the continuing isolationist–interventionist debate. See George Creel, "Beware the Superpatriots," *American Mercury*, 51 (September 1940), 33–41; Kathleen Norris, "Victory For the President," *Commonweal*, 33 (Dec. 20, 1940), 230–31; Theodore Dreiser, *The Dawn is in the East* (New York, 1940), a broadside re-

she had discussed with him. Another publisher took over the manuscript, which eventually appeared as *If War Comes to the American Home.* Several other of these projects came to fruition in the coming months. Kathleen Norris became one of the most prolific and vociferous opponents of the administration's firm attitude toward the Axis.

At the same time, the embassy was lending assistance to the "Make Europe Pay War Debts Committee" in its campaign against aid to the Allies. (It will be recalled that Goebbels, as early as 1933, had instructed Nazi propagandists to dwell on the war debts issue in order to rankle American opinion.) One of the highlights of this group's work, and one for which Thomsen proudly claimed partial credit, was Charles Lindbergh's radio address on June 15, in which he denied as always that there was any danger to the New World from Hitler's conquest of the Old.[11]

By late June the German embassy was able to inform Berlin that the first stage of the campaign to defeat Roosevelt had been completed with the distribution of the Warsaw documents. Agents had taken up 50,000 copies of the first edition from Howell and Soskin and sent them to prominent persons in all walks of life, while "tens of thousands" were distributed through the American book trade. All Senators, Representatives, newspapers, and radio outlets were by now in possession of the documents, as were most of the politically influential citizens. In addition a "suitable Congressman," Republican Representative Jacob Thorkelson of Montana once more, had placed five documents from the German White Paper in the *Congressional Record.* Prominent isolationist Senators dealt with the papers in some detail in speeches to the upper chamber, timing their remarks to influence developments at the Republican convention.

> I think I can report that this propaganda campaign has been carried through with the success we envisaged . . . Thanks to the varied methods of camouflage and the extreme caution observed by our agents, it is to be hoped that up to now nothing has come to the knowledge of the American authorities which they could exploit for their own ends.[12]

The rapid disintegration of French defenses before the Nazi rampage and suspicious German activities in the Western Hemisphere combined to

---

printed from *Common Sense* for December 1940; and *America is Worth Saving* (New York, 1941). On the Porter case, see Rogge, *The Official German Report,* pp. 325–46.

11. Thomsen to Berlin, June 15, 1940, *DGFP–D, 9,* 575–76.

12. Thomsen to Berlin, June 19, 1940, ibid., pp. 624–25.

sustain a general anxiety in the United States during the summer of 1940. The Nazi consulate general in New Orleans had earlier offered to support the German departments in the University of Tampa and certain other schools, provided the faculty members were "satisfactory." Now the consul general, von Spiegel, remarked sinisterly that Germany would not forget that the United States was aiding her enemies. Later he declared that he had been misquoted and that he had spoken confidentially, but neither statement seemed very reassuring to the public. The Governor of Louisiana approached the State Department to request an investigation of Spiegel's activities.

At the same time, investigators of the House Special Committee on Un-American Activities began to look into the work of the German consul in Boston, who was known to be submitting reports to Nazi agencies on the conduct of anti-Nazi Germans in New England. Press agitation continued over Consul General Wiedemann in San Francisco, whom many believed to be on special assignment and to have authority over the embassy itself. Likewise, German Commercial Attaché Westrick, whose activities had touched off a storm in April, remained in the news.[13]

For many months the United States had been shifting gradually toward positive action to defend the hemisphere. In May President Roosevelt approved the dispatch of military liaison officers to a number of Latin American countries. On June 15 a Joint Resolution of Congress authorized military and naval assistance to other American republics. Three days later a similar resolution reaffirmed the non-transfer dictum of the Monroe Doctrine, which had been "Pan-Americanized" by the twenty-one nations at the Panama Meeting of Foreign Ministers. That same day the State Department delivered to the Reich an appropriate caveat on the subject. The American chargé d'affaires in Berlin, Donald Heath, notified the German Foreign Ministry that the United States would not recognize the transfer of any geographic territory in the Western Hemisphere from one non-American power to another, obviously referring to the possessions of states which the Nazis had just conquered. In July, as we have seen, the second consultative meeting of American foreign ministers took substantially the same position by adopting the Act of Havana and related resolutions.[14]

13. On the Spiegel incident, cf. the *New York Times,* June 19, 1940. See also *HR Investigation,* Appendix, parts 2 and 7 for an indication of the reaction against the Nazi menace. Also Thomsen's dispatch to the Foreign Ministry, June 18, 1940, *DGFP–D, 9,* 603.

14. Heath's note to the Foreign Ministry, June 18, 1940, ibid., p. 596 f.; Ribbentrop's reply, July 1, 1940, ibid., *10,* 78. See also above, Chapter 7.

Faced with increasing firmness by the United States government and growing antagonism toward the Reich among the American people, the German embassy continued to avoid overt activity. Thomsen emphasized the importance of letting the isolationists do the Germans' work for them. In view of the anti-Nazi hysteria in some quarters, the fears of a German victory in Europe, and the mistrust of Nazi propaganda, he reported to the Foreign Ministry that it would be most effective "if American politicians themselves provide enlightenment regarding our political aims and the mistakes of Roosevelt's foreign policy."

Bearing this in mind, the embassy's press representative devised a scheme whereby the American people themselves helped pay a large part of the expenses for a major propaganda campaign in support of the common aim of Nazi Germany and the isolationists, i.e. to keep the United States out of the war at all costs. The Nazi agent maintained discreet contact with several Senators and Representatives in order to guarantee extensive circulation of their speeches, either in Congress or over the radio, arguing the isolationist case.

> These speeches, whose aim is to prevent America's entry into the war and to ward off all attacks by interventionist politicians, will be printed each time in the official American parliamentary publication, the *Congressional Record,* by these Senators and Congressmen, and then an edition of 50,000 to one million copies will be sent by them to specially chosen persons. In this manner, German influence is not visible to the outside, and thanks to the privilege of free postage enjoyed by American Congressmen, the cost of this large-scale propaganda can be kept disproportionately low, since, at the very least, mail expenses amounting to many tens of thousands of dollars would be saved. Up to the present nearly a dozen such operations have been or will be carried out during the Republican party convention.[15]

One such project involved Senator Gerald Nye of North Dakota. On April 25, 1939, Nye had delivered a lengthy address in the Senate on the danger that pro-Allies propaganda would lead to United States involve-

15. Thomsen's report to the Foreign Ministry, June 19, 1940, ibid., 9, 625–26. Also see his dispatch of July 18, 1940, ibid., 10, 243. As discussed subsequently, the Germans had a special interest in material from Senator Gerald Nye. It is impossible to say how deeply Nye himself was implicated in these arrangements, since the German documents reveal only the bare details summarized here.

ment in a European war. He incorporated most of the arguments advanced in Sidney Rogerson's book *Propaganda in the Next War* (London, 1938). In addition to its entry in the *Congressional Record,* Thomsen reported that Nye permitted 100,000 copies to be printed and distributed under his own frank. In the summer of 1940, after extended negotiations with Nye's office, embassy agents circulated a second edition of 100,000 through the same channels. It is not known just how long these arrangements persisted, nor how extensive they became, but this instance seems typical of the astonishing exploitation of American isolationists by the German diplomatic corps.

The Germans viewed the results of the Republican convention with mixed emotions. The nomination of Wendell Willkie surprised and disturbed the Nazis, for they knew that he was not a member of the party's isolationist wing. Thomsen informed Berlin that although the Republican candidate had pledged himself to embrace the nonintervention program of his party, there was no doubt that he saw America's best defense in supporting England by all means short of war. The embassy was greatly aroused by confidential reports that Willkie had been a charter member of the White Committee. The chargé d'affaires also feared that Willkie's nomination would weaken the German attempt to bring about the downfall of Roosevelt because the presidential campaign would now center around domestic issues, since the candidates' foreign policies differed only in methods and not in essence.

Nevertheless, Thomsen did claim a substantial success in regard to the Republican platform's foreign policy planks, which declared: (1) the Republican Party is firmly opposed to involving this nation in a foreign war; (2) the Republican Party stands for Americanism, preparedness, peace. In Thomsen's judgment these central principles reflected the efficacy of Nazi propaganda efforts most directly, for they came virtually verbatim from the conspicuous full-page newspaper advertisements which had been published during the convention at the embassy's instigation.[16]

In spite of their disappointment over Willkie's selection as the Republican standard-bearer, the Nazis remained optimistic during the summer that Roosevelt would be defeated, especially if the surprising course of the war continued. They were confident that should the war end before the

16. Cf. the text of the advertisement in the *New York Times,* June 25, 1940, p. 19. Thomsen's reports to the Foreign Ministry, June 28 and July 3, 1940, *DGFP–D, 10,* 48 f. and 101 f.

election the President's quest for a third term would be doomed. The German embassy also realized that were American authorities to discover that it was cooperating with the isolationists, it would mean political ruin for the Reich's friends in this country. Therefore Thomsen destroyed all receipts and other evidence linking the legation with the opponents of Roosevelt. He took the further precaution of burning the embassy's copies of all incriminating reports to Berlin, but, thanks to the capture of the Wilhelmstrasse's archives, one can now read the story of Nazi attempts to manipulate to their advantage the United States presidential election of 1940.

Their partial success during the Republican convention encouraged the Germans to attempt a similar effort at the Democratic convention in Chicago the following month. Here again the principal goal was incorporation of at least a formal pledge of nonintervention in the Democratic platform. The Nazi press adviser and DNB representative, Kurt Sell, arranged for several unidentified Congressmen to attend the convention on embassy funds to exert their influence in this direction. He also financed a number of prominent antiwar advertisements, notably one in the *Chicago Tribune* on July 15, the opening day of the convention. For these undertakings the embassy disbursed $4,500.

It is difficult to estimate the impact of the Nazi strategems, but isolationist views certainly evoked wide sympathy among the delegates, and the platform announced: "We will not participate in foreign wars, and we will not send our army, naval or air forces to fight in foreign lands outside of the Americas except in case of attack."[17] It could hardly have been expressed more happily, from the Nazi point of view, had it been composed in Berlin.

As the summer waned, the ubiquitous Sell remained active, especially among American journalists. He sounded out a number of prominent reporters at the Havana Conference at the end of July and discovered a widespread opinion that Roosevelt would seek to declare war shortly in order to promote his reelection. In view of that prospect, Sell reported that the radio commentator Fulton Lewis, Jr., with whom he had been friendly for more than a decade, contacted the press adviser while they were both in Havana. Lewis was already strongly identified with American isolationists.

According to Sell, Lewis proposed that Germany could score a propa-

17. Thomsen's dispatches of July 4, 5, and 19, 1940, ibid., 119 ff., 125 f. and 250.

ganda coup in its battle with the President by a simple expedient: Hitler should send Roosevelt a brief telegram urging that Washington exert influence on Churchill to reach a settlement and obviate the destructive invasion of Great Britain. This would demonstrate the Fuehrer's reasonableness and place Roosevelt in an awkward position. At the very least, the maneuver would embarrass the Chief Executive and aid his opponents in bringing about his downfall.

> Lewis added that Roosevelt would, of course make a rude and spiteful reply; that would make no difference. Such an appeal would surely make a profound impression on the North American people and especially on South America and would not be interpreted as a sign of weakness at all by responsible circles.[18]

Thomsen, however, advised against the proposed appeal, fearing it would suggest weakness. He dismissed Lewis as of no political importance and said similar suggestions often came from well-meaning but uninfluential individuals. Still, if one credits Sell's account, the incident is an interesting revelation of a well-known American publicist's apparent readiness to cooperate with the Nazis in discrediting the United States President.

The role of another Lewis, the labor leader John L., was of much greater interest to the German government. One of Lewis' friends, William R. Davis, was an oil promoter who had supplied fuel to the German armed forces for some years prior to the war. In the fall of 1939 Davis visited Berlin for discussions with Hermann Goering and other Nazi officials, but the subjects seem to have included considerably more than just business arrangements. Davis is said to have described plans to defeat Roosevelt in 1940 by exploiting Lewis' influence to split the labor vote. The prospect immediately excited Goering, who later told an American interrogator that "for such a purpose I would have spent $100 million to $150 million."[19] The Reichsmarschall assigned one of his aides, Joachim Hertslet, to follow up the lead. From his station in Mexico City,

---

18. Memorandum by Sell, July 26, 1940, ibid., 297–98. See also Thomsen's dispatch on the subject, Aug. 8, 1940, 435.

19. Quoted by Rogge, *The Official German Report*, p. 248. The same author treats this episode at length on pp. 238–58, also recording von Ribbentrop's postwar statement that "in the 1940 elections we placed our faith on Lewis, that he would oppose the reelection of Roosevelt. In attempting to influence the 1940 election against Roosevelt, we made use of oil man Davis. Davis and Hertslet worked with Lewis." It is of course possible that Ribbentrop had an exaggerated impression of the influence the Germans were able to exert through these channels. It seems unlikely that Lewis would have acted differently even if there had been no such contacts.

Hertslet reportedly managed to maintain contact with Davis, Lewis, and other American isolationists.

In early 1940 Hertslet notified the German embassy in Washington that Lewis had informed him and Davis that the labor leader would certainly oppose Roosevelt's reelection. Hans Thomsen observed that Lewis' opposition could be of critical importance, controlling perhaps eight to ten million votes. But the chargé d'affaires found fantastic Hertslet's notion that the Germans might somehow supply millions of dollars to support the labor leader's effort. While Lewis seemed determined to make ruthless use of his influence in favor of strict isolationism, Thomsen calculated that the American was acting "not indeed because of any pro-German sentiments, but because he fears that America's involvement in a war would mean the establishment of an American dictatorship and the placing of his organization under emergency laws."[20]

Goering, however, could not refrain from trying to cultivate Lewis. He instructed Hertslet to raise with Lewis the possibility of organizing a general strike in the United States if American intervention in the war appeared likely. Hertslet reported on June 25 that he had met with Lewis but gave no indication of the outcome of any discussions on Goering's proposition. Meanwhile, more positive reports were reaching Berlin concerning other endeavors by William R. Davis to defeat Roosevelt. Seeking to build up delegate strength to prevent the president's renomination, Davis had reportedly distributed over $160,000 to various groups within the Democratic Party. When that attempt failed he joined the larger effort to defeat FDR at the polls. It was apparently Davis who paid for a climactic nation-wide broadcast by Lewis on October 25.[21]

Vehemently denouncing Roosevelt and asserting that his reelection could very well mean both war and dictatorship, Lewis declared for Willkie and placed his personal prestige squarely on the line in support of the Republican nominee. If Roosevelt received a third term, Lewis vowed to consider it a vote of no confidence in his own leadership of the Congress of Industrial Organizations, a promise he was to keep by resigning the C.I.O. presidency after the election. Whether the Germans had significant influence on Lewis is debatable, but that they attempted to obtain such influence is unquestionable.

20. Thomsen to Berlin, July 4, 1940, quoted in ibid., p. 254.

21. See Friedlaender, *Hitler et les Etats-Unis*, pp. 97–98; also the report of Minister Ruedt in Mexico City to Berlin, July 8, 1940, *DGFP–D, 10,* 159; and Rogge, *The Official German Report*, p. 256. Marquis Childs reported that Davis paid $55,000 for the broadcast time used by Lewis.

While Hans Thomsen was directing a variety of special measures against Roosevelt's reelection, the German Library of Information and the German Tourist Information Bureau guided their regular propaganda along the same lines. The Library, operating independently since the outset of hostilities, stepped up its efforts substantially after May 1940 when it received an additional $15,000 monthly to increase the size and distribution of *Facts in Review*, its weekly bulletin. The periodical quadrupled in length and circulation swelled to 360,000 a month. The library also began to distribute 25,000 copies each week of a program guide for German shortwave broadcasts, spending another $3,000 a month beyond its regular budget.[22] To justify the Reich's actions in Europe the agency mailed out sundry other publications, including reports on alleged Polish atrocities against the German minority in Poland and another White Book on Britain's "Designs on Norway." To add a note of levity to the content of its material the Library also monitored and circulated the caustic anti-British commentary of the notorious German broadcaster, Lord Haw Haw.

Even though transatlantic tourism had ended with the beginning of war, the German Tourist Information Bureau continued to spend several hundred thousand dollars to promote a favorable disposition toward the Reich, both through politically slanted advertising and through its weekly publication, *News Flashes from Germany*. Here, too, the tenor of the propaganda meshed with Thomsen's program to defeat Roosevelt at the polls in November.

During the late summer and early fall the embassy instituted additional intrigues. Thomsen reported to Berlin on the continuing literary campaign and described five books "in the production of some of which the embassy has had a share and the distribution of which it is at present promoting to the greatest possible extent." These included *Country Squire in the White House* (New York, 1940) by the "renowned and widely read journalist" John T. Flynn, which Thomsen considered the most harmful attack on Roosevelt to date; *The Dynamics of War and Revolution* (New York, 1940) by Lawrence Dennis, in which the fascist intellectual predicted an antidemocratic revolution in the United States; a compilation of neutralist views from Borah, Hoover, Lindbergh, and other isolationists, edited by Paul Comly French and entitled *Common Sense Neutrality* (New York, 1939); an elementary proposal of collaboration by the United States with the totalitarian states, *America! Wake Up* (New York, 1940) by An Beneken (pseudonym); and a sharp indictment of Ameri-

22. Thomsen recapitulated the changes in the Library operation in a lengthy dispatch of October 4, 1940, *DGFP–D, 11*, 243–44.

can Jews by a "patriotic American" writing under the pseudonym Cincinnatus, *War, War, War—Veritas Vincit* (1940), which was privately printed and unavailable through the regular book trade.

The embassy had already bought limited numbers of the second, third, and fourth books and sent them to a carefully selected group of individuals. Thomsen said it had become evident that Flynn's book had the heaviest impact of all on American readers. He now planned to distribute 50,000 copies of the work during the election campaign, always carefully concealing the German hand in the operation, and he requested $25,000 to initiate the project.[23] The precise relationship of these authors to the Nazi efforts is impossible to assess on the basis of present documentation, but there is no doubt that Thomsen and his associates were prepared to support virtually any native propagandist whose work gave promise of serving the Reich's own purposes.

Early in September Thomsen arranged another collaboration with Roosevelt's isolationist opponents. Senator Rush Holt had delivered a lengthy address condemning British propaganda in the United States. The speech, accompanied by four articles attacking Lord Lothian and other English spokesmen, had already been distributed to 100,000 interested persons. "Senator Holt has, however, through an intermediary also declared himself prepared to circulate the speech and articles as a reprint in 250,000 copies." The Foreign Office allocated $3,000 to help defray the costs of this operation.

At the same time the German chargé reported that embassy officials

---

23. Thomsen to Berlin, Aug. 7, 1940, *DGFP–D*, 10, 427. Several of these authors contributed other labors to the isolationist, anti-Roosevelt campaign. The book by Cincinnatus went through three editions and gained forty pages of text before the end of 1940. A writer using the same pseudonym published another important article, "Running For Office: A Confession," *New York Times Magazine*, Sept. 8, 1940, pp. 10 ff. Rogge, *The Official German Report*, p. 315, identifies Cincinnatus as Arthur Peter, a Washington attorney. Some material for later editions of his book reportedly was supplied by the German embassy and was drawn from William Joyce's *Twilight Over England*, a volume which no U.S. publisher would agree to handle.

Through 1940 Lawrence Dennis was also circulating his authoritarian message via a privately printed news sheet, *The Weekly Foreign Letter*. During 1940 and 1941 John T. Flynn produced a veritable barrage of articles condemning Roosevelt and any suggestion of intervention in the European imbroglio. For but a few examples, see John T. Flynn, *Can Hitler Beat American Business?*, a pamphlet reprinted from *Harper's Magazine* (February 1940); "Coming: A Totalitarian America," *American Mercury*, 52 (February 1941), 151–57; "Can Hitler Invade America?," *Readers Digest*, 38 (April 1941), 1–6. Paul Comly French also added another expression of his views as a conscientious objector to any war in *We Won't Murder* (New York, 1940).

had come under closer surveillance by American authorities. He feared that the Dies Committee would publish the mailing lists used for *Facts in Review* and other German propaganda material in hopes of discrediting those persons who still maintained contact with Reich agencies. The illustrated paper *P.M.* had been particularly venomous in its attacks on isolationist and German propaganda activities.

As one counterattack against such undesirable publicity, Thomsen planned to provide $3,000 to the "Make Europe Pay War Debts Committee" for publication of a pamphlet directed against *P.M.* The Committee would distribute 200,000 copies of the tract and it would also appear in the *Congressional Record*. Although German agencies in this country were under heavy fire, the embassy advised Berlin not to retaliate against American concerns in Germany, at least for the time being.

One other German ploy proved abortive. Thomsen had found Malcolm Lovell, a prominent New York Quaker and dedicated opponent of Roosevelt's foreign policy, to be one of his best and most resourceful contacts, "partly because of his inner conviction of the necessity of a German-American settlement, and partly in expectation of later personal advantages." His connection with the embassy had been camouflaged as consultations in regard to various humanitarian causes, but Thomsen considered his political suggestions quite valuable, especially those for radio propaganda. The chargé d'affaires arranged for Lovell to visit Berlin for conferences with the appropriate offices concerning future propaganda work in the United States. The reason for the trip was, of course, kept secret. However, late in September other Quakers intervened with the State Department to argue that the journey was purposeless, and the government withdrew Lovell's passport.[24]

While the German propaganda engine ground out a steady stream of information designed to thwart Roosevelt's reelection, Axis diplomacy was working feverishly to reinforce the isolationist impulse in this country. Through September Germany, Japan, and Italy hastened negotiations for a new agreement to protect their interests against U.S. intrusions. Both Berlin and Tokyo believed that a strengthened alliance among the totalitarian states would pose the greatest possible constraint on Roosevelt's attempts to assist the victims of aggression, for it would confront the United States with the clear danger of a two-ocean war. As Ribbentrop told Count Ciano on September 19, "the isolationists would gain a very

24. This discussion relies on a number of Thomsen's dispatches to Berlin during September, *DGFP–D*, *11*, 1–4, 12–14, 41–42, 91–92, 108–10, 157–60.

powerful argument in the campaign if they explain that under these circumstances the risk of war for America is too great."[25]

The desire to ward off American intervention was the principal motive for the Tripartite Pact of September 27, which committed its signatories "to assist one another with all political, economic, and military means when one of the three Contracting Parties is attacked by a power at present not involved in the European War or in the Sino-Japanese conflict." The Fuehrer himself was confident that "seeing the possibility of a two-front war would have quite a dampening effect on America."

In fact, however, the new agreement served to confirm the Roosevelt Administration's view that the aggressors were in league with one another and that still greater efforts to stop them were called for. Announcement of the Tripartite Pact, though apparently bolstering the arguments of isolationists, helped the American public to see the totalitarian menace as a global one and strengthened this country's resolve to meet it. But these effects were only to reveal themselves gradually during the next year.

Initially, the Germans could take satisfaction in the pessimism which the Pact engendered in some American circles. On September 30 Hans Thomsen informed State Secretary Weizsaecker that on the day the Pact was signed, Ambassador Joseph Kennedy had sent one of his gloomiest reports from London.[26] An unidentified but highly placed informant, with whom Thomsen had apparently been in touch before, provided the German diplomat with an accurate summary of the Ambassador's dire assessment of Great Britain's prospects and his warnings to Roosevelt not to take irreparable steps that might leave the United States fighting alone after England's collapse.

25. Quoted in Theo Sommer, *Deutschland und Japan zwischen den Maechten, 1935–1940* (Tuebingen, 1962), p. 411. Sommer's study is a definitive treatment of German-Japanese relations during this period; he aptly characterizes the partners as "accomplices without complicity," for the alliance was always disjointed and marked by independent, uncoordinated action by all parties. See also the German record of Ribbentrop's conversation with Ciano on September 19, 1940, and Hitler's remarks to Mussolini, October 4, 1940, *DGFP–D, 11,* 113–21 and 245–59; and Ernst L. Presseisen, *Germany and Japan: A Study in Totalitarian Diplomacy, 1933–1941* (The Hague, 1958), pp. 250–80.

26. Kennedy had wired the President, "I cannot impress upon you strongly enough my complete lack of confidence in the entire conduct of this war," alluding to the new German pact with Japan as one more "nail in the coffin." His telegram of September 27, 1940, appears in *FR, 3* (1940), 48 f. An unresolved question, smacking of high treason in the American government, is how Thomsen came to have such complete information on Kennedy's reports; see Thomsen to Berlin, Sept. 30, 1940, *DGFP–D, 11,* 227.

By early October the embassy had depleted its special press fund, for which it had received $50,000 the preceding April, and Thomsen sought an additional $50,000. He reminded the Foreign Office that the fund was vital for press policy activities, exertion of influence on newspapers, informants, and similar enterprises. Since this sum would suffice only to maintain press work already undertaken by the embassy, the chargé reserved the right to make special requests in certain cases.

In the weeks leading up to the presidential election Thomsen was moderately encouraged by the progress of the isolationist campaign. Both he and the military attaché, General Boetticher, had high praise for the statements of Charles Lindbergh, but they cautioned Berlin against any mention of his speeches or connections with leading German personages. They noted that the interventionist forces were attempting to portray Lindbergh and his associates as vassals of Germany and that any reference to the isolationists in the German press or official comments might contribute to such suspicions.

Thomsen also warned that anonymous leaflets like those some German agencies distributed had only negative effects in the United States. This was particularly true since British control of the seas made it necessary to route materials from Germany via the Far East and they were hopelessly obsolete by the time they reached America. It was far better to prepare and publish propaganda in the United States, camouflaging the German role so far as possible. For example, "in the case of pronounced anti-British propaganda an American publisher could always be found who would bring out the publication under his name."[27]

In spite of Thomsen's efforts to work behind the scenes, the embassy's activities had not escaped notice. The Dies investigation began to produce evidence of improper behavior on the part of Reich representatives. Only a strong German protest to the State Department had prevented the House committee from ordering Riggs National Bank to produce all its records, ledgers, and vouchers concerning the embassy's accounts. Even without this information the investigators had learned that several German consular officials were also agents of the Party's *Auslandsorganisation*.

Although Consul General Draeger in New York insisted to Thomsen that he had always forbidden the Nazis under his jurisdiction to engage in any political activity, the chargé d'affaires wired Weizsaecker that the mere semblance of Nazi organization in the United States would be interpreted

27. See reports from Boetticher and Thomsen, Oct. 16 and 22, 1940, ibid., pp. 307–09 and 361–62.

by the government and people as a violation of previous German assurances that all Party apparatus here would be disbanded. No matter how innocuous the Nazis considered their activity, a strong public reaction to these discoveries was unavoidable.

As the outcry over the improprieties of Reich diplomats and other representatives grew to new proportions, the Germans sought to administer a coup de grâce to Roosevelt's campaign for reelection. Early in October Ribbentrop discussed with Hitler the possible publication of a damaging report concerning Roosevelt which the Polish ambassador to the United States, Count Jerzy Potocki, had allegedly sent his government in March 1939. The document, suggesting that Roosevelt had been planning American intervention in the war long before Germany attacked Poland, was published in Germany on October 28.

In the United States Thomsen did his best to time the appearance of the document so as to gain maximum influence on the election. He found difficulty in carrying out the plan. The persons who had aided in publication of the earlier volume of Polish documents were now under surveillance, so Thomsen had to seek out new intermediaries. Although he approached a number of leading isolationist newspapers in the Midwest and elsewhere, they turned down publication of the Potocki report, both because they felt it would be treasonable and unpatriotic to use Nazi propaganda material and because they thought the document added nothing sensational to the Warsaw documents already published. "The Republican election committee likewise held on similar considerations that it could not make use of the report."[28]

Nevertheless, two days before Americans went to the polls, the *New York Enquirer* carried the verbatim text of the so-called Potocki report. In an enlarged edition of 250,000 copies New York's only Sunday evening newspaper gave the material prominent headlines on page one.[29] Thomsen was particularly anxious to disguise his role in this episode for he feared that discovery of the embassy's interference in American internal

28. Thomsen to the Foreign Minister, Nov. 4, 1940, ibid., pp. 463–64; see also his reports of Oct. 20, 22, 26, and 30, 1940, pp. 337–38, 362–63, 404, and 431–32. Thomsen assessed the outcome of the balloting in a dispatch of Nov. 6, 1940, pp. 476–78.

29. Rogge, *The Official German Report,* p. 312, states that William Griffin, publisher of the *Enquirer* had other relations to the embassy's propaganda agent, G. S. Viereck. Griffin reportedly requested the Germans to ban his paper in the Reich in order to enhance its respectability in this country. A German version of Potocki's report appears in the Reich Foreign Ministry's collection, *Roosevelts Weg in den Krieg* (Berlin, 1943), no. 19, pp. 73–75.

politics and direct personal attacks on Roosevelt might lead to rupture of diplomatic relations.

When Roosevelt swept to a comfortable victory on November 5, Thomsen could only console himself and his superiors in the Wilhelm-strasse with the feeble observation that at least the President's margin had been reduced to a mere five million, as compared with eleven million in 1936. Summarizing recent trends in this country's attitude toward the European war, he dolefully conveyed the stern reality to Berlin: "As to the whole American people's determination to come to the aid of England with all means, there can be no doubt; this was clearly expressed in the course of the election campaign." The differences between the candidates had been only on points of emphasis. All Germany's devious artifices had been for nought.

The extent and effect of the Reich's propaganda activities in the 1940 campaign will never be fully known, but it is obvious that they consti-tuted one of the most massive interferences in American domestic affairs in history, far surpassing in cleverness and intensity the French attempts to bring about the downfall of the Federalists in the presidential election of 1796. Alluding to efforts by the French Directory to see that he was not elected President, John Adams remarked in his inaugural address:

> If an election is to be determined . . . by foreign nations by flattery or menaces, by fraud or violence, by terror, intrigue, or venality, the Government may not be the choice of the American people, but of foreign nations. It may be foreign nations who govern us, and not we, the people, who govern ourselves.[30]

Neither in 1796 nor in 1940 would the election of the defeated candi-date have produced the results hoped for by the foreign meddlers who supported them, for Thomas Jefferson and Wendell Willkie were, first of all, Americans, earnestly intent on promoting the interests of the United States. But, regardless of the merits of the opposing candidates in these contests, the American people must take satisfaction in the fact that the outcomes represented serious defeats for the foreign powers who tried to manipulate this country's political processes for their own purposes.

---

30. The story of French interference in the 1796 presidential elections has been told by Samuel Flagg Bemis in his classic article, "Washington's Farewell Address: A Foreign Policy of Independence," *American Historical Review*, 39 (January 1934), 250–68. It must be stressed that, in both 1796 and 1940, the central goal of the foreign plotters was really the defeat of incumbent administrations, rather than the election of specific individuals from whom they expected special favors.

CHAPTER 10

Propaganda in Retreat

The reelection of President Roosevelt, following the actions taken at Havana to protect the Western Hemisphere against invasion and subversion, left Nazi propagandists fighting a rearguard action. Their basic goal remained to prevent American interference in the German conquest of the Old World, but the growth of U.S. assistance to Great Britain and the trend toward hemispheric solidarity against totalitarian inroads obliged Berlin to modify its tactics. German propaganda in the New World now crystallized around a set of major themes prepared by the Foreign Ministry in late November 1940.

In references to the United States, German publications and broadcasts were to observe restraint, hoping to allay American concern over the Reich's ultimate intentions. At the same time, "by indirect and camouflaged actions" the instruments of Nazi propaganda would seek to undermine the psychological bases for Anglo-American collaboration. The Wilhelmstrasse's information experts judged that they could achieve the greatest impact on U.S. public opinion by influencing the moods of neutral areas (South America, Iberia, East Asia) that were important to this country.

Although the German military attaché in Washington, Boetticher, had recently been revising his disparaging estimates of America's military potential, Berlin found it expedient to stress the qualitative and quantitative inadequacy of U.S. forces. Through "neutral" radio stations Anglo-American weakness would be hammered into the public consciousness in Latin America and elsewhere, reinforcing the impression that Nazi victory was inevitable.

The successes of anticapitalist Europe would be contrasted with unemployment, farm problems, and other social ills in the United States. German propaganda would characterize Americans and others who enlisted to fight for Great Britain as agents of reaction rather than of progress. This thesis would be buttressed by the argument that the true purpose of the Anglo-Saxon nations was not the liberation of Europe but the suppression of the new and dynamic culture which was emerging on the continent. To counter the U.S. tendency to portray its actions as a crusade in the name of Christianity, the Reich would call attention to the highly un-Christian method of the food blockade under which Europe now suffered. The Germans also hoped to exploit the religious sentiments of Quakers in the United States, as well as the sympathies of Irish and Italian Catholics.

The Nazi propaganda strategists doubted that atrocity stories like those circulated in the years after 1914 would have a constructive effect in the Western Hemisphere. They planned to apply a more "objective" veneer to such tales, disguising German intentions in publishing them and, hopefully, enhancing their credibility. In both North and South America, German planners thought they could profitably emphasize the latent economic antagonisms between England and the United States, highlighting their conflicting interests in matters of currency, markets, and so forth. The "plutocratic opposition" to Roosevelt in the United States might be aroused by playing on the danger that the President was leading the country toward socialism.[1] Similar themes had been heard before, but now, realizing that they were losing ground in the psychological theater, the Germans determined to drive these points home to citizens of the American republics.

From Washington Hans Thomsen discerned new opportunities for Germany in the ambivalence of American opinion. By this time the country had begun to polarize into clearly defined camps, symbolized, on the one hand, by the Committee to Defend America by Aiding the Allies, and, on the other, by the America First Committee. Formed in the autumn of 1940, the latter group sought to coordinate the efforts of the estimated seven hundred isolationist organizations actively engaged in propaganda against Roosevelt's policies. By December 1941 the committee claimed some 450 chapters and subchapters across the country with membership exceeding 800,000, almost two-thirds of it concentrated near Chicago.

The Committee to Defend America by Aiding the Allies, under the leadership of William Allen White, quickly became anathema to German interests. Desperate to counter the work of White's group, the German embassy saw the America First Committee as a godsend. How better to reverse the interventionist tendencies emerging in the United States than by collaborating with a group of respected and patriotic American citi-

1. Memorandum by an official of the Information Department, Nov. 19, 1940, DGFP–D, 11, 624–28.

zens who sincerely believed in the wisdom of their isolationist professions? Within weeks after the American First Committee began to function Thomsen reported that he and his confidential operatives had already established close and constant contact with a number of the movement's leading figures. He was further heartened in December 1940 when another isolationist organization, the No Foreign Wars Committee, entered the fray. The chargé d'affaires informed Berlin that "we have good relations with both isolationist committees and support them in various ways. In order that this cooperation be not compromised I request that the work of the committees be passed over in silence in the German press and radio."[2]

While the embassy now placed its hopes primarily on the efforts of these groups, other projects also went forward in the German campaign to frustrate Roosevelt's program of aid to Great Britain. Ribbentrop was hopeful that Irish-American antipathy for the British would serve as an important constraint on Roosevelt and the German Foreign Minister instructed his agents to cultivate relations with the Irish hyphenates.

Thomsen was not sanguine about Irish influence on the U.S. government. Although he thought their hatred of the English was undiminished, he wired Berlin that the Irish Catholics no longer looked to Germany as a liberator and opposed the Reich on ideological grounds. Still they might serve to retard all-out American support to Great Britain. For this reason the embassy press attaché had long been active among the Irish-American press and related organizations.

> For example, by spending considerable sums from the War Press Fund, we make use of the Irish-American newspaper, *The New York Enquirer,* whose circulation and (one group garbled) we have in various ways greatly increased. Moreover, the *Enquirer* arranges for us cooperation with other Irish newspapers, such as the *Gaelic American* and *The Leader,* which is published in California. Also, through Consul General Kapp, we maintain relations with Father Coughlin and his newspaper, *Social Justice.*[3]

2. Thomsen to Berlin, Dec. 25, 1940, ibid., pp. 949–50. Wayne Cole has written a comprehensive account of the most important isolationist organization, *America First: The Battle Against Intervention, 1940–1941* (Madison, Wis., 1953). His study complements the earlier history of the White Committee by Walter Johnson, *The Battle Against Isolation* (Chicago, 1944).

3. Thomsen's summary of his efforts among Irish-Americans went to Berlin on January 26, 1941, *DGFP–D, 11,* 1213–14. Karl Kapp was consul general in Cleveland.

American assistance to Great Britain had so far consisted of relatively modest commerce in arms, the destroyers-for-bases trade, and similar cooperative gestures. By late December 1940, however, Roosevelt's concept of the United States as the "arsenal of democracy" had matured in his plan for the Lend-Lease program. The Germans now faced the imminent probability of a massive flow of American arms and other manufactures to the British. The Lend-Lease bill, H.R. 1776, rapidly gained irresistible political momentum. Handicapped by ever-tighter surveillance of its staff and operatives, the German embassy nevertheless brought all its resources to bear in hopes of postponing passage of the legislation.

Thomsen's agents secretly helped to organize and finance public protests against the bill and sought to induce as many Americans as possible to write their congressmen and senators in opposition to Lend-Lease. They persuaded a group of German-Americans in the Middle West to form the German-American National Alliance in support of the America First Committee's active campaign to defeat H.R. 1776. The Nazis also drew on the labor of their emotional allies, several anti-Semitic groups, to organize floods of letters to members of Congress.

In a dispatch of February 9, 1941, Thomsen summarized several of these efforts:

> In various cities demonstrations of protest were held through the Peace Mobilization Committee, which is closely allied with us. Such a demonstration took place on February 1 before the Capitol and on February 2 before the White House. . . . In addition, there is being prepared, with our financial support, a women's march on Washington, accompanied by sensational publicity, planned in a way similar to the march of war veterans on the Capitol in 1932. It is being organized under the motto "Mothers' Crusade to defeat H.R. 1776."[4]

Father Charles Coughlin, organizer of the Union for Social Justice, was one of Roosevelt's most vehement adversaries. Besides his written attacks on the Administration, Coughlin was a prominent radio commentator for some years, although his standing had waned considerably by this time. See Schlesinger, *The Politics of Upheaval*, pp. 16–28, 553–59, 626–30, and Charles J. Tull, *Father Coughlin and the New Deal* (Syracuse, 1965). In April 1942 Coughlin's *Social Justice,* which had once enjoyed a circulation of 1,000,000 was barred from the mails on charges that its contents were seditious. Michael Sayers and Albert E. Kahn, *Sabotage! The Secret War Against America* (New York, 1942), p. 251.

4. Thomsen to Berlin, Feb. 9, 1941, *DGFP–D, 12,* 60–62. Cole, *America First,* pp. 111–22, describes the conscientious, but not entirely successful, attempts of the America First Committee to avoid association with German agents and sympathizers.

To support these activities large quantities of isolationist literature were being distributed. The chargé d'affaires recognized that these measures would not prevent the adoption of Lend-Lease, but he calculated that they would contribute to lengthening the debate, to strengthening the opposition to the bill, and to displaying before the world the divisions among American citizenry.

As action on the bill neared completion, the embassy bitterly informed the Foreign Ministry and the Wehrmacht that passage of Lend-Lease would mean that "the Jewish ideology will have prevailed to a very considerable extent in the United States." Boetticher took some comfort from the existence of what he thought were sympathetic circles in the American officer corps, who, he claimed, considered Lindberg their great protagonist.

Analyzing the situation from Berlin, Ambassador Dieckhoff noted that public opinion polls showed 85 to 90 percent of Americans favoring aid to England short of war but 70 to 80 percent opposing outright U.S. entry into the contest. It was imperative to consolidate the latter sentiment for, contrary to the facile assumption held by many in the Reich Government, a U.S. declaration of war would be of the utmost significance, ensuring a prolongation of the conflict and permitting Roosevelt to mobilize tremendous forces against the Axis. The Germans hoped to intensify the reluctance of most Americans to enter the war by secretly promoting a campaign "which several Senators of the opposition are going to launch all over the country in the coming weeks."[5] Dieckhoff emphasized that progress of the war itself would have a decisive impact on American opinion. Prompt defeat of the English would tend to squelch any U.S. disposition to get into the war, while an extended period of desultory combat would involve grave risks of encouraging American intervention.

Neither the embassy's operations nor those of the isolationists were helped by Berlin's failure to heed repeated warnings against comments from Germany on the domestic political situation in the United States. In January 1941 a Nazi shortwave broadcast commended the America First Committee as "truly American and truly patriotic," further stimulating the suspicion that the committee was actually, if not intentionally, abetting the Axis. Some time later Hitler himself cited remarks by the committee's

---

5. Memorandum by Dieckhoff, Mar. 10, 1941, *DGFP–D, 12,* 258–59. He had previously outlined implications of a U.S. declaration of war in a trenchant critique of the prevailing Nazi complacency toward that contingency; see his memorandum of Jan. 9, 1941, *DGFP–D, 11,* 1061–63.

chairman, General Robert Wood, to prove that Britain was really responsible for the European conflict. Try though they might to disengage themselves from the leprous touch of Nazi propagandists, the isolationists could not disguise the fact that, from however divergent motives, they shared the Reich's goal of keeping the United States out of war.

For some time German diplomats throughout the Americas had been calling for another authoritative declaration by Hitler, like his earlier "interview" with Karl von Wiegand, repudiating all suggestions that Germany might harbor aggressive intentions toward the New World. In May 1941 Hitler again attempted to calm American apprehension on this point.

The United States was pondering President Roosevelt's inclination to provide escorts for Lend-Lease convoys across the Atlantic. John Cudahy, former U.S. ambassador to Belgium, was one of many Americans who feared that convoying would certainly draw this country into a war. He thought a clear declaration by the Germans that they would fire on such escorts would alert the American public and bolster opposition to Roosevelt's policy. To seek such a declaration Cudahy called on both Ribbentrop and Hitler.

The Fuehrer told him that "in his opinion American escorts meant war." At the same time, however, Hitler and Ribbentrop were disdainful of the rumors that Germany might invade the Western Hemisphere, dismissing such a notion as "childish" and "absurd." In response to Cudahy's candid statement that most Americans considered Germany a ruthless aggressor Hitler blandly denied responsibility for the war and said he would assure peace, prosperity, and happiness for Germany's neighbors. "He [the Fuehrer] was afraid that he would also not be spared being praised by the professors of economics who had attacked his economic views in the past."[6] Hitler disclaimed any desire to undercut the Western Hemisphere through employing slave labor from the conquered countries, although he did think the United States would probably have to adopt the superior economic principles practiced by Germany.

With the Fuehrer's concurrence Cudahy proposed to release to the press the substance of the conversation. He did so on his return to the United States, but Hitler's reassurances were lost in the uproar over another declaration: on May 27 President Roosevelt had proclaimed an unlimited

6. German memoranda of Cudahy's conversations with Ribbentrop and Hitler on May 4 and May 23, 1941, *DGFP–D, 12,* 704–10, 854–61. Cudahy's report of the discussions is summarized in the *New York Times,* June 19, 1941.

National Emergency, declaring that the Nazis were engaged in a world war for world domination and that "unless the advance of Hitlerism is forcibly checked now, the Western Hemisphere will be within range of the Nazi weapons of destruction."

The President's speech underscored his belief that the threat to the New World was materializing first of all in the work of Nazi propagandists and advance agents in both North and South America. As an example to other American republics, the United States now adopted stringent provisions to suppress such agents. On June 14 German assets in this country were frozen. Two days later Under Secretary of State Welles notified the German embassy that the United States had learned of improper and unwarranted activities of the Reich's agencies in this country. Welles, acting on instructions from the President, then demanded the closing of the German Library of Information, the German Railway and Tourist Agencies, the Transocean News Service, and the German consulates. All German nationals affiliated with these agencies were to be withdrawn from the United States by July 10.[7] The order did not apply to the embassy, but Thomsen and his staff were henceforth under close scrutiny.

The Germans had anticipated a crackdown for some time and had taken precautions to minimize its effects. Several months before, after a U.S. grand jury had indicted Manfred Zapp and Gunter Tonn of Transocean News Service for failure to register as agents of a foreign government, the Germans had taken reprisals against several American citizens in Europe. Among those arrested were reporters Richard Hottelet of United Press and Jay Allen of the North American Newspaper Alliance. It soon became apparent that the Americans were being held as hostages for German operatives in the United States. Now, after many weeks of delay, the Reich agreed to exchange Allen, Hottelet, and two other Americans for Zapp and three other Nazi agents being held in the United States. To Welles' démarche of June 16 Berlin replied by advancing parallel charges against U.S. consular officials in Germany and the zones of occupation, as well as against offices of the American Express Company.[8]

In spite of these developments Ribbentrop counted on the German em-

---

7. Welles' memorandum of a conversation with Dr. Wilhelm Tannenberg, first secretary of the German embassy, June 16, 1941, *FR,* 2 (1941), 626–30. Though fully aware of the justifications for the U.S. accusations, Germany rejected them in a note of June 18, p. 630. President Roosevelt's address of May 27, 1941, is conveniently reproduced in S. Shepard Jones and Denys P. Meyers, eds., *Documents on American Foreign Relations, 1940–1941* (Boston, 1941), pp. 48–58.

8. For details on these events see *FR,* 2 (1941), 597–635.

bassy in Washington to carry forward the campaign against U.S. intervention. On July 19 the Foreign Minister transmitted new instructions to Thomsen, directing him to circulate the theme that American Jews actually had the most to lose from U.S. entry into the war. American involvement, he reasoned, could only lead to an authoritarian regime in the United States and eventually to retaliation on the "Jewish warmongers." To Ribbentrop's inquiry concerning the extent to which such ideas had begun to emerge in the United States, Thomsen shortly replied that he thought some Jews had already become sensitive to such charges. But the chargé d'affaires cautioned that he saw no early prospect for any successful anti-Semitic movement in the United States. Thomsen also had to disappoint Ribbentrop's hopes of acquiring control over some newspapers in the United States. The embassy saw no chance for this at the moment. It did, however, foresee a possibility of later purchasing some Hearst journals, which might be sold after the owner's death to meet his debts.[9]

The same month the Nazi Foreign Minister conceived another scheme to discredit American and British leaders. He proposed to disseminate each day "one or two mendacious reports . . . concerning the intentions of Roosevelt or of Churchill."[10] Depending on the circumstances these would be planted in the foreign press, published or broadcast in Germany or abroad, or circulated through occasional remarks and press conferences of appropriate officials. As an example, Ribbentrop suggested that the arrival of U.S. forces in British Guiana (under an occupation agreement between Britain, Brazil, and the United States) should be portrayed as the prelude to American landings in Venezuela or annexationist attempts elsewhere in Latin America.

With the closure of German consulates and other agencies the embassy found it difficult to initiate propaganda intrigues, but Thomsen had already launched a number of endeavors which continued through the summer and early fall. Unknown to many of the Congressmen and other prominent citizens who were involved in various isolationist groups, the Germans had provided funds to several of the committees which continued the battle against U.S. intervention. Among others, these groups included the War Debts Defense Committee and the Islands for War Debts

---

9. Ribbentrop to Washington, July 19, 1941, and Thomsen's reply, July 25, 1941, *DGFP–D, 13,* 201, 213 f. Regarding the possible acquisition of U.S. papers, see the summary of Thomsen's dispatch no. 2639, August 8, 1941, in Friedlaender, *Hitler et les États-Unis,* p. 264.

10. Memorandum by Ribbentrop to his Secretariat, July 24, 1941, ibid., p. 206 f.

Committee, reportedly conceived by George Sylvester Viereck. A paid German agent, Prescott Dennett, was chief administrator of several such committees, as well as of the Columbia Press Service.

A visitor to Dennett's Washington office in the summer of 1941 found business flourishing. Working with George Hill, assistant to Congressman Hamilton Fish, Dennett had obtained large quantities of congressional envelopes for use in distributing isolationist materials. In addition to mailings under Fish's signature, Dennett was using envelopes bearing the franks of Clare Hoffman, Henry Dworshak, Bartel J. Jonkman, Harold Knutson, John G. Alexander, James C. Oliver, Gerald P. Nye, D. Worth Clark, and Robert R. Reynolds. Through Dennett the Germans were also paying George Hill to obtain reprints of suitable speeches and articles that appeared in the *Congressional Record*. From March to September 1941 Hill purchased more than half a million reprints from the Government Printing Office.[11]

A related operation of which the embassy was particularly proud involved mass mailings of propaganda postcards. Heribert von Strempel, the press officer, reportedly arranged and financed the distribution of a dozen such cards, each in quantities of one hundred thousand to one million copies. All bore congressional letterheads and urged recipients to write their representatives expressing opposition to U.S. participation in the war. The themes were familiar: sarcastic attacks on Roosevelt and the alleged warmongers in his cabinet, reminders of the President's campaign promise to keep the country out of the European conflict and of the American sacrifices in the last great war, appeals to American mothers to save their sons from the bloody ordeal.

A notable sample was an isolationist card sent out by Senator Burton K. Wheeler in July 1941. Some of the million copies distributed reached members of the armed services, provoking a public controversy between the Senator and Secretary of War Stimson, who strongly condemned the potential damage to military morale. Wheeler's abuse of the franking privilege also brought a rebuke from one of his colleagues, Senator Alben Barkley. Barkley pointed out that it was unlawful to permit the frank to be used by a committee, organization, or association and that

11. See Sayers and Kahn, *Sabotage*, pp. 167–211. This discussion also draws on Wayne S. Cole, *Senator Gerald P. Nye and American Foreign Relations* (Minneapolis, 1962), pp. 176–201; Cole, *America First*, pp. 111–31; John Roy Carlson (pseud.), *Under Cover* (New York, 1943), pp. 126–31, 409–16. Carlson's real name was Avedis Derounian. He had been chief investigator for Friends of Democracy, Inc., a group which passionately denounced America First as the "Nazi transmission belt."

Wheeler had clearly violated the statute by lending his frank to the America First Committee.[12] But Congress continued to tolerate such infringements.

In addition to Prescott Dennett's distribution of such items, sizable quantities were processed through the Washington headquarters of the America First Committee, again employing franked envelopes. Less respectable organizations like the Silver Shirts, the Christian Front, and the Christian Mobilizers also collaborated in this activity, often inserting their own anti-Semitic and authoritarian materials.

A key figure in these undertakings was G. S. Viereck, a principal intermediary for the embassy in a host of matters. Viereck had successfully cultivated cordial relationships with a number of Senators and Congressmen, among them Senator Ernest Lundeen and Congressman Hamilton Fish whose offices he often used as bases of operations on Capitol Hill. Viereck himself had sometimes dictated speeches for Lundeen, openly using the Senator's telephones to obtain material from Hans Thomsen at the embassy. Lundeen's death in a 1940 air crash had cost Viereck and the Germans one of their most important contacts.

Not all isolationists were prepared to deal with Viereck, whose sentiments and previous work for the Germans in World War I were widely known. Viereck had, for example, aroused the suspicions of Senator Gerald Nye and his staff by requesting permission to order "six or seven million" copies of one of Nye's speeches. When Nye refused to cooperate, the German agent was obliged to obtain the material indirectly. His associate Dennett requested a smaller mumber in behalf of the "Make Europe Pay War Debts Committee" and Nye complied, evidently unaware that the committee was little more than a front for Viereck.

Viereck's other projects had also flourished. By early 1941 Flanders Hall, the New Jersey publishing concern whose establishment he had engineered in 1939, had published a dozen books and booklets, mainly directed against the British. At least four of these publications had been supplied directly by Berlin, often as hasty and crude translations of polemics that had originally appeared in German. One such tract was *Inhumanity Unlimited*, "from the French of Jeanne D'Arc Dillon la Touche;" it was in fact Reinhard Frank's *Englands Herrschaft in Indien*. Other

12. Thomsen described these projects in dispatches of July 29 and July 30, 1941, *DGFP–D, 13*, 234 and n. 2; on the Wheeler episode see also Rogge, *The Official German Report*, p. 355, and Henry L. Stimson and McGeorge Bundy, *On Active Service in Peace and War* (New York, 1947), p. 378.

Flanders Hall titles reflected Viereck's developing ties in the U.S. Congress. A lengthy speech by Senator Lundeen appeared under the firm's imprint as *Lord Lothian Versus Lord Lothian,* with editorial comment by "James Burr Hamilton," a rather flamboyant pseudonym for Viereck.

He also claimed credit for the expanded circulation of the German Library of Information newsletter, *Facts in Review,* which he helped to edit. This publication had grown to 16 pages an issue and by 1941 was reaching at least 100,000 readers. Viereck's motives seem to have been financial as well as political. In a letter of January 25, 1941, to Matthias Schmitz, the former Smith College professor who now directed the Library of Information, Viereck complained that he was grossly underpaid and that he should be getting at least $2,500 a month for his contribution to *Facts in Review.*

Certainly Viereck's diligence, if not his effectiveness, seems to have justified a handsome salary. Apart from his editorial duties, he also helped develop or obtain mailing lists with hundreds of thousands of names. And through much of this period he was filing weekly intelligence reports, press and propaganda analyses with Ambassador Dieckhoff in Berlin. For his multiple services Viereck was judged the "most valuable liaison agent" of the Foreign Office's Information Section.[13]

Meanwhile, Thomsen was helping to finance the activities of Laura Ingalls, a frequent speaker at isolationist rallies during the latter half of 1941. Miss Ingalls, a socialite and aviatrix who had earned notoriety some months earlier when she "bombed" the White House with antiwar leaflets, now went on the embassy payroll. Her instructions from Baron Ulrich

13. Viereck's activities during 1940 and 1941 are detailed in Sayers and Kahn, *Sabotage,* pp. 167–95. An extended description of the congressional speeches and reprints in which Viereck had a part appears in Rogge, *The Official German Report,* pp. 130–72. The latter work is a somewhat revised version of a 1946 report by a Justice Department lawyer who prosecuted Viereck and others for sedition. Rogge concludes that at least four members of Congress "collaborated" with Viereck: Senators Rush Holt and Ernest Lundeen and Congressmen Stephen Day and Hamilton Fish. He lists twenty other members of Congress whom Viereck managed to exploit in his lengthy campaign: John G. Alexander, Philip A. Bennett, Usher L. Burdick, D. Worth Clark, Cliff Clevenger, Henry C. Dworshak, Clare E. Hoffman, Edwin C. Johnson, Bartel J. Jonkman, Harold Knutson, Robert M. La Follette, Gerald P. Nye, Robert R. Reynolds, Paul W. Shafer, Henrik Shipshead, William G. Stratton, Martin L. Sweeney, Jacob Thorkelson, George H. Tinkham, Burton K. Wheeler. Sayers and Kahn add to the list the names of Congressmen James Oliver, Dewey Short, and John M. Vorys. A number of these individuals, including Wheeler, Nye, and Holt, were soon repudiated by the voters, perhaps because of public revelations concerning their relationships with Viereck and his associates.

von Gienanth, the embassy's second secretary, were simple: "The best thing you can do for our cause is to continue to promote the America First Committee."[14]

But the net drew tighter around the Nazi maneuvers. In September a grand jury began an investigation of foreign propaganda which was to lead to the eventual conviction of Viereck, Hill, Ingalls, and others. Well before the Japanese attack at Pearl Harbor resolved the great debate over America's attitude toward the Axis, strong security measures had effectively subdued the German propaganda machine in the United States. Within hours of the Japanese assault Hans Thomsen was reporting to Ribbentrop that "there is no such thing as an opposition any more. . . for the first time all segments of political life are joined in eagerness for war, hatred of Japan, and desire for unity."[15]

German efforts to foster American isolationism had perhaps enjoyed limited and temporary success, but failure to prevent U.S. intervention was to prove decisive in the Axis defeat.

The Nazis had fared less badly in Latin America. Just prior to the Havana Conference in July 1940 illness had forced the resignation of Argentina's moderate president, Roberto Ortiz. Ramon Castillo now assumed power as Acting President, the first of a series of Argentine leaders who were to prove more amenable to Nazi cajolery. Through the autumn of 1940 legal action continued against a group of Germans who had been implicated in alleged subversive activities that summer. After Ambassador von Thermann lodged a number of sharp complaints against the proceedings, however, the Castillo government began to have second thoughts. Whether as a sop to the Germans or from lack of evidence, the indictments were quashed. In discussions with the German diplomat, who repeatedly emphasized the great opportunities a Nazi victory in Europe would bring for Argentina, Castillo expressed a decided inclination to build friendly relations with the Third Reich. The anti-German tendencies which had flared briefly in the summer of 1940 now began to recede in Argentina.

Serious economic difficulties increased Argentina's unwillingness to an-

14. Quoted by Johnson, *The Battle Against Isolation*, p. 164; see also pp. 147–84. Von Gienanth had succeeded Richard Sallet as the PROMI attaché in Washington and also served as a Gestapo agent.

15. Thomsen to Berlin, Dec. 8, 1941, *DGFP–D, 13,* 978 f. The lengthy sedition trials of Viereck and some thirty others are traced in Rogge, *The Official German Report,* pp. 173–218.

tagonize Berlin. In 1940 the country's balance of payments deficit swelled to 360 million pesos; the decline in Argentine exports was worse than that of the deep depression of 1932. Castillo was seeking to ease the nation's economic crisis by forming a customs union with Brazil. For this arrangement to be feasible the Germans would have to waive their right under existing treaties to demand most-favored-nation treatment. The Castillo regime felt it necessary to court German support for this scheme. This consideration, along with Castillo's expectation that Hitler would win the war, prompted Argentina to relax pressure against German activities during 1940 and early 1941.[16] Not surprisingly, Berlin welcomed the proposal for a customs union, hoping it would be a counterweight to U.S. influence in the region.

By the spring of 1941 Thermann, acting on instructions, was preparing new propaganda efforts in conjunction with the economic inducements Germany was holding out to Buenos Aires. The ambassador laid the groundwork for "a society for the purpose of influencing Argentine policy more effectively, which is to have important Argentine politicians, parliamentarians, and businessmen as members."[17] The official purpose of the organization would be to promote the broadest possible trade between Germany and Argentina. Thermann proposed to invest 250,000 pesos in this effort during 1941.

This scheme was impeded, however, by a renewed outcry against the embassy's political activities. Influential members of the Argentine Chamber of Deputies did not share Castillo's lenient attitude toward the role of Thermann and other German representatives. Under the chairmanship of Damonte Taborda, a special legislative commission conducted an extensive investigation of Nazi activities in the country, uncovering evidence that generated renewed currents of public alarm over the propaganda efforts of German diplomats. By September 1941 Thermann feared that he would be declared persona non grata and, indeed, the Castillo govern-

16. Memoranda byWeizsaecker, Dec. 10, 1940, and by Wiehl, a Foreign Office economics expert, Jan. 23, 1941, *DGFP–D, 11*, 933–37, 1176–77; memorandum by Freytag of the Foreign Office Political Division, Feb. 9, 1941, and dispatch from Ambassador von Thermann, Mar. 6, 1941, *DGFP–D, 12*, 65–67, 228 f.; Wiehl to embassy in Buenos Aires, July 25, 1941, *DGFP–D, 13*, 217 f.

17. Thermann to Berlin, Apr. 9, 1941, ibid., p. 496. In the next two years the German embassy was also to contribute some $200,000 to Juan Perón and other leaders of the 1943 coup d'état that firmly established an authoritarian regime in Argentina. Alejandro Magnet, *Nuestros Vecinos Justicialistas* (Santiago de Chile, 1953), pp. 135–38. See also Isidoro Ruiz Moreno, *Historia de las Relaciones Exteriores Argentinas* (Buenos Aires, 1961), pp. 316–18.

ment felt obliged to ask Berlin if the German ambassador might not be recalled or take an extended leave from his post.[18] The Reich Foreign Ministry indignantly refused to consider such a suggestion and its determined stand apparently cowed Buenos Aires.

Although Argentina would make sporadic efforts to control German activities, Buenos Aires was to remain until 1944 the principal base of operations in the Nazi effort to seduce the countries of Latin America. These intrigues, together with the admiration some Argentine military officers felt for Hitler's totalitarian model of politics, figured prominently in the country's drift toward military dictatorship.

Elsewhere in Latin America during these months, Germany's prospects fluctuated. In Uruguay the trial of the German conspirators who had been discovered in the summer of 1940 focused hostile attention on the Nazis. A Nazi named Fuhrmann had worked out a plan for partitioning the country. For such a flagrant act of treason there was no chance of acquittal, but the Germans did hope to have him declared insane. The Reich secretly provided defense counsel for Fuhrmann and his associates, hoping to minimize the damage the episode would inevitably do to Germany's posture in South America.

That posture suffered further from incidents in two other countries during the summer of 1941. On July 19 the Bolivian government announced a state of siege, claiming to have discovered proof of an intended putsch by pro-Nazi circles. The Bolivians also charged the German minister, Ernst Wendler, with complicity in the affair and declared him persona non grata. Wendler protested his innocence, as did the Bolivian military attaché in Berlin with whom he had supposedly been implicated. German propagandists counterattacked by asserting that the President of the United States had instigated the episode to poison relations between the Reich and Latin America.[19] The facts of the case remain obscure, and it is possible that the affair was staged by the Bolivian regime to justify strong action against its opponents. But this possibility seemed less plausible

18. See the memorandum by State Secretary Weizsaecker, Aug. 27, 1941, and dispatches from Thermann to Berlin on Sept. 3 and 9, 1941, *DGFP–D, 12,* 401–02, 443–44, 467–70. Results of the Taborda Commission's inquiry have been cited here as *Argentine Investigation:* see above, especially Chapter 8.

19. The minister in Bolivia (Wendler) to Berlin, July 20, 1941, *DGFP–D, 13,* 195 f. and n. 5, p. 196; see also the memorandum by the Director of the Political Department in the Foreign Ministry, Aug. 14, 1941, pp. 314–15 and n. 1, p. 314. On the Uruguayan developments see the memorandum by Freytag of the Foreign Ministry, Oct. 31, 1940, *DGFP–D, 11,* 441–43.

when on August 10 Chile announced the arrest of several Nazi party members, also in connection with an alleged subversive plot. Recurrent crises of this nature served to sustain public anxiety over a potential fifth column in this hemisphere.

Yet Germany retained a major advantage in Latin America—the wide-spread belief that the Fuehrer was invincible. This view persisted in many quarters long after Germany had begun its Russian campaign in June 1941.[20] Some American governments were compelled to walk a political tightrope, avoiding irrevocable commitment to the bold policies being advanced by Washington and holding open the possibility of a rapprochement with Berlin, should a final Nazi victory preclude any other choice. This was particularly true in Brazil, where Getulio Vargas, without the knowledge of his foreign minister, was quietly carrying on discussions with German Ambassador Pruefer.

Although Vargas, trapped in an excruciating dilemma, remained intolerant of Nazi propaganda or political activities in Brazil, he was anxious to safeguard his relations with the Reich. One of his principal motives was to encourage Germany to deliver the arms Brazil had purchased under a 1938 agreement with Krupp. To this end Vargas readily portrayed Brazil as "the bulwark against the inclusion of South America in Roosevelt's anti-German policy." Pruefer urged Berlin to continue weapons deliveries in order to help the Brazilian President withstand North American pressure.

As one token of his good faith toward the Reich, Vargas assured the ambassador that he would not hamper the movement of German ships laid up in Brazil, although he did express interest in the possible purchase of some vessels. On June 6, 1941, Vargas raised another idea with Pruefer. For some time, he declared, he had been evading U.S. requests to reciprocate Roosevelt's visit to Rio de Janeiro several years earlier. He was now afraid he would have to commit himself to make the trip, although the timing would be most awkward since Vargas' visit would be interpreted as an endorsement of Roosevelt's policy toward the Axis. To avoid this appearance, Vargas inquired if the Germans might agree to his going

20. See Sumner Welles, *Seven Decisions That Shaped History* (New York, 1950), pp. 94–123. The attack on the Soviet Union did, however, catalyze many left-wing elements in Latin America. Where they had observed an uneasy silence regarding the German threat, the rupture of the Nazi-Soviet nonaggression pact brought forth a flood of anti-Nazi antagonism from Russia's ideological allies and sympathizers. This tendency was offset to some degree by the feeling among Catholics and others that a crusade against atheistic Communism should be welcomed.

to Washington with a proposal of mediation rather than as a presumed ally of the United States.

Ribbentrop would have none of this. Any initiative in this respect would have to come from the other side. Vargas was disappointed, but he soon recognized that deteriorating relations between Washington and Berlin made his plan inopportune.[21] While Vargas hesitated to burn the bridges between Brazil and Germany, the demands of hemispheric defense led him increasingly to align his nation with the United States. Even as he offered sympathetic gestures to the Germans, the Brazilian President was undertaking positive measures to aid the United States in protecting South America.

Neither Vargas nor any other Latin American leader could adopt the forward policy against the Axis which the United States was following in 1941. But apart from Argentina, the American republics had by this time made substantial progress in controlling Nazi propaganda and subversion, and the German government had few avenues of influence open to it in the Western Hemisphere. The alarms of 1940 and 1941 had prompted most of the countries to snuff out or bring under close surveillance the agencies of Axis penetration. When Hitler declared war on the United States four days after Pearl Harbor, the New World still felt considerable trepidation over the danger of subversion, but, as events were to prove, the actual threat posed by the Nazi agents in this hemisphere had been brought under reasonably effective control.

Joseph Goebbels had once voiced his contempt for representative government by commenting, "It will always remain the best joke made by the democratic system that it provided its deadly enemies with the means of destroying it."[22] The American republics had demonstrated that, under vigorous and enlightened leadership, the system could also provide its defenders with the means of protecting it.

21. Pruefer's reports to Berlin, June 7 and June 18, 1941, minute by Wiehl of the Foreign Office, June 10, 1941, Ribbentrop's instruction to Pruefer, June 11, 1941, *DGFP–D, 12,* 974 f., 993–95, 1046. Also Pruefer's dispatch of Nov. 29, 1941, *DGFP–D, 13,* 895–96.

22. Quoted by Carlson, *Under Cover,* p. 500.

CHAPTER 11

Hitler and the American Hemisphere

Having examined the widespread Nazi activities in the New World, what significance can we attribute to them? In attempting to answer this question, no factor is more illuminating than Adolf Hitler's own basic attitude toward the Western Hemisphere. A distinguished English student of the Fuehrer and his Reich, H. R. Trevor-Roper, has called attention to the paucity of reliable sources bearing on Hitler's most intimate opinions.[1] In spite of the fact that the Nazi bureaucracy was a phenomenal "paper factory," only a handful of documents afford useful information on the dictator's private thoughts. Yet there is an internal consistency and continuity among these few sources interspersed through more than a decade that lend added weight to conclusions based upon them.

While *Mein Kampf* provides extensive material for an analysis of Hitler's political ambitions in Europe, it offers little more than a negative clue to the author's views on the Western Hemisphere. That the Americans merit only passing mention in the gigantic volume suggests that they did not figure prominently in his early schemes for the resuscitation of a Greater Germany. Although he praises the United States for restrictive immigration policies conducive to a high degree of racial purity, Hitler condemns what he sees as growing Jewish control of the country's financial and governmental power. He describes America's favored position, "with its enormous wealth of virgin soil," but one cannot be sure whether his tone is envious, covetous, or admiring.

1. See Hugh R. Trevor-Roper, "Hitler's Kriegsziele," *Vierteljahrshefte fuer Zeitgeschichte,* 8 (April 1960), 121–34. This address, delivered at the *Institut fuer Zeitgeschichte* in Munich, supplements the author's earlier and equally excellent analysis of Hitler in the introduction to *Hitler's Secret Conversations, 1941–1944* (New York, 1953). Also notable is the "explanatory introduction" by Percy Ernst Schramm, in Henry Picker, *Hitlers Tischgespraeche im Fuehrerhauptquartier, 1941–1942,* ed. Percy Ernst Schramm in collaboration with Andreas Hillgruber and Martin Vogt (Stuttgart, 1963), pp. 13–119. Of special interest is the painstaking study by Guenter Moltmann, "Weltherrschaftideen Hitlers," in *Europa und Uebersee: Festschrift fuer Egmont Zechlin,* ed. Otto Brunner and Dietrich Gerhard (Hamburg, 1961), pp. 197–240.

More ominous are general statements of Hitler's fundamental plans to rejuvenate Germany on a racial basis: "A State which, in the epoch of race poisoning, dedicates itself to the cherishing of its best racial elements, must some day be master of the world."[2] Combined with the first plank of the Nazi Party program, calling for the "union of all Germans to form a Great Germany," such declarations were hardly calculated to comfort any country, especially those with substantial elements of German blood among their population.

Hitler gives greater prominence to the United States in a second book which he wrote in 1928 but never published. In this rambling discourse, which did not appear in print until fifteen years after his death, the Fuehrer reveals more clearly than in any other document his appreciation of the selective immigration policies pursued by the American Union. Confronted with this young, racially select people, he thought old Europe was in danger of losing its superior status.

But Hitler invokes the American example only for the familiar purpose of goading Germans to safeguard their own racial purity: "In the future only the state which has understood how to raise the value of its folkdom and to bring it to the most expedient state form for this, through its inner life as well as through its foreign policy, will be able to face up to North America."[3] To meet the impending challenge of the United States he rejects the possibility of a coalition or fusion of European peoples in favor of Teutonic domination of the continent. After all, had not the United States itself recognized the distinctive qualities of Nordic-German elements by granting them the largest fraction of immigration quotas?

Hitler's second book also expresses admiration for America's industrial capacity and admits that U.S. entry into the war in 1917 had been an im-

2. Adolf Hitler, *Mein Kampf* (New York, 1939), p. 994. Also disturbing were Hitler's lengthy discourses on the uses of propaganda and subversion in destroying foreign nations from within; cf. Chapter 6, "War Propaganda," pp. 227–42, and Chapter 11, "Propaganda and Organization," pp. 846–68.

3. *Hitler's Secret Book,* introduction by Telford Taylor, transl. Salvator Attanasio (New York, 1961), p. 106. Gerhard L. Weinberg discovered and identified the manuscript in 1958; see *Hitlers Zweites Buch: Ein Dokument aus dem Jahr 1928,* ed. Gerhard L. Weinberg (Stuttgart, 1961). The book is an extensive exposition of his views on foreign policy. By the time Hitler wrote it, he had begun to seek an aura of legality and respectability in his efforts to gain power. One surmises that the intemperance of portions of the manuscript, together with its turgid language, argued against its publication thereafter. Weinberg notes, however, that the book's treatment of the United States parallels many of the passages in Hitler's public speeches during these years; see his article, "Hitler's Image of the United States," *American Historical Review,* 69 (July 1964), 1008–09 and n. 7.

portant factor in the outcome, second only to the treasonable collapse of
Germany's homeland. Even that collapse was not unrelated to American
intervention, for it stemmed in large part from "the infection of German
thinking by the fraudulent declarations of Woodrow Wilson," a view
Hitler often repeated in later years.

He sees the emergence of North America as an unprecedented threat
to England's supremacy on the seas. To the Hitler of 1928 England's only
sensible policy would be collaboration with Germany against France and
Russia in Europe and against the United States in the rest of the world. He
prophesies that America, once fully colonized, will turn outward as
Europe's principal rival in imperialism. "It is frivolous, however, to believe that the contest between Europe and America will always be only
of a peaceful economic nature, if economic motives develop into deter-
mining vital factors."[4] Thus, for all his apparent admiration of the United
States, Hitler uses this country to arouse the competitive instincts of Germans and other Europeans, emphasizing conflict between the continents
as inevitable.

In his numerous public addresses Hitler was careful never to attack the
American people, although several themes recur in his speeches which
offer interesting glimpses into his attitude toward this country. For example, the United States played an important role in the Fuehrer's efforts to
convince the German people that the Allies had deceived but not defeated
them in the First World War. As early as 1923 he was declaring that
America's entry into the conflict had been the product of Jewish war
profiteers' influence, assisted by a Jewish-dominated press. Hitler echoed
this theme repeatedly in subsequent speeches, bolstering it by references
to the investigations of the Nye Committee in the United States and to the
writings of revisionist historians:

> Germany did not attack America, but America attacked Germany,
> and, as the Committee of Investigation of the American House of
> Representatives concluded, from purely capitalist motives, without
> any other urgent cause.[5]

4. *Hitler's Secret Book,* p. 107; see also pp. 83, 91–106, 117, 156 f., 200–09. In
these passages the English version, a hasty translation that is occasionally unreliable,
adequately conveys Hitler's basic meaning; cf. the German text in *Hitlers Zweites Buch,*
pp. 123–32.

5. Speech of Jan. 30, 1939, in Berlin, translated and printed in Gordon W. Prange,
ed., *Hitler's Words* (Washington, 1944), p. 349. Hitler's references to affairs in the
United States are notoriously imprecise and such is the case here, for he was apparently
referring to the Senate investigation of the munitions industry in the First World War,

And again:

> it has been proved conclusively by American teachers of constitu-
> tional law, historians, and professors of history that Germany was
> no more to blame for the outbreak of the war than any other peo-
> ple.[6]

In addition to the betrayal of Germany's armies which Hitler glibly
attributed to traitors on the home front, he publicly laid much of the
blame for the armistice of 1918 and the subsequent settlements at Versailles on Woodrow Wilson, "an American medicine man who found the
formula that deceived the German people."[7] He made no secret of his
antipathy for Wilson, whom he denounced as treacherous and unfaithful
to the guarantees for which Germany had laid down her arms.

Nor did he conceal his similar attitude toward Franklin D. Roosevelt,
even before the outbreak of war in 1939. In his public reply to Roosevelt's
peace appeal of April 15, 1939, Hitler's references to the President reflected strong contempt both for the person and the accomplishments of
the American leader. Alluding to the "immeasurably easier task" which
the President had inherited in the United States, as compared to his own
difficulties when he came to power in the Reich, the Fuehrer crowned his
oration with raw sarcasm, expressing his understanding that Roosevelt's
comfortable status in a vast and wealthy nation allowed him "to feel responsible for the whole world and for the fate of all peoples."[8]

After Pearl Harbor, when there was no longer any need to moderate
his remarks on Roosevelt, Hitler did not hesitate to charge the President
with primary responsibility for the European war in the first place. In the
German Chancellor's version Roosevelt had incited the Poles to start the
war and had prolonged the French agony by promising assistance if the
Reynaud government continued to resist. Surrounding himself with Jews,

---

conducted by Gerald Nye and his committee in the nineteen-thirties. At another point,
Hitler mentioned such an investigation as one carried out by a committee appointed by
President Roosevelt himself. Konrad Heiden has illustrated how certain references to
the United States were often changed or eliminated in published versions of Hitler's
speeches; see Heiden's *Der Fuehrer* (Boston, 1944), pp. 138–39.

6. Speech of Apr. 28, 1939, Prange, *Hitler's Words*, p. 351.

7. Cf. speeches at Munich, Nov. 8, 1940 (from which the quoted phrase is taken),
and Berlin, Nov. 11, 1941, ibid., p. 231 ff. See also Raoul de Roussy de Sales, ed.,
My New Order (New York, 1941), pp. 871 ff., for a different translation. H. R.
Rudin has refuted such interpretations of Germany's collapse in the First World War
in his *Armistice 1918* (New Haven, 1944).

8. Speech of Apr. 28, 1939, Prange, *Hitler's Words*, p. 363.

the President himself had become "Judaised" and had then contrived to bring on the war to divert attention from the domestic failures of his administration.

> While an unprecedented revival of economic life, culture, and art took place in Germany under National Socialist leadership within the space of a few years, President Roosevelt did not succeed in bringing about even the slightest improvement in his own country. Yet this work must have been unquestionably easier in the United States, where there live scarcely 15 persons on a square kilometer, as against 140 in Germany.[9]

The Fuehrer harbored bitter personal animosity for the American Chief Executive. Still Hitler directed these remarks against the individual occupying the presidential office and one cannot construe them as general expressions of low esteem for the United States. As a matter of fact, on more than one occasion Hitler declared his peaceful intentions regarding the Western Hemisphere and proclaimed his support for the Monroe Doctrine, on condition that a comparable doctrine for Europe be respected by the American nations. While these statements are worth noting, Hitler's public speeches contain little of value for the present investigation except an indication of themes which neo-revisionists soon adopted. We must seek further information in more confidential materials.

A useful perspective on Hitler's attitudes toward America is afforded by Ernst Hanfstaengl, the Harvard-educated German who was a member of the Fuehrer's inner circle from 1922 until the mid-thirties. Hanfstaengl saw his own task as that of correcting Hitler's "wildly superficial" views about the United States, but he confesses that the Fuehrer never comprehended the importance of this country as an integral factor in European politics. According to Hanfstaengl, Hitler tended to regard America merely as part of the Jewish problem, but one with which he could not deal immediately. The only American he respected was Henry Ford and even he was seen "not so much as an industrial wonder-worker but rather as a reputed anti-Semite and a possible source of funds."[10] He

9. Speech of Dec. 11, 1941, ibid., p. 369.

10. Ernst Hanfstaengl, *Hitler, The Missing Years* (London, 1957), p. 41. Heiden, *Der Fuehrer,* claims that Hitler tried to obtain money from Ford; Hitler denied this in a court proceeding of 1930, and Heiden asserts that he could have been sent to prison for perjury had a certain witness not been too frightened to produce the incriminating documents. That witness was presumably Kurt G. W. Ludecke. In 1923 Hitler had told Robert Murphy, then a young consular official in Munich, that "unfortunately

seemed to think that the Ku Klux Klan was a political movement with which the Nazis might make some kind of pact.

Hanfstaengl reports that Hitler never understood the decisive character of U.S. intervention in the war of 1914–1918, and that he believed the Americans could never bring their power to bear effectively in any European conflict. He quotes Hitler as saying "you would only have to blow up the Panama Canal and they would not be able to exert pressure either way with their navy."[11] Hitler was also impressed by stories of gangsterism in the United States, commenting disdainfully that any country that could not master its own police problems could scarcely hope to play a part in foreign affairs.

After he became Chancellor, Hitler's prejudices seemed to harden and he scoffed at Hanfstaengl's suggestion that it might be useful to visit the United States: "What is America but millionaires, beauty queens, stupid records and Hollywood. . . ." Hanfstaengl did not find Hitler really anti-American but a pronounced contempt for the United States grew stronger with the passage of time, as did the undertone of hatred for what he considered the overprivileged American Jews.

By far the most explicit and incriminating remarks on the Western Hemisphere are ascribed to Hitler by Hermann Rauschning, former Nazi President of the Danzig Senate. They afford an interesting comparison with the developments we have chronicled in the preceding chapters.

In conversations with Rauschning during the years 1932–1934, the Fuehrer expressed goals for Nazi activity in North and South America fully as incredible as those he had earlier sketched for German expansion into Eastern Europe. If Latin America was to develop, the vigorous leadership of Germany would be required and on this subject Hitler waxed prolific a few months after he came to power. He was especially interested in Brazil, which he was convinced was ripe for revolution and which he vowed to transform, within a few decades or even years, from "a corrupt mestizo state into a German dominion."

"We shall create a new Germany there," he cried. "We shall find everything we need there."[12]

Mr. Ford's organization has so far made no money contributions to our party." *See* Murphy, *Diplomat Among Warriors* (Garden City, N.Y., 1964), p. 26; cf. Kurt G. W. Ludecke, *I Knew Hitler* (New York, 1937), pp. 192 ff.

11. Hanfstaengl, *Hitler*, p. 135; also see pp. 74, 121, 188, 210–11, 222.

12. Hermann Rauschning, *The Voice of Destruction* (New York, 1940), pp. 61 ff. Rauschning's reliability, though questioned in some quarters before the war, was largely vindicated by the course of events during the late thirties and early forties. His

The new Chancellor was confident that Germany would succeed Spain and Portugal as the cultural leader of Ibero-America. He was equally sanguine about displacing the United States from its position of influence among its Latin neighbors, for he was positive that the other American republics were fed up with Yankee exploitation. German supremacy would be established on the totalitarian, National Socialist model; there was no place where democracy was more senseless than in South America. Working toward this goal, dedicated Nazis must enable the people of Latin America to overthrow both their liberalism and their democratic systems. External force would not be necessary to accomplish this.

> We shall not land troops like William the Conqueror and gain Brazil by strength of arms. Our weapons are not visible ones. Our conquistadores . . . have a more difficult task than the original ones, and for this reason they have more difficult weapons.[13]

Nazi strategy would be to destroy the enemy from within, to conquer him through himself. In this modern scheme of aggrandizement, propaganda would take the place of artillery; it would weaken the enemy psychologically before military units even began to function. Such tactics would find effective employment in Brazil and elsewhere in the New World, notably in Argentina and Bolivia, where Hitler thought Nazi prospects to be particularly good.

A year later, after the "blood purge" of June 30, 1934, had reinforced Hitler's position as master of the Nazi Party and of Germany, his thoughts turned again to the Americas, focusing this time on Mexico. Sir Henry Deterding of Royal Dutch Shell, which had been engaged in developing petroleum deposits in Mexico, had greatly influenced Hitler's view of that country. He was convinced that Mexico was "the best and richest country in the world with the laziest and most dissipated population under the sun." No doubt German vigor and initiative would be required to realize the enormous potential of the territory. Pondering what he considered to be Germany's urgent need for *Lebensraum*, Hitler speculated that all his nation's difficulties would vanish if he but had control of Mexico.

> Mexico is a country that cries for a capable master. It is being ruined by its government. With the treasure of Mexican soil, Ger-

---

testimony has received additional independent confirmation by the remarkable identity of views recorded in the *Bormann Vermerke,* to which we shall have reference shortly, with those described by Rauschning. His credibility is now generally accepted among students of Nazi history; see Moltmann, "Weltherrschaftideen Hitlers," p. 236, n. 10.

13. Rauschning, *The Voice of Destruction,* p. 63.

many could be rich and great! Why do we not tackle this task? . . .
You could get this Mexico for a couple of hundred million.[14]

It occurred to him that a first step might be to make an alliance with
Mexico, both for defensive and for customs purposes. But his plans pre-
supposed "much longer periods of time" than his schemes for European
continental dominion, and he was not proposing immediate and direct
action in the Western Hemisphere. He made it clear that the Third Reich
would not need to gain its ends by force, once its invisible weapons of subversion and propaganda had full opportunity to work their insidious
effects.

As far as the United States was concerned, Hitler rambled on at length,
contending that this nation was constantly on the brink of revolution, and
that with little effort one could produce turmoil in its venal democracy.
One method of disruption which he weighed was bacterial warfare; this
would be sure to bring unrest and revolt, and would keep the ruling "gen-
try" occupied so that they would have no time or inclination to interfere
once again in European affairs. The existing North American government
represented to Hitler "the last disgusting death-rattle of a corrupt and out-
worn system which is a blot on the history of this people." In his opinion
the United States had steadily deteriorated since the Civil War. That conflict had destroyed the foundations of a great new society based on the
principles of slavery and inequality. Had the outcome of that contest been
different, a true *Herren*-class would be ruling America instead of the
decrepit and moldering caste of tradesmen who now held power.

Yet Hitler believed that certain sections of the American middle class
and farming population retained a fighting spirit worthy of the early settlers, and he depicted the widespread prejudices against Negroes and the
colored races, including the Jews, as a "wholesome aversion." He was certain that the United States would never again take part in a European war;
therefore, Germany could plan its maneuvers in the Old World with little
concern for repercussions across the Atlantic. The Reichschancellor supplemented this conclusion with the contention that the American was no
soldier anyway, as the Yankee had shown in 1917 and 1918, and that the
United States need not be feared as a military power. "The inferiority and
decadence of this allegedly new world is evident in its military ineffi-
ciency."[15]

It was in June 1933 that Hitler made the most direct remarks bearing

14. Ibid., p. 67.
15. Ibid., p. 70. Cf. also the same author's *Hitler and the War* (Washington,
1939), pp. 4 f.

on his own intentions toward the United States. He was determined to awaken the "sound elements" in that country, a phrase whose reference he immediately made clear.

> National Socialism alone is destined to liberate the American people from their ruling clique and give them back the means of becoming a great nation. . . . I shall . . . undertake this task simultaneously with the restoration of Germany to her leading position in America. . . . The German component of the American people will be the source of its political and mental resurrection. The American people is not yet a nation in the ethnographical sense; it is a conglomerate of disparate elements. But it is the raw material of a nation. And the Yankees have failed to create a nation from it! They have instead kept their noses in their moneybags. Today this is being avenged. Their difficulties will become insuperable.

At this point, Rauschning, who, along with Joseph Goebbels, had been attentively following the Fuehrer's discourse, interrupted to ask: "Do you mean . . . that the German-American, rejuvenated by National Socialism, will be called to lead a new America?" Hitler replied:

> That is exactly what I mean. . . . We shall soon have an S.A. in America. We shall train our youth. And we shall have men whom degenerate Yankeedom will not be able to challenge. Into the hands of our youth will be given the great statesmanlike mission of Washington which this corrupt democracy has trodden under foot. . . . I guarantee, gentlemen, that at the right moment a new America will exist as our strongest supporter when we are ready to take the stride into overseas space. We have the means of awakening this nation in good time. There will be no new Wilson arising to stir up America against us.[16]

German language and culture would replace Anglo-Saxon influence as a preliminary to the incorporation of the United States into a Germanic world empire. But neither in the United States nor elsewhere in the West-

---

16. Ibid., pp. 68 f. The "S.A." mentioned by Hitler was the private army of Storm Troopers organized by the Nazis during their campaign for power in Germany. The reader will recall that during this very period—the summer of 1933—the Nazis were attempting to launch the *Bund der Freunde des neuen Deutschlands* to mobilize German-Americans. And as late as 1938 Ambassador Dieckhoff was warning the Party against its efforts to form "native assault troops" for the "crucial moment" in the United States. See above, Chapters 3 and 4.

ern Hemisphere did Hitler plan early and direct action. His first objective was to dominate the world island of Eurasia and only thereafter did he intend to turn his full attention across the Atlantic.

Since the eventual European conflict did not end as the Nazis antici-pated, Hitler never had an opportunity to concentrate on the New World. This hemisphere played only a secondary role in his calculations as he moved Germany toward and into the great holocaust. The records of the famous meeting of November 5, 1937, at which Hitler first outlined in detail the steps by which he was determined to seize additional living space for Germany, do not indicate that the German dictator even considered the position or possible intervention of the United States. On May 23, 1939, when final plans to initiate hostilities against Poland were set, the role of the United States again appears to have been ignored. Even when the Nazi conspirators weighed the possibilities of prolonged conflict, the records fail to mention the contingency that America might ally herself with the Euro-pean democracies.[17] The United States was just not a significant factor in the immediate designs of the modern Alexander.

This was probably due to a combination of several things—Hitler's certainty that the United States would never again participate in a Euro-pean struggle; his disdain for America's martial prowess; his conviction, which we shall explore momentarily, that Washington coveted Canada and was anxiously awaiting the final collapse of the British Empire—but its principal foundation was sheer ignorance of the power which the American government might throw against him. With an understandable faith in Germany's traditional military greatness, the Fuehrer apparently believed his own public comments on the *Dolchstossfrage* and did not appreciate the fact that American industry and troops had actually turned the tide against the Reich in 1918. This fatal misconception, in conjunc-tion with the enhanced sense of invincibility which he acquired in the opening phases of the war, played a major part in Hitler's prompt and foolhardy declaration of war on the United States after Pearl Harbor.

Even though he repeatedly disclaimed any interest in gaining territory or political power in the Western Hemisphere, and in spite of the fact that no specific directives for action against the Americas have been discovered in the captured German archives, the Nazi dictator and his associates were not completely oblivious to the possibility of future conflict with the

17. Records of these momentous conferences are in *DGFP-D*. The Hossbach min-utes of the 1937 meeting may be found in *1*, 29–30; minutes of the 1939 conference are in *6*, 574–80.

United States. Speaking to a group of aircraft manufacturers on July 8, 1938, Hermann Goering called for daring technical innovations, mentioning a rocket engine or a high-altitude bomber which could reach New York with a payload of five tons. The Reichsmarschall remarked that he would be quite pleased with such a weapon "in order to shut up those arrogant people over there."[18]

By the autumn of 1940, when Hitler was virtual master of Europe, and before he had turned his attention toward the Soviet Union, he began to consider the prospects for a subsequent assault of the Western Hemisphere. On his instructions, German military and naval advisers started deliberations looking toward occupation of the Azores and Canary Islands; these were to serve as advance positions for the prosecution of the war against the United States at a later date. One should note that the conditions which the advisers deemed essential to any such venture, viz., no other operational commitment, Portuguese neutrality, and the support of France and Spain, were never satisfied.[19] This demonstrates conclusively that American apprehensions about possible seizure of the Atlantic islands sometime during 1940 or 1941 were not unjustified.

Already, in the summer of 1940, the office of Heinrich Himmler had adopted a long-range view to prospects in the Americas. Looking toward future expansion of the *Waffen S.S.,* Himmler's staff devised plans for the recruitment of new divisions of German stock in the United States after 1953. On August 7, 1940, the recruiting service's director provided Himmler with estimates of available reserves: "we have these additional racial Germans at our disposal: In North America and Canada, approximately five and one half million." After listing other sources of racial raw material for the elite corps, including the other large groups elsewhere in the New World, the officer concluded that "the recovery of these people, who would be exceptionally suited as settlers later on, should be started."[20] It takes little imagination to fathom the assumptions on which such plans rested, and even less to appreciate their implications for the United States.

While these preparations were proceeding, a principal task of Nazi

18. Quoted in Boehm, "Policy-making of the Nazi Government," pp. 414 f.

19. This is the substance of the famous Falkenstein Memorandum, Oct. 29, 1940. First given prominence at Nuremberg, it is conveniently printed in *Nazi Conspiracy and Aggression* (Washington, 1947), 3, 288–90.

20. This document was introduced in the trial of Ernst von Weizsaecker and is cited by Trefousse, *Germany and American Neutrality,* p. 15. Trefousse's opening chapter, "The Problem of Hitler's Ultimate Aims," is a scholarly exposition only recently surpassed by the works of Moltmann and Weinberg.

diplomacy and propaganda remained that of keeping the United States out of the conflict in order to facilitate the elimination of Germany's opponents one by one. Berlin adopted a policy of extreme restraint, even to the point of tolerating various excesses by the supposedly neutral United States, but there should be no misunderstanding of Hitler's motives during the first two years of the European conflagration. In the words of one highly placed observer, State Secretary Ernst von Weizsaecker of the Foreign Office, "For opportunist reasons Hitler wanted to avoid a conflict with the U.S.A."[21] The credit for Germany's prolonged passivity in the face of America's progressively un-neutral conduct after March 1941 Weizsaecker gives to the career members of the *Auswaertige Amt* and certain other departments in Berlin who appreciated the massive force the United States could bring to bear against the Reich.

Even as the Fuehrer was extending the olive branch to Washington, he was secretly giving continued thought to occupation of the Azores and Canaries as a base for long-range bombers to operate against the United States. On May 22, 1941, Hitler informed his naval staff that the occasion for action against America might arise by the following autumn, by which time he expected the Soviet Union to succumb. Two months later, after German divisions had driven deep into Russia, he told the same group that, upon completion of the Eastern Campaign, he reserved "the right to take severe action against the U.S.A. as well."[22] Thus it is clear that the idea of an attack on the United States was not absent from Hitler's mind, and one should remember that the proposal for preliminary establishment of bases in the Atlantic islands originated sometime in 1940, long before such provocative American actions as President Roosevelt's declaration that the United States must become the "arsenal of democracy," Lend-Lease, and the order for U.S. destroyers to shoot on sight when they encountered German submarines in the Atlantic.

So far as we know, the Nazi war lord first began to consider serious incursions into the Atlantic at just the time one would have expected, when he had secured the continent, when Italy had allied itself with him and Franco Spain and Vichy France appeared likely to do so at any moment, when Great Britain tottered near collapse, and when he had grown confident of easy victory in the impending *Drang nach Osten*. Hitler directed

---

21. Ernst von Weizsaecker, *Memoirs* (Chicago, 1951), p. 261.

22. See *Fuehrer Conferences on Matters Dealing with the German Navy* (Washington, 1947), 2 (1941), 13, for a report of the conference of July 25, 1941; see also *1* (1941), 65, for the record of the May 22nd meeting.

that studies preliminary to a thrust against the Western Hemisphere be initiated precisely at the moment when it appeared certain that he would be completely successful in the Old World and thus would be free to concentrate on a new adventure.

The sequence of developments during this period is crucial. We have seen that, at least as early as October 1940, Hitler began seriously to ponder future hostilities with the United States. Why were his directives regarding an occupation of the Azores and Canary Islands never implemented? The records offer no definitive answer, but they do reveal a number of factors which no doubt bore heavily upon Hitler's portentous decisions of December 1940. First of all, the final phase of his western campaign had not come off on schedule and the Fuehrer found himself stymied for the moment. Mr. Churchill and the weather had conspired to reinforce the heroic resistance of the British people, and Hitler had been compelled, reluctantly and secretly, to postpone the intended invasion of the English homeland until spring 1941.

The unexpected resilience of the English had produced other, perhaps even more critical repercussions for the German leader. He had been unable to carry out his plan to destroy the British bastion at Gibraltar, because Franco, owing partly to conflicts between his territorial aims and those of Mussolini and partly to Spain's economic dependence on England and the United States, had procrastinated in associating himself actively with the Axis. At the same time, Pétain had evaded an alliance against France's former ally and had begun to resist the blandishments and advice of the arch-advocate of collaboration with the Nazis, Pierre Laval. All these developments had come during October 1940 and were complicated by Italy's ill-fated aggression in Greece on the 24th of that month, which came on the heels of Mussolini's ineffectual undertakings in North Africa. In short, the very month in which Hitler was contemplating eventual engagements with the United States witnessed a series of temporary setbacks which necessitated a delay in Nazi schemes for action in the Atlantic.[23]

But even more decisive in turning the Fuehrer's thoughts away from involvement with the United States was his growing determination to take early action against the Soviet Union. Having swept away the opposition in the West, Hitler briefly contemplated a strike against Russia in 1940, but abandoned the notion because of the obvious logistical difficulties of

---

23. Among the ablest treatments of this period is Langer and Gleason, *The Undeclared War* (New York, 1953), Chapter 3, "Hitler and the West," pp. 53–101; and Chapter 4, "Mussolini and the Mediterranean," pp. 102–18.

shifting his armies to an eastern campaign. From July 1940 onward, however, preliminary plans for Operation Barbarossa were being developed. Hitler's geopolitical conceptions linked the United States and the Soviet Union together as integral parts of Germany's strategic problem. As he remarked to his army chief of staff:

> Britain's hope lies in Russia and the U.S.A. If Russia drops out of the picture, America, too, is lost for Britain, because the elimination of Russia would greatly increase Japan's power in the Far East. . . . Decision: Russia's destruction must therefore be made a part of this struggle. . . . If we start in May 1941, we will have five months in which to finish the job.[24]

It appears that even without a conclusive defeat of the British Hitler was already prepared to move against the Russians. Until this campaign was completed, he was not anxious to engage the United States.

Through these months the Fuehrer's perception of the United States and its likely behavior remained a cloudy mass of personal ignorance and prejudice. Much of Hitler's thinking on the United States was marked by the sort of projective processes which psychiatrists readily associate with a pathological mind. He was utterly confident that American leaders shared motives similar to his own and was always prepared to expand its *Lebensraum,* by fair means or foul. After all, had he not found this to be true of Stalin, Mussolini, Franco, Matsuoka? Why should Roosevelt be any different?

In March 1940, several weeks prior to the blitzkrieg on Western Europe, Hitler had inquired of Colin Ross, one of the Nazi "experts" on the Americas, whether Washington's imperialistic tendencies did not buttress the presumed American desire to annex Canada and consequently produce an anti-English attitude in the United States. Ross replied that the Americans expected *Anschluss* to come of itself with the advancement of Americanization in Canada, but this mildly negative answer did not seem

24. Diary of General Franz Halder, entry of July 31, 1940, quoted in Bullock, *Hitler,* p. 598. Planning for Barbarossa was well advanced by the time Soviet Foreign Minister Molotov visited Berlin in November 1940. Hitler and Ribbentrop could scarcely conceal their antipathy for the Russian diplomat; the discussions were marked by intense mutual suspicion. Yet the Germans still hoped to extract diplomatic advantage from their relations with Moscow. They had sought an earlier visit by Molotov, believing that a dramatic Russo-German conference would reinforce the intended effects of the Tripartite Pact on the U.S. presidential contest. Stalin, however, had delayed the meeting until after the election. See Friedlaender, *Hitler et les Etats-Unis,* p. 150. Weinberg, *Germany and the Soviet Union, 1939–1941,* provides a comprehensive background to the attack on Russia.

to register with the Fuehrer. Hitler heartily endorsed other remarks by Ross, depicting Roosevelt as the Fuehrer's personal enemy and describing the growing anti-Semitism which Ross thought he had detected in his recent journeys to the United States. Hitler also took to heart the advice Ross tendered on German propaganda toward the New World:

> If Germany succeeded in convincing the Americans that it was in accordance with our German and National Socialist principles that the Western Hemisphere belonged to the Americans . . . then the Americans could develop very much understanding for our struggle since they would, after all, divine a clear profit from it.[25]

This was almost certainly Hitler's goal two months later when he authorized the planted interview with Karl Wiegand of the Hearst newspapers. Despite Ross' transparent sycophancy, a trait nearly universal among officials of the Third Reich, his views impressed Hitler who strongly identified himself with them and who expressed his high regard for Ross, "a very intelligent man who certainly had many good ideas."

Hitler's projective conception of the United States found renewed expression after Germany began the campaign against the Soviet Union, and his enmity toward America became increasingly apparent. To his dinner companions at field headquarters in the East, Hitler confided a number of his private opinions. "If America lends her help to England, it is with the secret thought of bringing the moment nearer when she will reap her inheritance," but she would find the crown of empire an uneasy one to wear. Alluding to an unspecified future date, he declared, "I rejoice on behalf of the German people at the idea that one day we will see England and Germany marching together against America."[26]

Two months later, and still before his declaration of war on the United States, the Fuehrer delivered a remarkable monologue:

25. Memorandum of conversation between the Fuehrer and Dr. Colin Ross, Mar. 12, 1940, *DGFP–D, 8,* 910–13. Ross had just returned from a lecture tour in the United States and had observed the prevalence of anti-German sentiments. However, he thought America's disillusionment with Europe would prevent any action by the United States.

26. *Hitler's Secret Conversations, 1941–44,* p. 22, recording remarks of Aug. 8–11, 1941. These summaries (officially known as the *Bormann Vermerke*) were made at *Wolfsschanze,* Hitler's field headquarters, by a Party official and then corrected by the Fuehrer's secretary, Martin Bormann. They are valuable not only in their own right, but also as a significant confirmation of the general reliability of Rauschning's earlier works, for many ideas attributed to Hitler by Rauschning reoccur in these later records.

If the English are clever, they will seize the psychological moment to make an about-turn and they will march on our side. By getting out of the war now, the English would succeed in putting their principal competitor—the United States—out of the game for thirty years. Roosevelt would be shown up as an impostor, the country would be enormously in debt—by reason of its manufacture of war-materials, which would become pointless—and unemployment would rise to gigantic proportions.[27]

Even more ominous for the United States were Hitler's forthright remarks on what he expected to come from Germany's dominance in Europe, recalling statements to Rauschning some years before. He explicitly asserted that the goal of his European maneuvers was to gain preponderance in the entire world. Once Germany controlled the four hundred million people of the New Europe, together with the continent's agricultural and industrial wealth, the Western Hemisphere would find itself in a radically altered position.

Turning to the current war situation, Hitler bemoaned the fact that the British Empire would fall before German arms, but that the Reich would reap no benefit from it. Russia would take India, Japan would inherit Eastern Asia, and the United States would seize Canada and British possessions in Africa. His confidence that just such a development would transpire was high, and he was already looking beyond it to analyze the expected new situation. "In the case of England's being sunk I would have no profit—but the obligation to fight her successors. At present, England no longer interests me. I am only interested in what's behind her."

As he weighed his future conflict with the American supporters of the dying British Empire, the Fuehrer did not blanch or quaver. "We need have no fears for our own future. I shall leave behind me not only the most powerful army, but also a Party that will be the most voracious animal in world history." In the course of the following year, as the United States entered the war and the Nazi war machine bogged down in the vast reaches of Great Russia, the Fuehrer's thoughts often turned to America. On January 7, 1942, immediately after the announcement of a "no-separate-peace" alliance between the United States, Great Britain, and twenty-four other nations, Hitler believed it would still be possible to negotiate a separate settlement with the English by offering to leave India in the reconstructed Empire.

27. Ibid., remarks of Oct. 26–27, 1941, pp. 76 ff., from which all quotations in this section are taken.

In that case, what would happen to the United States? They would be territorially intact. But one day England will be obliged to make approaches to the Continent. And it will be a German-British army that will chase the Americans from Iceland. I don't see much future for the Americans. In my view, it's a decayed country. . . . My feelings against Americanism are feelings of hatred and deep repugnance. I feel myself more akin to any European country, no matter which. Everything about the behavior of American society reveals that it's half Judaised, and the other half negrified. How can one expect a State like that to hold together—a State where 80% of the revenue is drained away for the public purse—a country where everything is built on the dollar? From this point of view, I consider the British State very much superior.[28]

As the summer months of 1942 rolled by, the Nazi autocrat was repeatedly disparaging the cowardly and unpredictable Americans, and, by comparison, praising the courageous British. "If only Britain had supported the Southern States in the American Civil War! And what a tragedy that God allowed Germans to put Lincoln firmly in the saddle!" He was even greatly incensed by the occasional criticisms which the American press directed at the British, who were much more nearly a pure Teutonic race than the vile inhabitants of that "melting pot." "In so far as there are any decent people in America, they are all of German origin." In no other source do we find Hitler speaking so specifically on these matters. In words both candid and grandiose, his fundamental antagonism toward the United States emerges distinctly.

Against the backdrop of Hitler's own comments on the United States, the testimony of Friedrich Gauss, Chief of the Foreign Office's Legal Division, acquires additional credibility. At Nuremberg Gauss declared that the German leaders welcomed the Japanese destruction of the American fleet at Pearl Harbor as the first step toward creation of a Great Germanic Empire.

28. Ibid., records of Jan. 7, 1942, p. 155; Aug. 6, 1942, p. 502; Aug. 28, 1942, p. 541, and Sept. 2, 1942, pp. 556 ff. The same intense hatred of Roosevelt, "the stooge of the Jews," and for "that monster which is called the United States," recurs in a brief but important series of transcripts of Hitler's comments which Bormann recorded in February and April 1945, when it was apparent that the Reich's end was near. Cf. *Le Testament Politique de Hitler*, ed. Martin Bormann (Paris, 1959), pp. 71–73 and 122–23, a most valuable addition to the scanty sources on Hitler. An English edition has appeared as *The Testament of Adolf Hitler: The Hitler-Bormann Documents, February–April 1945*, ed. François Genoud (London, 1960).

> This Empire was intended not only to rule Europe, but to be the decisive factor in the steering of world events in their entirety. . . . The triangular coalition of Berlin-Rome-Tokyo, Ribbentrop had tried to establish as early as 1936 through his Anti-Comintern Pact and then above all through the Tripartite Pact of autumn 1940. . . . It was intended that the United States should thereby receive a position of second rank, excluded from the heritage of the British world empire and her sphere of power and influence limited to the northern part of the American continent.[29]

In sum, the United States would be eliminated as a world power. And this is perhaps a generous interpretation of the fate which was being concocted for the United States within the fertile depravity which was the mind of Adolf Hitler.

Hitler realized that the technical problems of invading the Western Hemisphere were presently difficult to surmount, but the Nazi leaders had great faith in the progress of military technology. As Ribbentrop told French Admiral Darlan on May 11, 1941, "The Fuehrer was no random conquerer, without a plan, such as had appeared in the past. He was sober in his calculations and was accustomed to think in terms of long periods of time."[30] Having advanced far beyond his original conception of a consolidated Germany, Hitler was now concentrating on securing the entire continent against other hemispheres. In another decade, the Reich Foreign Minister declared, aircraft should be flying at 1500 to 2000 kilometers an hour, shrinking the world still further and opening new possibilities for global action. In this perspective the national interest of the United States, and that of her sister republics, clearly lay in the balance of the struggle in Europe.[31]

29. Quoted by Trefousse, *Germany and American Neutrality*, p. 19. In 1943 Hitler was still expressing confidence to Goebbels that the Reich would emerge victorious as the master of all Europe. "Thereupon the way to world domination is practically certain. To dominate Europe will be to assume the leadership of the world." Cf. *The Goebbels Diaries*, ed. Louis Lochner (London, 1948), p. 281. The Gauss testimony receives further confirmation from Japanese documents on the origins and purposes of the Tripartite Pact; see Sommer, *Deutschland und Japan*, pp. 509–14.

30. Memorandum of conversation between Ribbentrop and Admiral Darlan, May 11, 1941, *DGFP–D, 12*, 755–63.

31. Gerhard L. Weinberg develops a similar theme in his article, "Hitler's Image of the United States," and Guenter Moltmann stresses that Franklin D. Roosevelt's place in history is best measured by his correct appraisal of Hitler's global ambitions. See his "Weltherrschaftideen Hitlers," pp. 232 ff.

CHAPTER 12

The New Order and the New World

It was Voltaire who once reflected, "Doubt is a very uncomfortable condition, but certainty is a ridiculous one." So it is with any appraisal of history as it might have been. The "ifs" of history offer a virtually unlimited set of possibilities, but very little opportunity for confident conclusions. Yet a sound assessment of the political wisdom of historic actions and decisions must often include evaluation of the hypothetical past, as well as of the real past, examining events that did occur, and events that might have occurred in the absence of those actions and decisions.

Comparison of what was with what might have been is not merely a pleasant pastime. It is an essential responsibility of the historian and political analyst, for only in this manner can one reach a balanced judgment concerning the objective merits of different courses of action.

Such comparisons are especially necessary if one is to gain an understanding of the subjective elements in past policy, since that policy, to the extent that it reflected a conscious design, involved implicit or explicit assumptions about how things might go in the absence of certain actions and decisions. To the policymaker there is not one future but many possible futures, some of which may appear decidedly preferable to others. For these reasons a just analysis of political behavior must give attention both to the actual results of policies that were adopted and to the potential results of alternative policies that were not. And such analysis must consider not only the outcomes that hindsight judges likely, but those that were perceived as likely by the decisionmaker at the time. If history is to help us judge the wisdom of past action, it must also help us comprehend other options that might have been chosen.

These general observations suggest the multiplicity of factors that must be weighed in evaluating the American policy of opposition to Nazi Germany and its Axis partners. The issues are not limited to the question of Hitler's real intentions regarding the Western Hemisphere. They are equally related to the expectations which American decisionmakers derived from the Fuehrer's past behavior and growing capabilities. It was in light of those considerations that Franklin Roosevelt and leaders of other American nations had to project the future relationships of the two hemispheres.

Much of the evidence concerning Hitler's fundamental policy and attitude toward the United States and other American republics is susceptible to various interpretations. One can marshal data either sustaining or refuting the contention that he would someday have directed his forces against the Western Hemisphere. It is clear that he and his associates never prepared a detailed plan for aggression against the New World. But was this due to pacific intentions toward the Americas, to an exclusively continental or hemispheric policy encompassing only Europe and Africa, or to the simple fact that he was too preoccupied with immediate conquests to give attention to an ultimate design for subjugation of transatlantic territories?

Would success in Eurasia, by providing both opportunity and capacity to threaten the Western Hemisphere, have led the Fuehrer to entertain schemes for attacking across the ocean? Would the defeat of his European opponents have sated his hunger for power? Or would continental hegemony have whetted his appetite for truly global dominion? The records to which one looks for answers abound in contradiction. And one can never be quite sure that the surviving expressions of Hitler's views and those of others in the Nazi system reflect their real thoughts and intentions; even private statements by the Fuehrer and his subordinates frequently appear to have been framed to influence or impress an audience, to bolster its morale, or for other reasons that raise doubts about the degree to which they actually reveal underlying attitudes and opinions.

Yet the irremediable ambiguity of the evidence does not obscure Hitler's latent hostility toward the United States and his confident, albeit condescending, expectation of growing German influence in Latin America. Furthermore, Nazi activities in the Western Hemisphere, not only among the colonies of German hyphenates but more generally in the domestic political processes of the American nations, were a convincing demonstration of the Reich's readiness to intervene politically. This tendency in itself posed an insidious and potentially vital threat to the stability and character of American political institutions. It is certainly reasonable to conclude that such intervention could have grown worse if the New Order had become firmly established in Europe. In that event a modus vivendi with Hitler's European empire may have been particularly imperative for the countries of Latin America—and on terms very costly to their national independence and security.

These political factors could have combined with the immense economic and military power of a Nazi Europe to become a continuing source of danger to the United States and its neighbors. Especially if Tokyo had acted on Berlin's repeated advice to move initially, not against the United States, but against either the Soviet Union or the British position in Southeast Asia,[1] the Axis might have been able to postpone U.S. intervention long enough to gain early victories in both Europe and the Far East. In this case, American power, acting alone, might well have proved insufficient in a later contest with the Axis, however it originated.

These were the prospects that confronted the leaders of the Western Hemisphere in 1939–1941 and retrospective appraisals of their actions during that extended crisis should give due weight to the disastrous consequences they feared might flow from inaction. Whether or not one is certain that inter-hemispheric war would have ensued, what responsible official could have viewed with equanimity a situation in which the Axis powers would have acquired impressive capabilities to engage in such a conflict at will against an isolated American hemisphere?

There is another group of factors which one can appreciate fully only from an ex post facto vantage point. We now know how soon technology was to present unprecedented opportunities for global warfare. One must reckon with the likelihood that if the Reich had not been burdened with the continuing drain of a long war—and without American support for Britain and Russia Hitler might have gained victory in 1942 or shortly thereafter—Germany's remarkable scientific and technical talents could have been concentrated on the perfection of the kinds of novel weapons that so excited the Fuehrer. More resources would have been available for Germany's technological endeavors, which would have been spurred by Hitler's professed determination to make Europe invincible. Such a concentration of effort might well have produced nuclear weapons at an early date, as well as systems to deliver them over transoceanic distances.

Indeed, subsequent progress in rocket technology by both the Soviet Union and the United States is attributable, to a significant extent, to concepts and hardware on which German scientists and engineers began work during the Nazi period. When the war ended, General Walter Dornberger and the staff of the German Rocket Research Center at Peenemuende already had on the drawing boards blueprints for a rocket known

---

1. Saul Friedlaender's useful work, *Hitler et les États-Unis, 1939–1941*, emphasizes the importance the Fuehrer attributed to preventing U.S. intervention during the opening phases of his aggression.

as the "America Project." It was nothing less than the pioneer concept for an intercontinental ballistic missile, designed to hit New York from a base near Hamburg.[2]

Granted the advanced status of German technology at the time, it is by no means clear that the United States could have outperformed the Third Reich in a research and development competition that might have followed a quick Nazi victory in Europe. It is difficult to believe that a Nazi Germany in control of all Europe, and with its economic and technological capacities unravaged by a major war on its own soil, would have been a lesser threat than the Free World subsequently encountered in a badly battered Soviet Union controlling but a fraction of Europe.

These are some of the more salient features of the hypothetical past. Only in consideration of these alternative outcomes can one approach a judgment on American policy toward the Axis powers. The policy toward which Franklin Roosevelt led the United States and its hemispheric neighbors after 1940, namely that of active opposition to the Axis, was rooted in a grave concern for the radical change in the world balance of power which seemed to be impending.

Roosevelt's reelection constituted a decisive reversal for Nazi efforts to influence the policy of the United States and other American nations. The President had already done much to promote integrated action by the twenty-one republics and his victorious bid for a third term made it certain that these cooperative endeavors would continue. More important was the fact that Roosevelt interpreted his success at the polls—correctly—as an endorsement of the developing U.S. assistance to the harassed British.

In September 1940, at what some observers considered exorbitant risk to his domestic political ambitions, the President had taken a major step to relieve Great Britain, and simultaneously to improve the United States' defensive position in the New World, by trading fifty over-age destroyers to England in exchange for bases in British possessions in this hemisphere. The month before the Chief Executive had joined Canada's Mackenzie King in establishing a Permanent Joint Board on Defense to consider the northern reaches of the continent. At the same time, the President had cultivated bipartisan support for preparedness by bringing Henry Stimson

2. Dornberger subsequently became a U.S. citizen and a prominent executive in the aerospace industry. The "America Project" is recalled in an article that deals primarily with a recent interview in which he expressed his views on future rocket and space technology; Claude Witze, "Let's Get Operational in Space," *Air Force and Space Digest*, 48, no. 10 (October 1965), 80.

and Frank Knox, both Republicans, into the War and Navy Departments. Working through Republican Representative James Wadsworth of New York and Democratic Senator Edward Burke of Nebraska, Roosevelt had maneuvered the first peacetime draft in American history through the Congress.

Now, with a substantial popular and electoral majority behind him, the President could move forward confidently to implement the measures he knew to be necessary. On December 29, 1940, he characterized to his fellow citizens the lowering prospects which faced this nation:

> If Great Britain goes down, the Axis powers will control the continents of Europe, Asia, Africa, Australia, and the high seas—and they will be in a position to bring enormous military and naval resources against this hemisphere. It is no exaggeration to say that all of us, in all the Americas, would be living at the point of a gun—a gun loaded with explosive bullets, economic as well as military.

A week later, acting on this conviction, Roosevelt sent to Congress the Lend-Lease bill.

We have seen in the previous chapter how precisely the President's appraisal accorded with the facts. Hitler had described his grandiose schemes to infiltrate and eventually to subjugate the countries of the New World. National Socialism would transform Brazil from "a corrupt mestizo state into a German dominion." With his advanced techniques of subversion, he would be able to get Mexico "for a couple of hundred million." The Fuehrer planned to "restore Germany to her leading position in America" and to begin the task of forging a new racial state from the "conglomerate of disparate elements" which made up "degenerate Yankeedom." Hitler's colossal ignorance of the American nations, magnified through the prism of his Napoleonic ego, led him to believe that National Socialism could conquer this hemisphere even more easily than the movement had gained power in the Reich and would soon master Europe. "Today Europe; tomorrow the whole world," as the Nazis chanted in their wartime song.

Contrary to Nazi expectations, the masses of the American peoples evinced no inclination to barter their pluralistic institutions for the perverted racial system being evolved in the Third Reich. The United States reacted immediately and consistently against any efforts to transplant Hitler's alien ideology to this country. Americans of German extraction almost unanimously rejected the Nazi myths and did not hesitate to denounce the vicious policies of the new Reich.

Only in the final months of his life does it appear that Hitler himself came to appreciate the true significance of America's ability to assimilate German immigrants. At last the painful realization seems to have dawned on him that German-Americans were not potential allies of the fatherland.

> I am deeply distressed at the thought of those millions of Germans, men of good faith, who emigrated to the United States and who are now the backbone of the country. For these men, mark you, are not merely good Germans, lost to their fatherland; rather, they have become enemies, more implacably hostile than any others. . . . Transplant a German to Kiev, and he remains a perfect German. But transplant him to Miami, and you make a degenerate out of him—in other words, an American.[3]

Thus, in the end, even the Fuehrer perceived, in his own perverse way, the unreality of Nazi expectations concerning the German-American community.

Unfortunately, certain countries of Latin America, where large colonies of culturally segregated German immigrants provided Nazi doctrines a likely breeding ground, remained impassive for several years to the threat posed by the Hitler movement. By 1936 Ernst Bohle could boast that his *Auslandsorganisation* had conquered these *Volksgenossen* (racial comrades) for the Reich—the initial step on the road to Nazi domination in the Americas. Rudolf Hess himself had publicly declared the Party's purpose to be that of using foreign Germans politically for the benefit both of themselves and of the Reich. And Goebbels had instructed his agents in great detail on the means of manipulating American governments through exploitation of public naïveté.

But early Nazi successes in Latin America, in combination with the Reich's aggressive European policies, so alarmed the American states that an unprecedented unity began to develop. Progressively after 1938 a recognition of their perilous position, threatened from within by Nazi subversion and from without by the waxing might of Hitler's Germany, brought them together. Brazil and Argentina, the two states most seriously

3. *The Testament of Adolf Hitler,* remarks of Feb. 7, 1945, pp. 45–46.

menaced by internal Nazi activity, took measures to break the local fascist movements. The beginning of firm efforts to control the Nazis in this hemisphere also marked the emergence of major political differences between the countries involved and the Reich. Tension became severe, especially between Buenos Aires and Rio de Janeiro, on the one hand, and Berlin, on the other.

Prohibitions on the Nazi Party did not eliminate the organization. It continued to exist and function under cover, and the Reich still pursued its goal of warding off any concerted action by the United States and its neighbors to interfere with Nazi expansion in Europe. German propaganda, diplomacy, and economic pressure sought to exploit fears of "Yankee imperialism" in Latin America and to attract the region into the Reich's orbit by stressing the material advantages of cooperation with the New Germany. In the United States, Germany did its utmost to pacify public anxieties, taking full advantage of isolationist elements. Furthermore, the Nazis waged one of their greatest struggles to defeat the incumbent American President.[4]

At the same time, leading Nazis had already begun preliminary preparations for possible military action against this hemisphere, long before it was engaged in the European conflict. In 1938, Hermann Goering called on the German aircraft industry to construct aerial weapons with transatlantic capabilities for use against "those arrogant people" in the United States. By the summer of 1940, Nazi military planners, on Hitler's orders, started the detailed studies precedent to an assault on the New World via the Atlantic islands. The Fuehrer was confident that he could keep the United States out of the war until he had worked his will in Europe. After he had enthralled the world island, the Western Hemisphere would be at his mercy.

> For me the object is to exploit the advantages of continental hegemony. It is ridiculous to think of a world policy as long as one does not control the continent. When we are masters of Europe, we have a dominant position in the world. A hundred and thirty million

4. Nazi hatred of Roosevelt became fully apparent in German propaganda only after Pearl Harbor. The standard descriptions of the President, as directed by Ribbentrop, were to be "the Chief War Culprit" and "the Lunatic of the White House." The Germans consistently depicted the conflict as "Roosevelt's War" and the prescribed themes for Nazi propaganda against the United States all sought to place responsibility for the world disaster on him. See *Standardthesen und Richtlinien fuer die Deutsche Auslandspropaganda,* Library of Congress, pp. 12 and 27–40; cf. also the introduction and documents in *Roosevelts Weg in den Krieg* (Berlin, 1943).

people in the Reich, ninety in the Ukraine. Add to these the other states of the New Europe and we'll be four hundred millions, compared with the one hundred and thirty million Americans.[5]

To assert, as neo-revisionists do, that American security would have been compatible with the existence of a Hitlerized Europe, seems myopic.

The events of 1940 and 1941 certainly did not signify the end of the threat to the American hemisphere. In some quarters Nazi germs had taken deep root and were to reveal their true virulence only later. This was particularly the case in Argentina, where failure to eliminate Nazi sympathizers from the army and police soon cost that country its democratic institutions. By May 1942 the Castillo regime in Buenos Aires had begun secret collaboration with the Axis, a policy pursued ever more vigorously by the military group which seized power in June 1943. Brazilian President Vargas' brief flirtations with the Reich remained cause for concern to the other American republics. But by 1941 the general trend toward hemispheric unity and opposition to the Axis was clearly discernible, not least to the Nazis themselves. The Havana Conference of July 1940, the suppression of the several Nazi plots in Latin America in the course of that summer and the following one, and the electoral victory of Franklin Roosevelt were highlights of this development.

When the great test of actual involvement in the momentous world contest came, the results of these trends soon emerged. Within weeks after Pearl Harbor, every state in the hemisphere, with the exception of Argentina and Chile, had either declared war on the Axis or severed relations with the totalitarian powers. By January 1943 even Chile, with her long, exposed coastline, took the risk of breaking with Germany and her partners. Argentina alone proved unsympathetic to the cause adopted by her sister states.[6] She was a pointed reminder of the authoritarian paths into which the others might have been lured but for their own alertness to the Nazi menace and the fortunate leadership of a perspicacious U.S. President.

The Nazis failed in their attempts to promote the Hitler ideology in the

---

5. *Hitler's Secret Conversations,* records of Oct. 26–27, 1941, p. 76.

6. Argentina's wartime collaboration with the Axis, a sad chapter in that country's history equaled only by the subsequent tragedies of the Perón regime, provides ample material for a separate study. A beginning has been made in the memorandum presented by the State Department to other American governments, *Consultation Among the American Republics with Respect to the Argentine Situation* (Washington, 1946). Even Argentina finally broke relations with Germany and Japan as a token gesture, and declared war on them a few days before the end came in Europe.

New World and to manipulate American governments through public opinion. They were unable to direct the policies of the American states into channels best suited to serve Berlin. And eventually the Fuehrer's plan for world domination, concerning which he expressed persistent optimism to Goebbels as late as 1943, ended ignominiously in the bunker beneath the Chancellery. It would be a distortion to portray military and political superiority over the Western Hemisphere as Hitler's principal goal. But that it formed an important part of his global ambitions cannot be questioned.

Elihu Root once observed that "every sovereign state has the right to protect itself by preventing a condition of affairs in which it will be too late to protect itself." It was this principle that dictated and justified the New World's precautions against the rampant expansion of Hitler's New Order. Had the United States and other American republics not responded as they did, posterity would have marveled at their folly.

BIBLIOGRAPHY

As indicated in the preface, this study relies principally on German Foreign Ministry archives and other captured documents of the Nazi regime. Progress through the literature pertaining to the subject left no doubt that published works illuminated only slightly the central problems with which the writer was concerned, a conviction strongly reinforced by research among the sources now available. Even a partial examination of the literature reveals that the entire matter of Nazi activities in the Americas has received insufficient attention by historians. To be sure, enormous quantities of books, articles, and pamphlets appeared during the late thirties and early forties, but they exhibit the unreliability typical of undocumented expositions. Few have proved truly useful, although they do give one a keener appreciation of the deep-seated alarm over Nazi penetration which many writers shared at the time.

In groping one's way through the immense oceans of Nazi papers to the substantial islands of pertinent materials, three major publications serve as indispensable navigational aids: (1) Gerhard L. Weinberg, ed., *Guide to Captured German Documents* (Maxwell Air Force Base, Ala., Human Resources Research Institute, 1952); (2) Gerhard L. Weinberg, ed., *Supplement to the Guide to Captured German Documents* (Washington, National Archives, 1959); and (3) the American Historical Association's Committee For the Study of War Documents, *Guides to German Records Microfilmed at Alexandria, Virginia* (Washington, National Archives, 1958–). Thirty-seven of the latter guides have appeared, of which the most valuable for this investigation proved to be number 3, "Records of the National Socialist German Labor Party," number 6, "Records of Nazi Cultural and Research Institutions . . . ," and number 9, "Records of Private German Individuals," including those of Karl Haushofer. Dr. Willard Fletcher of the A.H.A. filming project generously permitted me to study the typescripts of several guides before they were released, notably numbers 21 and 22 on the DAI and PROMI papers at Alexandria. Although there remain vast files through which no one has even glanced, these several finding guides repay diligent perusal by leading one to the important documents already processed.

The use of the Foreign Ministry's archives has certain shortcomings that should be indicated. The foremost limitation is the fact that serious gaps exist in the files; especially disappointing in this investigation has been the absence of all but a fragment of Ribbentrop's personal files and of all the secret files of the Press Department. There is also the necessary observation that most career diplomats did not enjoy the Nazi hierarchy's confidence. They were not always in a position to know what the German government's actual policies on a given subject were.

The archives of Goebbels' Propaganda Ministry would have been preferable in many instances, but that agency began grinding its important documents into pulp as early as November 1944 to prevent their capture. Of those believed to have survived, including an extensive diary by Goebbels, virtually none are available in the Free World and the Russians are presumed to have seized them. Consequently, the Foreign Ministry files are the best available for an inquiry such as this. Their reliability as indicators of Nazi policy and practice increases perceptibly after February 1938, when Joachim von Ribbentrop became the first dedicated National Socialist to be German Foreign Minister. There is the additional consolation that Ernst Wilhelm Bohle, upon whose papers the work has drawn liberally, served simultaneously after 1937 as State Secretary in the Foreign Ministry and as chief of the Party's *Auslandsorganisation,* a duality of roles which permits his files to make up in part for the deficiencies of the purely diplomatic documents.

Microfilmed copies of selected Foreign Ministry records are being deposited in the U.S. National Archives, and a smaller selection has been published from the films. Extensive reading of both the published documents and the microfilms gives one great confidence in the competence of the international team of scholars who have edited the various published series of German Foreign Ministry documents. They have done a most admirable and thorough job in preparing the many volumes in series C and D.

It is, unfortunately, quite a different matter when one comes to the system adopted for organizing the microfilms themselves. The only data sheets for these materials are at the National Archives (and presumably at the official depositories in France and Great Britain), and one must report that they are inordinately difficult to use. Written as they are in three languages (English, French, and German), with at least two languages commonly appearing on the same page, it certainly would have been better to avoid the frequent and obscure abbreviations. The data sheets are often illegible, being carbon copies on transparent paper. More serious is the failure to indicate on many sheets the time period to which the documents refer. One can frequently date the year of a paper only through knowledge of the changing organizational structure of the Foreign Ministry, e.g. after September 1936, Section IX of the Political Department was responsible for the Americas. Finally, the film serial numbers given in the appendices to the printed documents are of little help in locating documents at the National Archives, for microfilms are arranged in that institution's Foreign Affairs Branch by container number and without special reference to the film serial number. In short, there are several obstacles to the easy and efficient exploitation of the unpublished Foreign Ministry materials which were so laboriously photographed. One would hope that an improved guide might be prepared, along the lines of the excellent finding aids of the A.H.A. Committee For the Study of War Documents.

In the following bibliography, publications are arranged chronologically, rather than alphabetically, in order to indicate more satisfactorily the development of the literature on the subject.

BIBLIOGRAPHICAL AIDS

GENERAL

Woolbert, Robert G. *Foreign Affairs Bibliography, 1932–1942,* New York, Harper, 1945.

Handlin, Oscar, and others. *Harvard Guide to American History.* Cambridge, The Belknap Press, 1954.

Roberts, Henry, and others. *Foreign Affairs Bibliography, 1942–1952.* New York, Harper, 1955.

SPECIALIZED

Lasswell, Harold D., Casey, Ralph, D., and Smith, Bruce Lannes. *Propaganda and Promotional Activities: An Annotated Bibliography.* Minneapolis, University of Minnesota Press, 1935.

Handbook of Latin American Studies. Cambridge, Harvard University Press, 1936–.

A List of Bibliographies on Propaganda. Washington, Library of Congress, 1940.

Farago, Ladislas. *German Psychological Warfare: Survey and Bibliography.* New York, Committee for National Morale, 1941.

Nazi Fifth Column Activities; A List of References. Washington, Library of Congress, 1943.

Smith, Bruce L., Lasswell, Harold D., and Casey, Ralph D. *Propaganda, Communication, and Public Opinion: A Comprehensive Reference Guide.* Princeton, Princeton University Press, 1946.

Dillon, Dorothy Rita. *Latin America, 1935–1949: A Selected Bibliography.* New York, United Nations, 1952.

Smith, Bruce L., and Chitra M. *International Communication and Political Opinion: A Guide to the Literature.* Princeton, Princeton University Press, 1956.

Humphreys, Robert A. *Latin American History: A Guide to the Literature in English.* Published under the auspices of the Royal Institute of International Affairs. London, Oxford University Press, 1958.

ARTICLES AND PAMPHLETS

Bemis, Samuel Flagg. "First Gun of a Revisionist Historiography for the Second World War," *Journal of Modern History, 19* (March 1947), 55–59.

Sachs, John H. *Hatchet Men.* New Oxford, Pennsylvania, Lincoln Way Booklets, 1947.

Morison, Samuel Eliot. "Did Roosevelt Start the War?—History Through a Beard," *Atlantic Monthly, 182* (August 1948), 91–97.

Historicus (pseud.). "History—Upside Down," *Prevent World War III, 41* (January 1953), 39–44.

Ferrell, Robert H. "Pearl Harbor and the Revisionists," *The Historian, 17* (Spring 1955), 215–33.

Morton, Louis. "Pearl Harbor in Perspective," *U.S. Naval Institute Proceedings, 81* (April 1955), 461–68.

Cole, Wayne S. "American Entry into World War II: A Historiographical Appraisal," *Mississippi Valley Historical Review, 43* (March 1957), 595–617.

Murdock, Eugene C. "Zum Eintritt der Vereinigten Staaten in den zweiten Weltkrieg," *Vierteljahrshefte fuer Zeitgeschichte, 4* (January 1956), 93–114.

May, Ernest R. *American Intervention, 1917 and 1941.* Washington, Service Center For Teachers of History, 1960.

Barnes, Harry Elmer. *The Struggle Against the Historical Blackout.* 9th ed., rev. No facts of publication given, but apparently published in 1948.

Select Bibliography of Revisionist Books Dealing With the Two World Wars and Their Aftermath. Oxnard, California, Oxnard Press-Courier, n.d.

THE UNITED STATES AND THE SECOND WORLD WAR

THE LITERATURE OF DEBATE

BOOKS

Berber, Friedrich. *Der Mythos der Monroe Doctrine.* Essen, Essener Verlags-buchhandlung, 1943.

———. *Die Amerikanische Neutralitaet im Kriege, 1939–1941.* Essen, Essener Verlagsbuchhandlung, 1943. Two Nazi contributions, clearly designed for propaganda value and consistently denouncing "the Lunatic in the White House" for launching "Roosevelt's War."

Sayers, Michael, and Kahn, Albert E. *Sabotage! The Secret War Against America.* New York and London, Harper, 1942. The best and most well-documented of contemporary reports on Axis penetration and native fascists in the United States.

Carlson, John Roy (pseud.). *Under Cover.* New York, Dutton, 1943. Surprisingly useful for a sensational exposé, this volume, which went through 27 printings in six months, documents the Nazi and anti-Semitic influences which sought to exploit the isolationist movement.

Johnson, Walter. *The Battle Against Isolation.* Chicago, University of Chicago Press, 1944. Thorough treatment of the Committee to Defend America by Aiding the Allies.

Beard, Charles A. *American Foreign Policy in the Making, 1932–1940: A Study in Responsibilities.* New Haven, Yale University Press, 1946.

Morgenstern, George. *Pearl Harbor: The Story of the Secret War.* New York, Devin-Adair, 1947. A neo-revisionist condensation and rewriting of the forty volumes growing out of the Congressional inquiry into the disaster.

Langer, William L. *Our Vichy Gamble.* New York, Alfred Knopf, 1947.

Bailey, Thomas A. *The Man in the Street.* New York, Macmillan, 1948. Plea for understanding of Roosevelt's difficult position in relation to public opinion.

Beard, Charles A. *President Roosevelt and the Coming of the War, 1941.* New Haven, Yale University Press, 1948.

Flynn, John T. *The Roosevelt Myth.* New York, Devin-Adair, 1948. An unbalanced display of personal invective.

Sherwood, Robert E. *Roosevelt and Hopkins: An Intimate History.* New York, Harper, 1948.

Chamberlin, William Henry. *America's Second Crusade.* Chicago, Henry Regnery, 1950.

Feis, Herbert. *The Road to Pearl Harbor.* Princeton, Princeton University Press, 1950.

Rauch, Basil. *Roosevelt: From Munich to Pearl Harbor.* New York, Creative Age Press, 1950.

Watson, Mark S. *Chief of Staff: Prewar Plans and Preparations.* Washington, Department of the Army, 1950. Important for strategic considerations regarding hemispheric defense.

Kennan, George F. *American Diplomacy, 1900–1950.* Chicago, University of Chicago Press, 1951.

Sanborn, Frederick C. *Design For War: A Study of Secret Power Politics, 1937–1941.* New York, Devin-Adair, 1951.

Trefousse, Hans L. *Germany and American Neutrality, 1939–1941.* New York, Bookman Associates, 1951. Concise treatment with provocative opening chapter on "Hitler's Ultimate Aims."

Langer, William L., and Gleason, S. Everett. *The Challenge to Isolation, 1938–1940* and *The Undeclared War.* New York, Harper, 1952 and 1953.

Tansill, Charles C. *Back Door to War: The Roosevelt Foreign Policy, 1933–1941.* Chicago, Henry Regnery, 1952.

Barnes, Harry Elmer, ed. *Perpetual War For Perpetual Peace.* Caldwell, Idaho, The Caxton Press, 1953.

Cole, Wayne S. *America First: The Battle Against Intervention, 1940–1941.* Madison, Wisconsin: University of Wisconsin Press, 1953.

Osgood, Robert E. *Ideals and Self-Interest in America's Foreign Relations.* Chicago, University of Chicago Press, 1953.

Bemis, Samuel Flagg. *A Diplomatic History of the United States.* New York, Henry Holt, 1955.

Drummond, Donald F. *The Passing of American Neutrality, 1937–1941.* Ann Arbor, Michigan, University of Michigan Press, 1955.

Cole, Wayne S. *Senator Gerald P. Nye and American Foreign Relations.* Minneapolis, University of Minnesota Press, 1962.

Friedlaender, Saul. *Hitler et les États-Unis, 1939–1941.* Genève, Droz, 1963. A thorough and competent evaluation of the importance Hitler gave to preventing U.S. intervention during the critical stages of the war in Europe.

Hoggan, David L. *Der erzwungene Krieg.* Tuebingen, Verlag der Deutschen Hochschullehrer-Zeitung, 1961. Latest in the neo-revisionist efforts.

Tull, Charles J. *Father Coughlin and The New Deal.* Syracuse, Syracuse University Press, 1965.

ARTICLES AND PAMPHLETS

Flynn, John T. *The Truth About Pearl Harbor.* Privately printed, 1944.

———. *The Final Secret of Pearl Harbor.* New York, privately printed, 1945.

Lubell, Samuel. "Who Votes Isolationist and Why," *Harper's Magazine,* 202 (April 1951), 29–36.

Cole, Wayne S. "America First and the South, 1940–1941," *Journal of South-ern History,* 22 (February 1956), 36–47.

Haight, John McVickar, Jr. "France, the United States, and the Munich Crisis," *Journal of Modern History,* 32 (December 1960), 340–58.

Nazi Exploitation of Isolationists

Books

Howe, Quincy. *England Expects Every American to do His Duty.* New York, Simon and Schuster, 1937.

French, Paul Comly, ed. *Common Sense Neutrality: Mobilizing For Peace.* New York, Hastings House, 1939. Statements by Hoover, Lindbergh, Harry Elmer Barnes and other isolationists; distributed in undetermined quantities by the Nazis in 1940.

Beneken, An (pseud.). *America! Wake Up.* New York, World Study Bureau, 1940. Disparaging discussion of social conditions in the United States under F. D. R. and proposals for American cooperation with the Axis.

Cincinnatus (pseud.). *War! War! War!: Veritas Vincit.* Privately printed, 1940. One of the more widely circulated anti-Semitic tracts during the campaign against Roosevelt. Author identified by O. John Rogge as Arthur Peter, a Washington lawyer.

Dennis, Lawrence. *The Dynamics of War and Revolution.* New York, The Weekly Foreign Letter, 1940. An American fascist's analysis of why democracy will fail in the United States.

Flynn, John T. *Country Squire in the White House.* New York, Doubleday, Doran, 1940. Another vitriolic attack on Roosevelt, thought by the Nazis to be the most damaging of all propaganda works in the 1940 campaign.

French, Paul Comly. *We Won't Murder.* New York, Hastings House, 1940. A contribution by a conscientious objector whose works the Nazis welcomed.

Articles and Pamphlets

Facts in Review. New York, German Library of Information, 1939–1941. The weekly newsletter which presented the Nazi version of the war to thousands of Americans.

Hoover, Herbert C. *Shall We Send Our Youth to War?* New York, Coward-McCann, 1939. A brief and passionate plea for isolationism.

Dennis, Lawrence. "Can Democracy Put Men Back to Work?" *Current History,* 50 (July 1939), 35–37. Another exposition favoring authoritarianism.

Flynn, John T. *Can Hitler Beat American Business?* Reprinted from *Harper's Magazine* (February 1940). Debunks fears that the spread of Nazi autarky through Europe would endanger American trade.

Cincinnatus (pseud.). "Running For Office: A Confession," *New York Times Magazine,* Sept. 8, 1940, pp. 10 ff. Sarcastic contribution to the 1940 program to defeat Roosevelt.

Creel, George. "Beware the Superpatriots," *American Mercury, 51* (September 1940), 33–41.

Dreiser, Theodore. *The Dawn is in the East.* New York, 1940? Reprinted from *Common Sense* (December 1940).

Norris, Kathleen. "Victory for the President," *Commonweal, 33,* (Dec. 20, 1940), 230–31.

Dennis, Lawrence. "Party-State and the Elite: Who Owns the Future?" *Nation, 152* (Jan. 11 and 25, 1941), 39–41 and 111.

Flynn, John T. "Coming: A Totalitarian America," *American Mercury, 52* (February 1941), 151–57.

———. "Can Hitler Invade America?" *Readers Digest, 38* (April 1941), 1–6. All works by authors whose writing was being encouraged by the Nazis through the William Lengel Literary Agency.

THE NAZI MENACE IN THE WESTERN HEMISPHERE

BOOKS

Directory of Newspapers and Periodicals. Philadelphia, N. W. Ayer and Sons, 1880–. Reveals trend toward extinction of German-language press in the United States.

Ludecke, Kurt G. W. *I Knew Hitler.* New York, Charles Scribner's Sons, 1937. Personal account by former Nazi propagandist in the United States; published after he tried to blackmail the Party, but adding little to what he had already made public.

Beals, Carleton. *The Coming Struggle For Latin America.* Philadelphia, Lippincott, 1938.

Giudici, Ernesto. *Hitler Conquista América.* Buenos Aires, Editorial Acento, 1938. Fears that fascist victory in Spain might mean transmission of Hitlerism to New World.

Motta Lima, Pedro, and Barboza Mello, José. *El Nazismo en el Brazil.* Buenos Aires, Claridad, 1938. One of the first major reports on the Nazification of the Germans in southern Brazil.

Tejera, Adolfo. *Penetración Nazi en América Latina.* Montevideo, Editorial Nueva América, 1938. A more general survey than the preceding one.

Dickmann, Enrique. *La Infiltración Nazi-fascista en la Argentina.* Buenos Aires, Ediciones Sociales Argentinas, 1939. An anti-Nazi Argentine of German extraction speaks out against the work of the AO.

The German Reich and Americans of German Origin. New York, Oxford University Press, 1939. Excellent collection of documents and statements from official Nazi sources.

Ibero-amerikanisches Institut. Alemania y el Mundo Ibero-americano. Berlin, *Ibero-amerikanisches Institut,* 1939. Symposium designed to foster good-will; many important Reich officials participated.

Spivak, John L. *Secret Armies: The New Technique of Nazi Warfare.* New York, Modern Age Books, 1939. An exposé of Hitler's undeclared war on the Americas.

Bernal de León, José. *La Quinta Columna en el Continente Americano.* Mexico City, Ediciones Culturas Mexicanas, [1940?].

Brena, T. G., and Iturbide, J. V. *Alta Traición en el Uruguay.* Montevideo, Editorial ABC, 1940. Two Latin American reactions to the rash of Nazi plots discovered in 1940 by South American countries; latter volume by members of the Uruguayan Congressional Committee on Nazi Activities.

Dies, Martin. *The Trojan Horse in America.* New York, Dodd, Mead, 1940. Popular report of the findings of the Dies Committee.

Fernandez Artucio, Hugo. *Nazis en el Uruguay.* Montevideo, Talleres Graficos Sur, 1940. Indictment which set off an official investigation leading to the discovery of a Nazi plot in Uruguay and prompting similar inquiries elsewhere in Latin America.

Lavine, Harold. *Fifth Column in America.* New York, Doubleday, Doran, 1940. Description of organizations and leaders of both fascist and communist groups in United States.

Macdonald, N. P. *Hitler Over Latin America.* London, Jarrolds, 1940. A British observer's warning of the fate the New World would face should Hitler win in Europe.

Chéradame, André. *Defense of the Americas.* Transl. from the French by George Challies. Garden City, New York, Doubleday, Doran, 1941. A Frenchman sounds the alert.

Gunther, John. *Inside Latin America.* New York, Harper, 1941.

Herring, Hubert C. *Good Neighbors: Argentina, Brazil, Chile, and Seventeen Other Countries.* New Haven, Yale University Press, 1941. Brief but useful sections on Germans in Latin America.

Mendoza, Juan C. *La Argentina y la Swástika.* Buenos Aires, Bruno de Campo, 1941. Few documents and many details on individual Nazi agents.

Strausz-Hupé, Robert. *Axis America: Hitler Plans Our Future.* New York, Putnam, 1941. Conscientious effort to arouse the American public to the dangers a victorious Nazi Reich would pose.

Bischoff, Ralph F. *Nazi Conquest Through German Culture.* Cambridge, Harvard University Press, 1942. Draws on author's experience as a student in Germany during the thirties. Most valuable on DAI, VDA, and related agencies.

Fernandez Artucio, Hugo. *The Nazi Underground in South America.* New York, Farrar and Rinehart, 1942. Expansion of author's study of Nazi threat in his native Uruguay. Includes copy of what is alleged to be "Hitler's Map of South America," perhaps the one mentioned by Roosevelt in his famous speech of October 27, 1941.

Kirk, Betty. *Covering the Mexican Front: The Battle of Europe versus America.* Norman, Okla., University of Oklahoma Press, 1942. Undocumented but readable contribution by an American reporter in Mexico City.

Problems of Hemispheric Defense. Berkeley, University of California Press, 1942. Most useful is a lecture by Russell H. Fitzgibbon, "The Axis Advance Guard in Latin America," pp. 25–52.

Ross, Colin. *"Die Westliche Hemisphere" als Programm und Phantom des amerikanischen Imperialismus.* Leipzig, F. A. Brockhaus, 1942. The Nazi "expert" on the Western Hemisphere raising the bogy of "Yankee imperialism."

Solari, Juan Antonio. *América Presa Codiciada.* 3rd ed. Buenos Aires, "La Vanguardia," 1942. Chairman of Argentine investigation of subversive activities summarizes findings; includes several maps detailing Nazi organization.

Bemis, Samuel Flagg. *The Latin American Policy of the United States.* New York, Harcourt, Brace, 1943.

Burden, William A. M. *The Struggle for Airways in Latin America.* New York, Council on Foreign Relations, 1943. Describes the imminent danger in 1938–1941 that German control of airlines in South America would threaten vital interests like the Panama Canal.

Chase, Allen. *Falange: The Axis Secret Army in the Americas.* New York, Putnam, 1943. Another consideration of Axis penetration via Franco Spain. Plausible but unsubstantiated.

Welles, Sumner. *The Time For Decision.* New York and London, Harper, 1944.

Ogden, August R. *The Dies Committee.* Washington, Catholic University of America Press, 1945. Good treatment of House Special Committee on Un-American Activities and its predecessors.

Mackenzie, Norman. *Argentina.* London, Victor Gollancz, 1947. Impressions of authoritarian influences and collaboration with the Axis.

Norman, John. "Influence of Pro-Fascist Propaganda On American Neutrality, 1935–1936," in *Essays in History and International Relations in Honor of George Hubbard Blakeslee.* Worcester, Mass., Clark University, 1949.

Welles, Sumner. *Seven Decisions That Shaped History.* New York, Harper, 1950.

Magnet, Alejandro. *Nuestros Vecinos Justicialistas.* Santiago de Chile, Editorial de Pacífico, S.A., 1953. A Chilean view of Argentine collaboration with the Nazis.

Wittke, Carl Frederick. *The German-language Press in America.* Lexington, Ky., University of Kentucky Press, 1957.

De Jong, Louis. *Die deutsche fuenfte Kolonne im Zweiten Weltkrieg.* Stuttgart, Deutsche Verlags-Anstalt, 1959. Originally published in Dutch in 1953, and without benefit of many documents subsequently available; tends to discount the fifth column.

Conn, Stetson, and Fairchild, Byron. *The Framework of Hemisphere Defense.* Washington, Department of the Army, 1960. Able treatment of military aspects of Nazi penetration in Latin America.

Schlesinger, Arthur, Jr. *The Politics of Upheaval.* Boston, Houghton Mifflin, 1960. Chapter 5, "The Dream of Fascism," 69–95, presents a concise discussion of native American fascists.

Logan, John A., Jr. *No Transfer: An American Security Principle.* New Haven, Yale University Press, 1961. Several chapters of this excellent history cover in detail the hemisphere's reaction to the Nazi threat.

Rogge, O. John. *The Official German Report: Nazi Penetration, 1924–42, Pan-Arabism, 1939–Today.* New York, Thomas Yoseloff, 1961. Rambling and disjointed work with no precise documentation. By a former Justice Department lawyer, it is a prosecutor's report, not a scholar's.

Brunner, Otto and Gerhard, Dietrich, eds. *Europa und Uebersee: Festschrift fuer Egmont Zechlin.* Hamburg, Verlag Hans Bredow-Institut, 1961. Distinguished by Guenter Moltmann's perceptive paper, "Weltherrschaftideen Hitlers."

Ruiz Moreno, Isidoro. *Historia de Las Relaciones Exteriores Argentinas.* Buenos Aires, Editorial Perrot, 1961. Terse and legalistic but some useful information.

Wood, Bryce. *The Making of the Good Neighbor Policy.* New York, Columbia University Press, 1961. Sound history of the policy that contributed so much to hemispheric unity during the Second World War.

Gruchmann, Lothar. *Nationalsozialistische Grossraumordnung: Die Konstruktion einer "deutschen Monroe-Doktrin."* Stuttgart, Deutsche Verlags-Anstalt, 1962. Brief but authoritative study of Hitler's special conception of a Monroe Doctrine for the Old World.

Dzelepy, E. N. *Franco, Hitler y Los Estados Unidos.* Mexico, D. F., Ediciones Era, S. A., 1963. A recent reminder of Franco's role in the totalitarian infiltration of the New World.

Besson, Waldemar and Frhr. Hiller v. Gaertringen, Friedrich, eds. *Geschichte und Gegenwartsbewusstsein: Historische Betrachtungen und Untersuchun-gen, Festschrift fuer Hans Rothfels zum 70. Geburtstag dargebracht von Kollegen, Freunden und Schuelern.* Goettingen, Vandenhoeck and Ru-precht, 1963. Among several relevant contributions is that by Gerhard L. Weinberg, "German Colonial Plans and Policies, 1938–1942."

Smith, Arthur L. *The Deutschtum of Nazi Germany and the United States.* The Hague, Nijhoff, 1965. Principally a review of the DAI and its rela-tions to German-Americans.

ARTICLES AND PAMPHLETS

Beals, Carleton. "Totalitarian Inroads in Latin America," *Foreign Affairs,* 17 (October 1938), 78–89.
———. "Swastika Over the Andes," *Harper's Magazine,* 177 (1938), 176–86. Two essays by an observant journalist to whom the incidents over Nazism in Brazil, Argentina, and Chile in 1938 seemed especially grave.

Contreras Labarca, Carlos. *América Latina Invadida por el Fascismo.* Santiago de Chile, Ediciones Antares, 1938. Describes fascist penetration of the Chilean Chamber of Deputies.

Inman, Samuel G. *Democracy Versus the Totalitarian State in Latin America.* Philadelphia, American Academy of Political and Social Science, 1938. Report of an American missionary-scholar-journalist.

Knop, W. G. J. *Germany's Economic Situation in 1939 and Her Challenge to the World.* London, Friends of Europe, n.d.

The Nazi International. London, Friends of Europe, n.d. Two undocumented but pertinent discussions of Nazi economic and political penetration of the New World.

Vivero, León de. *Avance del Imperialismo Fascista en el Peru.* Mexico City, Editorial Manuel Arévalo, 1938. A sample of the left-wing counterpropa-ganda circulating in Latin America at this time.

Behrendt, Richard F. "Foreign Influences in Latin America," *Annals of the American Academy of Political and Social Science,* 204 (July 1939), 1–8. A warning from a German exile teaching at the University of Panama.

Bidwell, Percy W., "Latin America, Germany, and the Hull Program," *For-eign Affairs,* 17, (July 1939), 374–96. Comments on the triangular rela-tionships of Germany, the United States, and Latin America, especially economic aspects.

Hitler Over Latin America: Why the Embargo Against Spain Must Be Lifted Now. New York, Lawyers Committee on American Relations with Spain, 1939. Last-minute plea for aid to the Loyalists in Spain as a means to pre-vent totalitarianism from infiltrating Latin America.

Schlesinger, Alfredo. *El Arma Secreta: La Quinta Columna.* Guatemala, Centro Editorial, 1940. Pamphlet whose widespread impact so worried the Nazis that they demanded its suppression by the Guatemalan government.

"Getulio," *Time, 36* (Aug. 12, 1940), 18–20. A wary appreciation of the Brazilian President and his apparent flirtations with the Axis.

Behrendt, Richard F. *Fascist Penetration in Latin America.* Washington, American Council on Public Affairs, 1941. Elaborates and brings up to date the article by the same author two years earlier.

Bidwell, Percy W. *Economic Defense of Latin America.* Boston, World Peace Foundation, 1941. Careful reflections on what might have proved the Achilles heel of the New World.

Hall, Melvin, and Peck, Walter. "Wings For the Trojan Horse," *Foreign Affairs, 19* (January 1941), 347–69. An early and anxious survey of Axis airlines in Latin America, notably Colombia and Ecuador.

Martin, L. and S. "Nazi Intrigues in Central America," *American Mercury, 53* (July 1941), 66–73. An attempt to appraise the extent to which Nazism, already observed in South America, was making progress in Central America.

Murillo, Gerardo. *A Los Pueblos de América.* Méjico, Col. Acción Mundial, 1941.

———. *La Victoria de Alemania y la Situación de la América Latina.* Méjico: Col. Acción Mundial, 1941. Two clever pro-axis propaganda publications, promising Latin America great rewards as a consequence of impending German victory and condemning Roosevelt as just another imperialist.

Prange, Gordon W. *Hitler's Speeches and the United States.* New York, Oxford University Press, 1941. Principally an explanation of the propaganda purposes of Hitler's speeches, revealing his disregard for the truth.

Loewenstein, Karl. "Legislation Against Subversive Activities in Argentina," *Harvard Law Review, 16* (July 1943), 1261–1306. Scholarly critique written without knowledge that the executive branch of government in Argentina had already begun to make a mockery of the legislature's desires in this matter.

Fuller, Helen. "Nazism in Latin America," *New Republic, 110* (Jan. 31, 1944), 141–43. Extremely brief and sketchy, but correct in its estimate of continued Axis influence in Buenos Aires and certain other quarters.

Remak, Joachim. "Hitlers Amerikapolitik," *Aussenpolitik, 6* (February 1955), 706–14. Sensible assessment of conflicting views of diplomats like Dieckhoff and the Fuehrer.

———. " 'Friends of the New Germany': The Bund and German-American Relations," *Journal of Modern History, 24* (March 1957), 38–41. Brief but useful note pointing out the continuity of Nazi-inspired organizations of German-Americans.

Weinberg, Gerhard L. "Hitler's Image of the United States," *American Historical Review, 69* (July 1964), 1006–21. A thorough assessment of the disabilities under which Hitler labored in evaluating American capabilities and intentions.

NAZI PROPAGANDA

BOOKS

Childs, H. L. *Propaganda and Dictatorship.* Princeton, Princeton University Press, 1936. General but competent exposition; important forerunner of Childs' later work with the Princeton Listening Center.

Rogerson, Sidney. *Propaganda in the Next War.* London, G. Bles, 1938. A much-discussed little volume which served isolationist orators as authoritative proof of British schemes to lure the United States into the conflict.

Alemania y El Mundo Ibero-Americano. Berlin, Ibero-Amerikanisches Institut, 1939. A volume of essays, 19 in Spanish and 4 in Portuguese, stressing the opportunities for cooperation between the Reich and Latin America.

Grandin, Thomas. *The Political Use of the Radio.* Geneva, Geneva Research Centre, 1939. Survey of legal thinking on the topic at the time.

Hambourger, René. *Goebbels, "Chef de Publicité" du IIIe Reich.* Paris, F. Sorlot, 1939. The most important early effort to depict Goebbels' machinations at home and abroad.

Klein, Herbert A., ed. *Propaganda!—The War For Men's Minds.* Los Angeles, Los Angeles City College Press, 1939. Most noteworthy for a thoughtful article by Thomas Mann.

Chakhotin, Sergei. *The Rape of the Masses: The Psychology of Totalitarian Political Propaganda.* Transl. from the 5th ed. by E. W. Dickes. London, G. Routledge and Sons, 1940. In many ways a preview of 1984. Still worth reading and with broader relevance than merely to Nazi Germany.

Lavine, Harold, and Wechsler, James. *War Propaganda and the United States.* New Haven, Yale University Press, 1940. Somewhat premature but an interesting preliminary study with many good reproductions.

McKenzie, Vernon. *Here Lies Goebbels!* London, M. Joseph, 1940. Detailed rebuttal of many specific claims of Nazi propagandists.

Wirsing, Giselher, ed. *The War in Maps, 1939–1940.* New York, German Library of Information, 1941. Nazi victories glorified in an impressively handsome propaganda volume.

Childs, H. L., and Whitton, John B. *Propaganda By Short Wave.* Princeton, Princeton University Press, 1942. From the files of the Princeton Listening Center the authors present a systematic and extensive analysis of Nazi techniques, themes, and purposes.

Sington, Derrick, and Weidenfeld, Arthur. *The Goebbels Experiment: A Study of the Nazi Propaganda Machine.* New Haven, Yale University Press, 1943. Inadequate but still a notable accomplishment, considering the limits of the authors' sources.

Kris, Ernst, and Speier, Hans. *German Radio Propaganda.* London, Oxford University Press, 1944. Though limited to Nazi domestic propaganda, highly interesting for comparative purposes.

Riess, Curt. *Joseph Goebbels: The Devil's Advocate.* New York, Doubleday, 1948. In some ways still the best biography of its subject. Mainly reconstructed from interviews with persons who knew Goebbels

Lerner, Daniel, ed. *Propaganda in War and Crisis.* New York, G. W. Stewart, 1951.

George, Alexander L. *Propaganda Analysis: A Study of Inferences Made From Nazi Propaganda in World War II.* Evanston, Ill., Row, Peterson, 1959. Though not directly relevant to the present study, George's work is of general value for any student concerned with Nazi propaganda. It is primarily a systematic critique of the usually unsystematic analyses made by the U.S. Foreign Broadcast Intelligence Service.

Zeman, Z. A. B. *Nazi Propaganda.* London, Oxford University Press, 1964.

Bramstead, Ernest K. *Goebbels and National Socialist Propaganda, 1925–1945.* East Lansing, Mich., Michigan State University Press, 1965. Two useful, though not yet definitive, additions to the voluminous general literature on the subject.

Articles and Pamphlets

Schaefer, Otto. *Sinn und Wesen des V.D.A.* Frankfurt, Volksbund fuer das Deutschtum im Ausland, 1933. Official VDA publication.

Alemania. Berlin, Comité Oficial Alemán de Turismo, 1934–. This monthly, some copies of which are available at the Library of Congress, appeared in Spanish, French, and English; it enjoyed substantial circulation in Latin America as a running account of the New Germany's accomplishments.

Carr, Edward Hallett. *Propaganda in International Politics.* Oxford, England, The Clarendon Press, 1939. A candid and acute appraisal of Nazi Germany's propaganda techniques is included in this brief pamphlet, based on a chapter in Carr's *The Twenty Years Crisis, 1919–1939.*

Wilson, Charles H. "Hitler, Goebbels, and the Ministry for Propaganda." Reprinted from *Political Quarterly* (January 1939). Like all essays of the period, handicapped by lack of documents, but rather more scholarly and reliable than most.

Kris, Ernst. "German Propaganda Instructions of 1933," *Social Research,* 9 (February 1942), 46–81.

White, Ralph K. "Hitler, Roosevelt, and the Nature of War Propaganda," *Journal of Abnormal and Social Psychology*, 64 (April 1949), 157–74.

NATIONAL SOCIALISM AND THE EUROPEAN ASPECTS OF THE SECOND WORLD WAR

BOOKS

Germany Speaks. Preface by Joachim von Ribbentrop. London, Thornton Butterworth, 1938. The long-planned symposium in which various leaders of the Nazi Reich explained the "miracle of National Socialism."

Organisationsbuch der NSDAP. Munich, *Der Reichsorganisationsleiter der NSDAP,* 1940. Useful handbook for sorting out the intricate Party structure.

Neumann, Franz. *Behemoth: The Structure and Practice of National Socialism.* New York, Oxford University Press, 1942. Of fundamental importance for a broad understanding of the internal characteristics of the Third Reich.

Kempner, Robert M. W. (pseud.) *Nazi Subversive Organization, Past and Future.* Lansdowne, Penn., by the author, 1943. An official of the Weimar Republic details the procedures and organizational weapons by which National Socialism came to power in Germany and warns of their potential use elsewhere.

U.S. Department of State. *National Socialism.* Washington, Government Printing Office, 1943. Particularly valuable are chapters and documents on Nazi organizations operating among Germans abroad.

Heiden, Konrad. *Der Fuehrer.* Boston, Houghton Mifflin, 1944. Long since superseded by Bullock's biography, but interesting for comparison at some points.

Namier, Sir Lewis. *Diplomatic Prelude, 1938–1939.* London, Macmillan, 1948.

Churchill, Winston S. *The Gathering Storm, Their Finest Hour,* and *The Grand Alliance* (vols. 1, 2, and 3 of *The Second World War*). Boston, Houghton Mifflin, 1948, 1949, and 1950.

Lerner, Daniel, and others. *The Nazi Elite.* Stanford, Stanford University Press, 1951. Uneven in parts, but perhaps the best contribution of political science to an understanding of the historical phenomenon of National Socialism.

Boehm, Eric H. "Policy-making of the Nazi Government." Unpublished Ph.D dissertation, Yale University, 1951. Superb mastery of the sources then available.

Namier, Sir Lewis. *In The Nazi Era.* London, Macmillan, 1952. Included are many reviews of German memoirs.

Craig, Gordon A., and Gilbert, Felix, eds. *The Diplomats, 1919–1939.* Princeton, Princeton University Press, 1953. Especially valuable are Gordon Craig's essay, "The German Foreign Office from Neurath to Ribbentrop," and Franklin L. Ford's "Three Observers in Berlin: Rumbold, Dodd, and François-Poncet."

Weinberg, Gerhard L. *Germany and the Soviet Union, 1939–1941.* Leiden, Brill, 1954. Still a solid analysis of the evolution of Hitler's decision on Operation Barbarossa.

Wheeler-Bennett, J. W. *The Nemesis of Power: The German Army in Politics, 1918–1945.* New York, St. Martin's Press, 1954.

Presseisen, Ernst. L. *Germany and Japan, A Study in Totalitarian Diplomacy, 1933–1941.* The Hague, Martinus Nijhoff, 1958. A superb dissertation surpassed only by the work of Theo Sommer.

Shirer, William L. *The Rise and Fall of the Third Reich.* New York, Simon and Schuster, 1960.

Sommer, Theo. *Deutschland und Japan zwischen den Maechten, 1935–1940.* Tuebingen, J. C. B. Mohr, 1962. Definitive history of relations between Berlin and Tokyo in the years leading up to the Tripartite Pact.

Taylor, A. J. P. *The Origins of the Second World War.* New York, Atheneum, 1962.

Trevor-Roper, Hugh R. *The Last Days of Hitler.* 3rd ed. New York, Collier, 1962. Particularly valuable is the author's updated introduction, which brings into focus many of the important recent findings on Hitler's final days.

Bullock, Alan. *Hitler: A Study in Tyranny.* New York, Harper Torchbooks, 1964. A completely revised and expanded edition of the outstanding biography of the Fuehrer.

Murphy, Robert. *Diplomat Among Warriors.* Garden City, New York, Doubleday, 1964.

ARTICLES AND PAMPHLETS

The Redistribution of the World: Adolf Hitler's Reichstag Speech (January 30, 1939). London, Friends of Europe, n.d. An estimate of Hitler's global aims.

Kecskemeti, Paul, and Leites, Nathan. "Some Psychological Hypotheses on Nazi Germany," *Journal of Social Psychology,* 26 (1947), 141–83; 27 (1948), 91–117; 28 (1948), 141–64.

Trevor-Roper, Hugh R. "Hitler's Kriegsziele," *Vierteljahrshefte fuer Zeitgeschichte,* 8 (April 1960), 121–34. A noted British scholar argues that Hitler's ultimate aims pointed toward Russia and that he would have been content with the conquest of Eurasia.

Weinberg, Gerhard L. "Der deutsche Entschluss zum Angriff auf die Sowjet-union," *Vierteljahrshefte fuer Zeitgeschichte*, 1 (April 1953), 302–14. A detailed review of the background to the assault on Russia.

Koehl, Robert. "Feudal Aspects of National Socialism," *American Political Science Review*, 54 (December 1960), 921–34. Offers support to the established opinion that Nazi Germany was governed to a remarkable degree by one man, in much the fashion of a medieval lord surrounded by vassals and slaves.

Watt, D. C. "Hitler Comes to Power," *History Today*, *13* (March 1963), 152–59. Contains a brief appraisal of Hitler's early thinking on the United States.

PRINTED PRIMARY SOURCES

MEMOIRS AND DIARIES

Rauschning, Hermann. *The Voices of Destruction.* New York, Putnam, 1940.

Strasser, Otto. *Hitler und Ich.* Buenos Aires, Editorial Trenkelbach, 1940.

Ambassador Dodd's Diary, 1933–1938. New York, Harcourt, Brace, 1941.

Von Hassell, Ulrich. *The von Hassell Diaries, 1938–1944.* Garden City, New York, Doubleday, 1947.

Semmler, Rudolf. *Goebbels—The Man Next to Hitler.* London, Westhouse, 1947. Diary of one of Goebbels' young assistants; interesting and occasionally important.

Goebbels, Joseph. *The Goebbels Diaries, 1942–1943.* Transl., ed., and with an introduction by Louis Lochner. Garden City, New York, Doubleday, 1948.

Hull, Cordell. *Memoirs.* 2 vols. New York, Macmillan, 1948.

Kordt, Erich. *Wahn und Wirklichkeit.* Stuttgart, Union Deutsche Verlags-gesellschaft, 1948. A German official's occasionally illuminating but not always trustworthy remarks. Of interest are the statements on the slight role of the United States in Hitler's calculations.

Dietrich, Otto. *12 Jahre mit Hitler.* Munich, Isar Verlag, 1955. Rambling but interesting memoirs by the Reich Press Chief.

Schacht, Hjalmar. *Account Settled.* London, Weidenfeld and Nicolson, 1949.

Weizsaecker, Ernst. *Memoirs.* Chicago, Henry Regnery, 1951. Rather disappointing recollections of a once able German diplomat who played a key role as State Secretary in the Wilhelmstrasse, 1938–1943.

Bormann, Martin. *The Bormann Letters.* London, Weidenfeld and Nicolson, 1954. Bormann's letters to his wife from January 1943 to April 1945.

Hanfstaengl, Ernst. *Hitler, The Missing Years.* London, Eyre and Spottis-woode, 1957. Convincing evidence of Hitler's ignorance and prejudice concerning the Western Hemisphere.

Doenitz, Karl. *Memoirs: Ten Years and Twenty Days.* Cleveland, World Publishing Co., 1959.

Warlimont, Walter. *Inside Hitler's Headquarters, 1939–45.* New York, Praeger, 1965.

Goebbels, Joseph. *Das Tagebuch von Joseph Goebbels, 1925/26,* ed. by Helmut Heiber. Stuttgart, Deutsche Verlags-Anstalt, 1960. Includes additional documents and an especially valuable introduction by the editor.

Documents and Other Source Materials

Les Instructions Secrètes de la Propagande Allemande. Paris, Le Petit Parisien, n.d. Invaluable for this study.

Documents on American Foreign Relations, 1938–1942. Boston, World Peace Foundation, 1939–1942.

Hitler, Adolf. *Mein Kampf.* New York, Reynal and Hitchcock, 1939.

The German White Paper: Full Text of the Polish Documents Issued by the Berlin Foreign Office. Foreword by C. Hartley Grattan. New York, Howell and Soskin, 1940.

The controversial papers released to aid the isolationists defeat Roosevelt in 1940. For photostatic copies of some of the original documents, see Auswaertiges Amt, *Polnische Dokumente zur Vorgeschichte des Krieges.* Berlin, Deutscher Verlag, 1940.

Argentina. Camara de Diputados. Comisión Investigadora de Actividades Anti-Argentinas. *Informes.* 5 vols. Buenos Aires, 1941. Among the most valuable sources of all for an evaluation of Nazi activities in Latin America. Cited as *Argentine Reports.*

Hitler, Adolf. *My New Order.* Ed. Raoul de Roussy de Sales. New York, Reynal and Hitchcock, 1941.

U.S. House of Representatives. Special Committee to Investigate Un-American Activities and Propaganda in the United States. *Hearings.* 16 vols. and appendix, parts 2, 3, and 4. 75th Cong., 2nd Sess.; 76th Cong., 1st and 2nd Sess., 1939–1941.

———. *Investigation of Un-American Activities and Propaganda.* 76th Cong., 1st Sess. Report no. 2, Jan. 3, 1939.

———. *Investigation of Un-American Propaganda Activities in the United States.* 76th Cong., 3rd Sess. Report no. 1476, Jan. 3, 1940.

———. *Investigation of Un-American Propaganda Activities in the United States.* 77th Cong., 1st Sess. Report no. 1, Jan. 3, 1941.

———. *Special Report on Subversive Activities Aimed at Destroying Our Representative Form of Government.* 2 parts. 77th Cong., 2nd Sess. Report no. 2277, Jan. 25, 1942.

———. *Index to Hearings, Volumes 1–14; Reports 1939–1941; Appendices I–V.* Washington, 1942.

Prange, Gordon W., ed. *Hitler's Words*. Washington, American Council on Public Affairs, 1944.

U.S. Department of State. *Consultation Among The American Republics With Respect to the Argentine Situation*. Washington, Government Printing Office, 1946. Detailed demonstration with documents that Argentina collaborated with the Axis in violation of her obligations to the inter-American system.

Nazi Conspiracy and Aggression. 10 vols. Washington, Government Printing Office, 1946. Valuable general records used at Nuremberg, some of which bear on the Western Hemisphere.

Roosevelts Weg in den Krieg. Berlin, Deutscher Verlag, 1943. Collection of documents issued by the German Foreign Ministry to demonstrate Roosevelt's culpability for the war.

Fuehrer Conferences on Matters Dealing With the German Navy, 1939–1945. 7 vols. Washington, U.S. Office of Naval Intelligence, 1947. Translated from the captured German naval archives, several of these documents point up the preliminary considerations being given to war in the Atlantic against the United States, before American entry into the conflict.

Documents on German Foreign Policy, 1918–1945. Series C (4 vols., 1933–1935) and D (13 vols., 1937–December 11, 1941). Washington, U.S. Department of State, 1949–. (Cited as *DGFP-C* and *DGFP-D*.)

Foreign Relations of the United States, 1933–1941. Washington: U.S. Department of State, 1949–. (Cited as *FR*.)

Henry Picker, *Hitlers Tischgespraeche im Fuehrerhauptquartier, 1941–1942*. Ed. Percy Ernst Schramm in collaboration with Andreas Hillgruber and Martin Vogt. Stuttgart, Seewald Verlag, 1963. Interesting both for comparison with the English version (based on different records) and for the introduction by Schramm.

Hitler's Secret Conversations, 1941–1944. New York, Farrar, Straus and Young, 1953. Of value specifically for revelations of the Fuehrer's basic hostility toward the United States and the Western Hemisphere.

Burr, Robert N., and Hussey, Roland D., eds. *Documents on Inter-American Cooperation*, vol. 2, 1881–1948. Philadelphia, University of Pennsylvania Press, 1955.

Le Testament Politique de Hitler. Notes transcribed by Martin Bormann. Paris, Librairie Arthème Fayard, 1959. An English edition has subsequently appeared as *The Testament of Adolf Hitler: The Hitler-Bormann Documents, February–April, 1945*. Ed. François Genoud. London, Cassell, 1961.

Hitlers Lagebesprechungen: Die Protokollfragmente seiner militaerischen Konferenzen, 1942–1945. Ed. Helmut Heiber. Stuttgart, Deutsche Verlags-Anstalt, 1962. Minutes of wartime conferences on the military situation, assembled and massively annotated by Heiber. Important evidence of Hitler's contempt for U.S. military capabilities.

Hitler, Adolf. *Hitlers Zweites Buch: Ein Dokument aus dem Jahr 1928*. Ed. Gerhard L. Weinberg. Stuttgart, Deutsche Verlags-Anstalt, 1961. This historic discovery by Professor Weinberg, with a thoughtful introduction by Hans Rothfels, is particularly notable for its revelations of Hitler's attitudes toward the United States. A rather hasty English translation, introduced by Telford Taylor, has appeared as *Hitler's Secret Book*. New York, Grove Press, 1961.

MANUSCRIPTS

UNITED STATES NATIONAL ARCHIVES

"Political and Cultural Propaganda in the USA, 1933–1936," Files of *Abteilung III* of the German Foreign Ministry. Foreign Affairs Branch. Microfilm serials K1052–K1054, frames K269085–271050, containers 4614–4616. The best single source for the early years of Nazi activity in the United States; include not only Foreign Ministry documents, but reports and correspondence to and from PROMI, the Gestapo, and numerous other agencies.

Files of the Head of the AO and State Secretary in the Foreign Ministry (Ernst W. Bohle). Foreign Affairs Branch. Micro-copy T-120, serials 72, 78, 102, containers 64, 75, 103. These papers relate to AO activities in Latin America and contain considerable information on Bohle's persistent friction with other Party and State officials. Especially interesting are materials discussing "The financial means of the Foreign Ministry for Cultural Politics," and those relating to the crucial conference of AO, Foreign Ministry, and other officials on Ibero-America in June 1939.

Files of Political Department 9 in the Foreign Ministry. Foreign Affairs Branch. Microfilm serial 4515H, container 2276. Several of the interesting unpublished dispatches from the German embassy in Washington during 1940, especially one dated June 27 in which Chargé d'Affaires Thomsen reports on the publicity maneuvers surrounding Hitler's interview with Wiegand, and on the cooperation of Congressman Thorkelson of Montana.

Files of Political Department 9 in the Foreign Ministry. Foreign Affairs Branch. Microfilm serial 4516H, container 2276. Supplementary documentation to that already published on the Reich's growing political difficulties in Latin America in the late thirties, these files cover at some length German relations with most countries in the region from May 1936 to July 1940. Most of the important items appear in *DGFP-D*.

Files of Political Department 9 in the Foreign Ministry. Foreign Affairs Branch. Microfilm serials 8129 and 8130, container 3302. These files pertain to Germanism in the United States, March 1938 to January 1940, and reveal the staunch efforts by the Foreign Ministry to get the Party and other agencies to temper their subversive activities in this country.

Files of the Press Department in the Foreign Ministry. Foreign Affairs Branch. Microfilm serials K2004, K2005, K2007, K2010, K2012, K2013, container 5389. Only a few frames really pertain to the United States: K516188–193; K516194–243; K516249–272; K516342–360; K516392–618; K516619–636. Although the secret files of this department were not captured, these papers provide ample evidence of the Nazi reaction to the hostility of American public opinion and indicate some of the counter-measures adopted for Nazi propaganda.

Rolf Hoffmann papers. Micro-copy T-81, rolls 25–31, 35–37. Comprising many thousands of documents, these materials represent the correspondence of Hoffmann of the *Amt Auslandspresse* in Munich with individuals and groups in many parts of the world. The greater percentage of the documents concern attempts to disseminate propaganda in the United States and other countries of the Western Hemisphere. They cover fairly completely the years 1933–1941 and also include many exchanges with PROMI and other important agencies in the Reich. A most important group of manuscripts.

Edmund Fuerholzer papers. Micro-copy T-81, roll 189. Though disorganized, these records of a Transocean correspondent in the United States are interesting mainly for a letter of September 16, 1930 (frames 33707–708), from Fuerholzer to Hitler in which the reporter recommends that a special Nazi news agency be established in the United States. This may well have been the origin of the later expansion of Transocean activities in this country, after the agency had been established mainly as a service to South American countries and the Orient.

Papers of the *NSDAP Kameradschaft USA*. Micro-copy T-81, rolls 139–45. This was an organization under Fritz Gissibl whose membership was made up largely of former members of the Nazi movement in the United States who had been repatriated to the Reich. Many of these materials are of little interest, being mainly applications for admission to the organization or to return to Germany, but they do reveal Gissibl's stout support for continuing to assist the German-American Bund and a Nazi underground in the United States. The documents reflect the difficulty the Foreign Ministry encountered in its attempts to moderate Party activities in America.

Files of the *Deutsche Akademie* (Munich). Micro-copy T-82, serial 11, rolls 10 and 11.

Karl Haushofer papers. Micro-copy T-253, serial 38, roll 49. Both these groups of papers contain extensive documentation of Haushofer's activities as head of the deutsche Akademie and later of VDA. At times they reveal him to have been a cantankerous busybody; they leave no doubt that his status was due to his special relationship with Rudolf Hess, for his friction with other Party and state officials and agencies is recurrently evident. Of particular interest is roll 11, folder 809, concerning the incident between the Academy's representative in the Argentine and the AO.

United States Library of Congress

"A List of Newspapers Principally Representative of German Groups Outside of Germany." Collected by the *Deutsches Ausland-Institut,* Stuttgart. 26956, G3D46, 1946a. Contains photostats of the DAI card file of German-language papers in foreign countries, including many in this hemisphere. Some annotations.

Standardthesen und Richtlinien fuer die Deutsche Auslandspropaganda (Nur Fuer den Dienstgebrauch). DD254. AS, 1943. This collection of directives governing Nazi foreign propaganda was prepared by Dr. Megerle, Ribbentrop's propaganda specialist, and is an enormously rich little volume.

German War Propaganda For Latin America. Prints and Photographs Division. 7666. Useful group of pamphlets, articles, broadcasts, postcards, etc., exemplifying Nazi propaganda in Latin America, 1939–1945.

Deutsche Akademie albums. Prints and Photographs Division. 3050 and 3145. Hundreds of photographs in album form depicting the Academy's operations in Latin America, its establishment of branches in dozens of localities, and its promotion of Germandom in the area.

Grossdeutschland im Weltgeschehen. Prints and Photographs Division. 2651. Published by the Nazi Propaganda Ministry, these albums relate to the Reich's progress between 1939 and 1942 and emphasize the global brotherhood of Germans.

DAI Archives. Manuscript Division. Accession number 8393, containers 135, 158, 279, and 282; accession number 52162, containers 137, 158 A-C, 329A, and 329B. These files and scrapbooks pertain to all sorts of DAI projects in Latin America and the United States; of special interest are lists and biographies of Germans who had made notable contributions to the various countries of the New World and who therefore became useful subjects of propaganda appeals. There is also considerable information on the VDA in the last two containers.

"List of NSDAP Members in Foreign Countries." Headquarters Berlin Command, Office of Military Government for Germany (US), Jan. 31, 1948. Manuscript Division. Accession number D.R. G1668, containers 748–767. Coded list of all Nazis in foreign countries, including the thousands in the New World.

"Miscellaneous Items From the Government of the Third Reich." *Gegen Amerika.* Manuscript Division. Accession number 11,522. Materials from the files of Dr. Karl Megerle of the Foreign Ministry, these are mainly drafts of articles disparaging the United States, and cover the period 1939–1941.

Rehse Collection. Manuscript Division. Accession numbers 11,564; 11,249; 11,280; 11,522. Rehse was in charge of the *Archiv fuer Zeitgeschichte und Publizistik* in Munich, and this far-ranging group of papers includes a great deal of anti-American propaganda, along with various Nazi Party publications, both for domestic and foreign consumption.

YIVO INSTITUTE FOR JEWISH RESEARCH (NEW YORK)

Report on the participation of the "Propaganda Weapon" in Wehrmacht war games 1937. G-93. PROMI complaints about military interference in propaganda activities.

Aufklaerungs-Ausschuss Hamburg-Bremen; propaganda abroad, 1938. PA-7. Papers detailing the origins, aims, and methods of this organization for camouflaged propaganda abroad. Includes diagrams of contacts with newspapers and agents in the Americas.

Papers of the Reich Ministry of Interior. NFI-18. Inside material on the official financial support of the DAI; also much on its annual celebrations in honor of foreign Germandom and its educational functions abroad.

Reichsministerium fuer Volksaufklaerung und Propaganda. G-1-10. Although only fragmentary, these are the most illuminating PROMI files available in the United States. Especially good are documents pertaining to the climax in 1939 of the Goebbels-Ribbentrop dispute over foreign propaganda.

UNITED STATES DEPARTMENT OF STATE

"Nazi Activity in the American Republics," Division of American Republics, February 1938– based on Reports received from the field as of Feb. 1, 1938. (Cited as "Nazi Activities.") A brief, but extremely helpful survey of United States diplomatic calculations regarding Nazi penetration. It reveals that even as late as 1938, in spite of all the signs of the Party's success in the area, the State Department was not yet seriously aroused.

Index